EMPATHY AND RAGE

Female Genital Mutilation in African Literature

About the Editors

TOBE LEVIN is Collegiate Professor at the University of Maryland University College in Europe; an Adjunct Lecturer at the University of Frankfurt; and an Associate of the W.E.B. Du Bois Institute, Harvard University. A Ph.D in Comparative Literature from Cornell University, she is the first in the world to have written a dissertation on Nobel Laureate Elfriede Jelinek (1979). Also among the first to publish essays on FGM in creative writing (in 1986), she has been an activist since 1977 and is a recognised expert on FGM, who has been invited to advise the British Parliament, the European Union and the Bundestag. Editor-in-Chief of *Feminist Europa. Review of Books* and Founding President of FORWARD – Germany, she translated Fadumo Korn and Sabine Eichhorst's *Born in the Big Rains. A Memoir of Somalia and Survival* (2006). Formerly a Scholar-in-Residence at Brandeis University and an Associate at the Five Colleges Women's Studies Research Centre at Mt. Holyoke College, she edited *Violence: 'Mercurial Gestalt'* (NY & Amsterdam: Rodopi, 2008), which includes her chapter on FGM in creative writing.

AUGUSTINE H. ASAAH Associate Professor of French, is currently Head of the Department of Modern Languages at the University of Ghana, Legon, where he teaches Francophone African literature. He focuses on the tension between the sacred and the profane, African feminist literature, and gender-based violence in African fiction. Recent articles have appeared in *Research in African Literatures, Journal of Black Studies, Présence Francophone,* and *Notre Librairie.* He has also authored several textbooks on the teaching of French in Ghana.

EMPATHY AND RAGE

Female Genital Mutilation in African Literature

EDITORS
Tobe Levin and Augustine H. Asaah

ayebia

An Adinkra symbol meaning
Ntesie matemasie
A symbol of knowledge and wisdom

Ayebia Clarke Publishing Limited gratefully acknowledges Arts Council SE Funding

Editors: Tobe Levin and Augustine H. Asaah

This edition first published by Ayebia Clarke Publishing Limited 2009
7 Syringa Walk
Banbury
OX16 1FR
Oxfordshire
UK

Distributed outside Africa, Europe and the United Kingdom exclusively by
Lynne Rienner Publishers, Inc.
1800 30th St., Ste. 314
Boulder, CO 80301
USA
www.rienner.com

Co-published in Ghana with the Centre for Intellectual Renewal
56 Ringway Estate, Osu, Accra, Ghana.
www.cir.com

British Library Cataloguing-in-Publication Data
A catalogue record of this book is available from the British Library.

Cover design by Amanda Carroll at Millipedia
Cover photographs © iStockphoto.com
Picture research by Amanda Carroll

Typeset by FiSH Books, Enfield, Middlesex.
Printed and bound in Great Britain by CPI Mackays, Chatham ME5 8TD.

Ayebia Clarke Publishing Limited gratefully acknowledges the support of
Arts Council SE Funding.

ISBN 978-0-9555079-4-6

Available from www.ayebia.co.uk or email info@ayebia.co.uk
Distributed in Africa, Europe & the UK by TURNAROUND at:
www.turnaround-uk.com

DEDICATION
IN MEMORY of OUSMANE SEMBÈNE
(January 1, 1923–June 9, 2007)
Pierrette Herzberger-Fofana
Translated and Edited by Augustine H. Asaah

An accomplished novelist, filmmaker and, in 2004, winner of Cannes' first prize in the category 'un autre regard' for *Moolaadé*, Ousmane Sembène, a Senegalese and Pan Africanist, gave the world numerous subversive *chefs d'oeuvres*. His last movie shot in Burkina Faso, dedicated to 'all mothers and women fighting to abolish [a] retardant relic of the past,' makes a strong case against Female Genital Mutilation which, Sembène is convinced, represents a clear act of violence against women.

The storyline revolves around Collé Gallo Sy, an excised mother, who had freed her only daughter from the so-called purification rites, or 'salindé', organised every seven years. In this particular season, four little girls run away and seek protection – called Moolaadé – from Collé, whose defiance is known. She protects the children but, by this act, revolts against her husband, his family, and the village as a whole. In conflict are the right to asylum and attachment to tradition that approves excision. For her opposition, Collé is subjected to a brutal public whipping, her enraged husband trying to force her to recant. His efforts elicit rapturous applause. 'Break her! Break her!'; the crowd shrieks. But the forces of change are too strong. Increasingly, women join Collé to triumph over male-authored repression symbolised by the edict to burn all radios, a source of enlightened ideas.

With his earlier screenings of *Faat-Kine* and *La Confédération des Rats* ('The Confederation of Rats'), *Moolaadé* forms a trilogy of politically and culturally incorrect footage crafted to critique injustice.

In honour of Sembène, our collection celebrates the first full-length feature film contesting FGM.

Contents

Dedication   v

Biographies of Contributors   ix

Painting: *Defiance of Pain 1*   xiii

Preface   xiv

Acknowledgements   xx

Tobe Levin
Assaults on Female Genitalia: Activists, Authors and the Arts   1

EMPATHIZERS
Elisabeth Bekers
From Women's Rite to Human Rights Issue: Literary Explorations of
Female Genital Excision since *Facing Mount Kenya* (1938)   15

Stephen Bishop
Oppositional Approaches to Female Genital Mutilation (FGM) in
African Literature   38

Tameka L. Cage
Going Home Again: Diaspora, Female Genital Mutilation (FGM)
and Kingship in *Warrior Marks*   52

Jennifer Browdy de Hernandez
'Mother' as a Verb: the Erotic, Audre Lorde and Female Genital
Mutilation (FGM)   64

ENRAGED
Augustine H. Asaah
Female Genital Mutilation (FGM): Ambivalence, Indictment and
Commitment in Sub-Saharan African Fiction   75

Anne V. Adams
The Anti-Female Genital Mutilation (FGM) Novel in
Public Education: An Example from Ghana   93

Tobe Levin
What's Wrong with Mariam? Gloria Naylor's Infibulated Jew   112

Marianne Sarkis
Somali Womanhood: A Re-visioning   126

ENGAGED
Pierrette Herzberger-Fofana
Excision and African Literature: An Activist Annotated
Bibliographical Excursion   142

Muthoni Mathai
Who's Afraid of Female Sexuality?   156

Nura Abdi and Leo G. Linder
Tränen im Sand / Desert Tears (Excerpts)   173

Notes & References   177

Index   214

Biographies of Contributors

NURA ABDI born in 1974 into the Lali clan of northern Somalia as the fourth of eight children, is author (with Leo G. Linder) of a well-received memoir *Tränen im Sand* (Desert Tears), which has been translated into French, Polish and several other languages (though not yet into English). Only four when subjected to the *halaleiso*, she chronicles the suffering that follows. When at 18 she finds herself a refugee in Germany, she learns that not all women are excised and writes her book to encourage abolition, dedicating it to activists against FGM.

ANNE V. ADAMS former Professor of African/Diaspora literatures at Kent State and Cornell Universities is now the Director of the W.E.B. Du Bois Memorial Centre for Pan African Culture in Ghana. Her research and publications focus on Gender in African/Diaspora literatures (*Ngambika: Studies of Women in African Literature*, co-edited with Carole Boyce Davies) as well as Afro-German Cultural Studies, which include translations of works from German (*Showing Our Colors: Afro-German Women Speak Out* by Katharina Oguntoye, May Opitz, Dagmar Schultz; and *Blues in Black and White* by the Ghanaian-German May Ayim). She is a consultant for the German publications of Toni Morrison.

AUGUSTINE H. ASAAH is associate professor of French at the University of Ghana, where he has widely researched into African feminist literature and gender-based violence in African fiction. Recent articles have appeared in *Research in African Literatures, Journal of Black Studies, Présence Francophone*, and *Notre Librairie*. He has also authored several textbooks on the teaching of French in Ghana.

ELISABETH BEKERS who teaches at the Free University of Brussels (VUB) and is an affiliated Research Fellow at the University of Antwerp, writes about African literatures from the continent and the Diaspora and has produced several articles on literary explorations of female genital excision (in volumes published by Africa World Press, Rodopi and L'Harmattan). Her book-length comparative study of four decades of African and African American creative writing on this theme will appear in 2009 with the University Press of Wisconsin. Co-founder of the Postcolonial Literatures Research Group (University of Antwerp), she co-directs the Platform for Postcolonial Readings (a joint venture with the University of Leiden).

STEPHEN L. BISHOP Associate Professor in the Department of Foreign Languages and Literatures and the Africana Studies Programme at the University of New Mexico, focuses on African literature and culture, law and literature, shame and guilt, feminism, and cultural studies. He has published a number of articles on African and Québécois literature, cinema, and law, as well as *Legal Oppositional Narrative: A Case Study in Cameroon* (Lexington Books, 2008). He teaches courses on African literature and culture, theories of law and literature, feminism, and legal and moral philosophy in literature and film.

JENNIFER BROWDY DE HERNANDEZ earned her Ph.D in Comparative Literature at New York University in 1994, specialising in personal narratives of the Americas and postcolonial theory. In 2004 she published *Women Writing Resistance: Essays on Latin America and the Caribbean* (South End Press), which has been adopted for use in many college-level courses around the country, and has co-edited a second volume in this series, *Women Writing Resistance in Africa and the African Diaspora*. She served for three years as a board member of the US Committee for UNIFEM (the United Nations Development Fund for Women) and has been Vice-President for Programmes of the Berkshire Chapter of UNIFEM/USA since 2002.

TAMEKA L. CAGE teaches issues of healing, reconciliation, and social change in American Literature and Literatures of the African Diaspora at the University of Pittsburgh. She has presented research on female 'circumcision' at regional and national conferences and is invested in using her position as an academic and human rights advocate to join forces with those who seek to eradicate the practice, while also employing understanding and 'empathy' in these efforts. She is completing her manuscript, *Painful Discourses: Borders, Regions, and Representations of Female Circumcision from Africa to America.*

PIERRETTE HERZBERGER-FOFANA city councilwoman in Erlangen and Board Member of FORWARD - Germany, teaches at the University of Erlangen and has published *Littérature Féminine Francophone Afrique Noire suivi d'un Dictionnaire des Romancières* (Paris: Harmattan, 2001), which won the 'Grand Prix du Président de la République du Sénégal pour les Sciences.' Author of the Kwanraa award-winning *Écrivains Africains et Identités culturelles* (Tübingen: Stauffenberg Verlag, 1989), she is a frequent contributor to www.afrology.com, www.grioo.com, www.renaf.org/RDC and www.africultures.com. Of special relevance is her obituary of Ousmane Sembène, 'Anwalt der Frauen,' at www.gtz.de. Dr Herzberger-Fofana has been honoured with the 'Grand Prix du Président de la République du Sénégal.' (See www.cis-online.org; click on Amo Wilhelm Anton).

CHRISTINE LECHE has won the American Academy of Poets Prize, the Deep South Writers Competition, and the Billy Murray and Denny Poetry Award. Her work has appeared in *Nimrod, The Mississippi Valley Review, Louisiana Literature, Sow's Ear,* and others. She currently teaches English and Creative Writing on Bagram Airbase, Afghanistan, for UMUC-Europe.

TOBE LEVIN is Collegiate Professor at the University of Maryland University College in Europe; an Adjunct Lecturer at the University of Frankfurt; and an Associate of the W.E.B. Du Bois Institute, Harvard University. A Ph.D in Comparative Literature from Cornell University, she is the first in the world to have written a dissertation on Nobel Laureate Elfriede Jelinek (1979). Also among the first to publish essays on FGM in creative writing (in 1986), she has been an activist since 1977 and is a recognised expert on FGM, who has been invited to advise the British Parliament, the European Union and the Bundestag. Editor-in-Chief of *Feminist Europa. Review of Books* and Founding President of FORWARD – Germany, she translated Fadumo Korn and Sabine Eichhorst's *Born in the Big Rains. A Memoir of Somalia and Survival* (2006). Formerly a Scholar-in-Residence at Brandeis University and an Associate at the Five

Colleges Women's Studies Research Centre at Mt. Holyoke College, she edited *Violence: 'Mercurial Gestalt'* (NY & Amsterdam: Rodopi, 2008), which includes her chapter on FGM in creative writing.

MUTHONI MATHAI is a psychiatrist with ten years of research experience in Kenya. She was active as a Lecturer and Consultant for FORWARD – Germany before becoming a Faculty Member at the University of Nairobi, School of Health Sciences in the Department of Psychiatry. She wrote *Sexual Decision-Making and AIDS in Africa: A Look at the Social Vulnerability of Women in Sub-Saharan Africa to HIV/AIDS.* (Kassel: Kassel University Press, 2006), and her chapter in this collection opens up the human side of her research.

MARIANNE SARKIS is an applied Medical Anthropologist and Director/Webmaster of the Female Genital Cutting Education and Networking Project (http://www.fgmnetwork.org). She has served as a cultural liaison between hospitals and Somali refugee communities and has trained nurses and physicians on culturally appropriate care for women who have undergone FGM. Her research interests include social network analysis, migration studies, refugee therapeutic networks, refugee identity in the Diaspora, and acculturation. Currently residing in Worcester, MA, she is collecting data for her dissertation on the relationship between fertility, citizenship, and African identity after migration.

© Godfrey Williams-Okorodus. *Defiance of Pain 1.* Oil on Canvas

Preface

One afternoon in Munich, with sharp rays slicing through the pane, I lost my innocence. It was 1977, and the third issue of a German feminist magazine had opened to a two-page spread. In 'Klitorisbeschneidung' (Clitoridectomy), journalist Pauline Caravello had just initiated me and *EMMA*'s 150,000 other readers to an aspect of women's oppression hitherto unknown to us. 'What?!' we asked. 'They do *what*?!'

Empathy and rage. Frankly appalled, involuntarily I crossed my legs and sought solace from a classic poster where, fondled by Supreme Court judges, who were dignified and robed, a woman lay prone and naked. The caption read: 'Die Würde des Menschen ist unantastbar.' 'Human dignity is inviolable,' quoting Germany's post-war constitution, evidence that the country has learned from its excruciating past. The collage, however, had been inspired by a Karlsruhe magistrates' 1974 decision restricting women's access to abortion. In Africa, societies denied women uninjured bodies. Many of us made the link.

A movement arose in Germany. Basketsful of letters reached *EMMA*'s office. Study groups sprang up. Armchair feminists, moved by genital sorority, posed the ur-socialist question, 'What is to be done?' We called out to lone African campaigners – Awa Thiam, Edna Adan Ismail, Nawal el Saadawi, Marie Assaad. The Babikar Badri Women's Studies Centre in Omdurman advised. In 1978, the German Women Physicians' Association invited Dr Asma el Dareer to speak. (Dareer would go on to publish the first epidemiological study of FGM in the Sudan, *Woman, Why Do You Weep?* [London: Zed, 1982].) National coordination of a network fell to my Munich committee. A modest book appeared (I. Braun, T. Levin, A. Schwarzbauer. *Materialien zur Unterstützung von Aktionsgruppen gegen Klitorisbeschneidung* [Basic Documents for Caucuses against Clitoridectomy] [Munich: Frauenoffensive, 1979)]. And then things petered out.

For in 1980, Copenhagen 'happened': African women at the UN Mid-Decade for Women conference, among them Marie-Angélique Savané of

AAWORD, reacted with outrage to Fran Hosken's workshop on the topic. Hosken (1920–2006), a sharp-tongued refugee from Hitler, made it her life's mission to eradicate the practice; she coined the term FGM. Ceaselessly, she researched, wrote, and lobbied international agencies. She was, however, also notoriously short on tact and anti-male. With few allies even among non-African activists, she probably served as a template for the 'white Western feminist' damned by so many indigenous campaigners who often wished 'us' to butt out.

Some simply could not. Nor would many of the prescient pioneers allow us to. In 1982, Awa Thiam asked a small group from Germany to participate in the inaugural conference of CAMS (Commission pour l'Abolition des Mutilations Sexuelles) [Commission to Abolition Sexual Mutilation] in Dakar (see my report with the provocative title 'Solidarische Rassistinnen' [Racist Solidarity?] *Emma*. February 1983. 63). In April 1983, the fledgeling German human rights group Terre des Femmes returned the invitation to Awa Thiam, who addressed their first annual meeting in Frankfurt. Later that spring, Thiam, Efua Dorkenoo, and I met in Paris. Dorkenoo had just founded FORWARD and all of us asked, 'How can we work together?'

That is indeed the question, how to approach an issue viewed as urgent by only a tiny trans-national minority. For, make no mistake: an enormous and powerful majority tenaciously defends the practice. For instance, as recently as June 2007, you might have read that 'as part of the routine practice of vote buying... female teens will have their clitoris and labia minora cut off at no cost to their families' (Bowers). The news refers to government promotion of excision in Sierra Leone where more than 90 per cent of females are cut. Such is the strength of the status quo in all excising cultures.[1] Opposing it in Freetown, Dr Irene Koso-Thomas, threatened and harassed, is a solitary voice, whose ideas, first published in 1988, face as much opposition now as then, and possibly more in future.[2]

The essays on female genital mutilation in creative writing that you are about to read arose from a desire first and foremost to protect girls from the harm that inevitably follows when genitalia are amputated, because no matter how strong the social rationalisations and peer pressure, FGM inflicts anguish on the body, risks short and long term side-effects, and can be lethal. All contributors agree on this point. Consensus is lacking, however, once we look for the 'words to say it': do we censure, blame, persuade, exhort, insult, cajole, seduce, emote – or entertain? In their analyses of the literature, most writers in this collection follow the IAC (Inter-African Committee), whose Bamako Declaration of 2005 (described in Chapter 1) sets out the parametres of their argument. Others do not. Eschewing the word *mutilation,* they prefer 'milder' labels yet apply them to the same agonising facts. Their choices add a controversial piquancy to this endeavour and suggest our grouping chapters into 'Empathisers,' 'Enraged,' and 'Engaged.'

Yet these emotions often overlap. One noteworthy instance emerges from a letter to the editor penned by activist Comfort Ottah that I borrow to conclude. (You can see Ottah in *Warrior Marks* demonstrating against a bill to legalise female 'circumcision' in Great Britain.) In the (now defunct) African American magazine *Emerge,* Harriet A. Washington argues that 'nearly 60 per cent of newborn boys in the United States undergo a similar ritual' to that of girls. Given this likeness, erroneous of course, FGM becomes 'a judgemental term that lumps together many types of female circumcision' such as 'clitoridectomy [in which] the clitoris is nicked...' In response to such trivialisation and its discouragement of solidarity, Comfort Ottah wrote to the editor:

20 September 1996

Dear Mr George Curry,
[Having] recently read...Harriet A. Washington on 'the rite of female circumcision,' I find it offensive and insensitive to the suffering millions of African women and girl children.

How can she compare male circumcision to Female Genital Mutilation? Does she know how many men go out to satisfy their sexual needs because it is impossible with their wives? Does she know how many women are abandoned by their husbands because they shrink away due to pain each time the husbands come near them for sexual relationship? Does she know how many broken marriages there are due to lack of sexual relationship between the man and his wife? Does she know how many men have become impotent simply because each time they approach their wives, they weep with agony? How can you be hurting the woman you love? They ask.

How many babies have died due to obstructed labour? How many women have been left in a morbid state after childbirth due to prolonged obstructed labour and damage to adjacent organs?...

Does she know how many schoolgirls go off sick every month because they cannot menstruate freely? Does she know how many schoolgirls spend 30–45 minutes trying to pass urine and are always in trouble with their teachers for being late to classes? Does she know how many schoolgirls are expelled from classes because they are described as disruptive and erratic in their mood swings? No one understands what they are going through as they have been sworn to secrecy never to mention their pain... to anyone else.

Does she know how many suffer from recurrent urinary tract infections?

I have met these women and girls in my daily work both in the community and in the hospitals.

In some African societies, stretching of ear lobes until they reached shoulder length was a culture but... is now a rarity. Knocking off two front teeth was a culture;... it is no longer the case today. Tribal marks that deformed the face [were part of] a culture in the past; people are now seeking plastic surgery to erase them.

... Killing of twin babies was a culture before but now twins live and are cherished. Binding of feet, chastity belts, burning of widows or burying them alive, denial of voting rights for women, slavery, are cultures [now] past because culture is dynamic and not static...

...Enough politics [has been played] with the blood, health and rights of African women and their daughters. Enough is enough.

Comfort I. Ottah, Midwife,
FORWARD, UK.

Tobe Levin
January 2009

Scene from Life, Female Circumcision

October 1991, p. 36

By Chris Leche

The girl from Cairo
is screaming into the eye
of the camera as if we
should help her out
of this page, as if
she is paralysed
into this act
for the purpose
of a photograph
that will sit
on coffee tables
in doctors' offices,
law offices, magazine racks
next to commodes
in luxurious American homes.

The unfortunate girl
from Cairo is dressed
in white cotton, black
hair woven into a crown.
She has flown, face
down, into a hammock
of women's arms
that hold perfectly
still while the doctor
pushes the dress up
to the girl's waist.

She is crying
out of this page
as he cuts that minnow
from the stream
of her body, raises
his brows and examines
the catch in the tiny
gauze net.

We cross our
legs in dismay.
Turn the page.
There is nothing
to be done. In Cairo,
it is already night,
months later.

(Used with the poet's permission)

Acknowledgements

Books are born of passion, patience, and people, this volume in particular owing its existence to the serenity and confidence of our contributors, whose interest dates from 2003, and to the inspiration of our mentors, of whom Tobe would like to thank Henry Louis Gates, Jr., Florence Howe, Shulamit Reinharz, Obioma Nnaemeka, and Frankie Hutton (in the USA), Hanny Lightfoot-Klein, Alice Schwarzer, Elfriede Jelinek, Pierrette Herzberger-Fofana, Linda Weil-Curiel and Waltraud DuMont du Voitel (in Europe). Other inimitable midwives to the project have been Marianne Sarkis for IT expertise; Anne Adams, for leading us to Nana Ayebia Clarke our Ghananian Publisher and for introducing Augustine and Tobe to each other; and FORWARD – Germany, whose team gives selflessly of time, energy, and financial resources: Anne von Gleichen, Christoph von Gleichen, Fadumo Korn, Heidi Besas, Ekaterina Filippenko, Angelika Köster-Lossack, Audrey Haynes, Regina Lange, and Yordanos Melake among many dedicated activists.

Most important, however, we thank those in Africa and the Diaspora who insist that the systematic mutilation of girls' genitals should come to a speedy end and often risk their lives to change tradition. For courage, leadership and perseverance we honour Ayaan Hirsi Ali, Owolabi Bjalkander, Fatoumata Coulibaly, Fatoumata Siré Diakité, Khadidiatou Diallo, Waris Dirie, Efua Dorkenoo, Fana Habteab, Etenesh Hadis, Adwoa Kluvitse, Khady Koita, Muthoni Mathai, Comfort Momoh, Naana Otoo-Oyortey, Comfort Ottah, Berhane Ras-Work, Mariame Racine Sow, Awa Thiam, Alice Walker, Joy Keshi Walker, Godfrey Williams-Okorodus and our friends in GAMS, FORWARD UK and the European Network FGM.

And finally, the volume pays tribute to a family. *Tobe* remembers her good-humoured father Morris William Levin (1921–1990), who she wishes were still with us to applaud this work; and her artist mother Janice Metz Levin (b. 1920), who claps with her one good hand.

Augustine is grateful to his wife Charlotte, their son Eugene and Augustine's brother Tony for all their support. He also thanks Ahmadou Kourouma and Yambo Ouologuem, who, with *Les Soleils des indépendances* and *Devoir de violence* respectively, were the first African writers to initiate him into the knowledge of FGM.

Tobe Levin

Assaults on Female Genitalia: Activists, Authors and the Arts

'Everyone has the right to life, liberty and security of person.'
Article 3, UN Universal Declaration of Human Rights

...Terrible images [I keep on seeing]: a cheap hotel room, cramped and with yellowing wallpaper. There's a girl lying on the bed, maybe ten years old. She can't be more than twelve. She is naked. Four women are standing around...holding her down. The child's legs are spread ... and an old woman sits in front of her with a scalpel in her hand. The sheet is soaked in blood. The girl lets out piercing screams. She keeps [on] screaming. Her screams go...through my heart. (Dirie)

This invented but plausible description of an event in Cardiff, Wales, opens Waris Dirie's *Desert Children*, the Somali ex-model's third chronicle of campaigns against female genital assault.[1]

As the empathic act of an imaginary witness, it also serves perfectly to open the first edited volume of essays on female genital mutilation as a literary theme. Although many critics have appraised the topic in fiction, experiential texts and film, most have done so from an academic, not an activist, standpoint. Detached from abolition movements and sometimes captive to impending decisions on tenure, they apply questions different from those that guide this book, and, sadly, many have censured artists' breaking of taboo rather than assessed the aptness of their work to increase knowledge and end the woe.

Criticised, often unfairly, Alice Walker is a prime example of academia's argument with activism.[2] For decades before Walker's advocacy, campaigns in Africa and the Diaspora had invested considerable energy opposing FGM. Results, however, had been dismal.[3] Gradual

1

improvement began in the mid-1990s soon after Walker placed the topic at the heart of a novel, *Possessing the Secret of Joy* (1992) and a documentary *Warrior Marks* (1993). Content that such a public personality had finally stepped forward, activists in Africa and Europe received Walker's solidarity with gratitude. Efua Dorkenoo, for instance, founder of the London-based Foundation for Women's Health Research and Development (FORWARD), responded to *Possessing the Secret of Joy* by writing to the author to congratulate her: the portrait of Tashi/Evelyn was superb. Efua 'knew' the woman[4]: in consultations she had met any number of Tashis who, like the literary figure, had accepted genital surgeries as a patriotic duty only to discover that, as women, they had been sacrificed to patriarchal needs. Their suffering, both physical and mental, was keen – yet overlooked.

Warrior Marks ends with the usual stream of credits where we meet Dorkenoo again, a resource person for the film together with Awa Thiam, Khady Thiam, and other African consultants. Bracketing out these adjutants, *Jenda: A Journal of Culture and African Women Studies,* fulminates against the Pulitzer-prize winning writer, vilifying her for 'language, discourse and epistemic modes of Western culture' (Nako[5]). A 'somatocentric' bias is said to skew Walker's viewpoint, her theory apparently 'under-gird[ing] social hierarchies, privileges, identities, and ultimately social interest... [that] derives from the body' (Oyewumi 3),[6] and this body-centredness, it is implied, is not 'African'.

Now, there is something disingenuous in such an argument. After all, where women are initiated into the only available form of prestige, status change derives from clitoral ablation and a perilous somatic shift. In other words, where cutting prevails, the socio-cultural significance of females is premised upon a physical act: clitoridectomy, excision or infibulation. Where then does 'social interest derive from the body' (Oyewumi 3)? Clearly in excising cultures.

Agreed, the West has its (asymmetrical) counterpart in a type of consumerism demanded by and performed on adults: female genital landscaping, designer vaginoplasty, laser vaginal rejuvenation and female genital cosmetic surgery (involving labia minora reduction, labia majora remodelling, vaginal reconstruction, pubic tuck, hymenoplasty) *inter alia*, as *Jenda* in Volume 1, Number 1 (2001) is delighted to note. After all, if in the highly advanced Western world demand now exists for these services, why lambaste FGM? The West does it, too; the West has, in fact, learnt from Africa.[7]

Leaving aside the agency (or impotence) of victims, wounded *children* grow into adults who seek help. They find it at Well Woman Clinics[8] or in therapeutic creativity. In *Warrior Marks*, Dorkenoo describes an activity undertaken by FORWARD. Somali immigrants meeting at the Africa Centre in Covent Garden worked through residual pain by writing a play based on their lives. Arranged marriages brought young infibulated women to the UK where, were they to confront the G.P. with an infibulated vulva, 'he would just freak out' (Dorkenoo in *Warrior Marks*). So the brides would be held down and then 'do it' – de-infibulate – in their homes, 'right here in the UK, by themselves.' To muffle the shrieks in deference to British sensitivities, television, radio, and stereo would be set to blare.

To underscore the veracity of torture before turning back to means of assuaging it, let us cross the channel and alight at the rue de Montreuil in Paris, where something similar takes place. Mid-wife Hawa Gréou, the first practitioner in Europe sent to jail, was initially uncovered by the howls emanating from her flat. A neighbour reveals: '...they received a large number of African visitors who then departed with weeping children. ...There was sometimes a queue leading all the way down the stairs. I was curious about the children's screams. They were truly piercing shrieks' (Henry *et al* 7–8: my translation). The witness, suffering a heart condition, felt it necessary on those afternoons to leave her home.

Although for some, injury primes courage within initiation rites, grieving babies are clearly not testing their mettle. Instead, their ordeal is quite different, an experience of powerlessness and excruciating *schmerz*, whose trauma affects neural pathways and effects psychological change. Many are the memoirists – Waris Dirie, Nura Abdi, Fadumo Korn, Khady in the aptly titled *Mutilée* – who report their transformation from blithe, frolicking children into subdued, saddened spirits, whose earlier robust rebelliousness has been quelled.

It is, after all, in order to transform a cheeky girl into an acquiescent woman that the surgery is performed,[9] an aim recognised by FORWARD's amateur playwrights. Once concluding their script, however, they realised that, for fear of audience retaliation, it could not be performed. 'We would be killed,' they told Dorkenoo who added, yes, 'women can be killed' (*Warrior Marks*). Indeed, Dorkenoo herself, Ayaan Hirsi Ali and Soraya Mire, to name just a few, have received death threats seriously disruptive to their productivity, not to mention their daily lives (Mire email 29 September 2007).[10]

From whom then does this bullying proceed? From the practicing communities, immortalised in lethal opposition by Ousmane Sembène in his prize-winning film *Moolaadé*. After all, only because the majority favours cutting is a protest movement called for, and, as Sembène stages his cautionary tale, traditionalists deploy the lash, the stake, and the mob to maintain the status quo. In the literature on FGM, it has become a shibboleth to point out how deeply-rooted and complex the custom is, how difficult to change behaviour, how hard to win over crucial stakeholders, and how fragile are the seeming victories already achieved, few as they are. What is less often stressed is the extraordinary courage demanded of and shown by the 'positive-deviants', mainly African women leaders who, as noted above, endanger themselves to improve the lives of coming generations. Thus, one aim of this anthology is to move the discourse from complacency, misplaced patience and under-estimation of the challenges African activists face to a more compassionate understanding, increased solidarity and, ideally, personal engagement on and at their sides.[11]

Nowhere have lines been so clearly drawn as at the 6th General Assembly of the Inter-African Committee, 4–7 April 2005, in Bamako, Mali, resulting in a 'DECLARATION: on the Terminology FGM,' a document linked ideologically to 'International 'Zero Tolerance' to FGM Day' first called into existence by the IAC in 2003. Representing 28 African countries with twenty-five years' experience, Bamako answered attempts by 'some UN specialised agencies and bi-lateral donors… [under the influence of] specific lobby groups largely based in Western countries' to modify the discourse, replacing 'female genital mutilation' with inadequate alternatives.[12] Hailed for alleged courtesy, these deficient synonyms trivialise the harm, weaken activism and endanger girls. Why is a blunt approach essential? 'African women in the front line of the campaign' in Africa itself chose frank wording to 'confront the issue head on with… practicing communities.' Wishing to avoid confusion regarding 'the nature and gravity of the practice,' they contend, '[only] struggle [can alter] mentality and behaviours' with unavoidable 'pain integral to' empowerment. At issue is winning control of women's sexuality and reproductive rights.

Activists, in turn, see themselves as 'change agents' enlisted to 'help communities...go through' a distressing process that requires admitting harm, revising beliefs, and taking risks. To facilitate this, Bamako insists, 'the term FGM [must be] retained' for it is 'not judgemental...A medical term [it] reflects what is done to the genitalia of girls and women. It is a cultural reality.'[13]

Thus, if FGM is a 'cultural reality,' culture should be drawn on to oppose it. Yet the connection is elusive. On 19 September 2007, for instance, the Bundestag invited experts to Berlin. Understandably concerned with crime and punishment, legislators failed to inquire into the advocacy role of the creative arts – literature, film, music, theatre and dance. Although all major political parties promised increased efforts to stop FGM on German soil, ease admission for asylum seekers fleeing excision, and hasten global attempts to spare girls from the knife, a major strategic element was missing ('Experten').

Not solely a medical, legal, and human rights problem, the custom is *inscribed in desires* of both women and men. FGM is therefore rooted in the affective domain, not in dry scientific judgement, a fact that escaped the assembly's notice. Nonetheless, if, as years of campaigning have shown, the 'ritual' remains largely impervious to 'dialectical argumentation' (not to mention defiant of law), culture promises supplementary aesthetic appeals, investment and engagement. As neuroscientist Antonio Demasio has pointed out, 'good decision-making in matters of personal and social importance requires an emotional component' (Robinson 73). In this regard, artists may be the mislaid key.

Confronted with Annie de Villeneuve's 1937 description of an infibulation, Benoite Groult wrote, 'On a mal au C...n'est-ce pas, quand on lit ca. On a mal au coeur de soi-meme.' 'Your own genitalia throb on reading that, don't they? And your heart aches' (Groult 100: my translation). Stirring in the reader is compassion, for 'compassion involves dwelling imaginatively on the condition of the other' (Lawrence Blum in Robinson 110). From a philosophical perspective, it 'not only... tak[es up] the other person's viewpoint and...vision of the world, but also [means] care and concern for that person as a fellow human being... like oneself in important ways: she is part of my group,...sect or society or language group or ethnic group or gender or species. She is in some sense one of 'my own'... [and] related to me' (Robinson 110).

Prized for its capacity to engender empathic identification, literature has been enlisted in many campaigns. For instance, successfully reducing the number of excisions in Senegal, TOSTAN values 'singing, dancing, theatre, music and poetry' (Melching 157). Drama is also deployed in Nigeria, as we learn from playwright Chuck Mike's work with SISTERHELP, an affiliate of the Performance Studio Workshop. This Theatre-for-Development uses mime, song, dance, and drama to educate against the practice. Performed 'in open stage community environments such as rural dwellings, market places, motor parks and schools' (Zabus 258), Mike's two plays, *Oyela, the Drum that Beats a Change* (1995) and *The Tale of Ikpiko or Sense of Belonging* (2002) have taken the message to larger crowds. The 1995 script opens with a baby's genitalia at risk. In the knick of time, a relative intrudes, initiating dialogue on excision's pros and cons. The audience is left to authorise, or not, the razor's task.

Mike's *Ikpiko*, about the abuse intact girls suffer in western Nigeria, includes a stirring scene as well. In it, the actress re-enacts an initiate's agony so convincingly that viewers are 'visibly shaken,'[14] as are 'the foundations of [their] belief' in the cut (Zabus 259). In fact, 'Theatre-for-Development... is, because of its participatory and experiential [aspect], considered the only approach... capable of negotiating difficult, often taboo subjects in conservative communities' (Dr Aida Opoku-Mensah in Zabus 259). Indeed, 'Stella Omoregie got so 'involved' that she became a member of the acting crew and was so moved by the play and the young woman's plight that she renounced her trade' (Zabus 259).[15] Such conversions are not unique. In addition to Hawa Gréou's spectacular change of heart, *Dabla! Excision* (Pomerance) shows midwives in Mali giving up their tools, a strategy promoted by Sini Sanumen as well.

Music and drama as didactic media have also found a home in Germany. 'In the Shadow of Tradition, or, They do It Because It's Done,' a play designed for enlightenment campaigns in schools, was first performed on 12 December 2006 at the national INTEGRA conference against FGM[16] sponsored by the German Association for Development Cooperation (GTZ) in Berlin (Bundesministerium). Written by FORWARD – Germany's girls' group under the guidance of theatre coaches Hélène Ekwe and Aicha Bah, the musical realised multiple aims.

For one, since most performers had come from West Africa as young children or were born to immigrant parents in Germany, preparation for scripting permitted them to learn more about a custom of which they were ignorant, but could expect to confront in the media, in school, and, possibly, as victims. The spectacle, including drummers and a breathtaking break dancer, dramatises in a hypothetical African village pressure to conform, the first act ending with a piercing shriek as the struggling initiate is taken by force; it then debates the theme in a *gymnasium* class where the girls essay to both condemn the cut and affirm their pride.

It is precisely such enriching ambivalence that makes the Arts so valuable, with artistic expression finding enactment in numerous genres beyond the stage. Among admirable novels written for youth, Rita Williams-Garcia's *No Laughter Here* deserves mention in its realistic portrayal of friendship between an African American adolescent and her Nigerian counterpart, the latter experiencing a sea-change in personality after a summer's return to Lagos and a clitoridectomy.[17] At least one textbook used for basic literacy has also been enlisted – *Mon destin est entre les mains de mon père* [My Destiny is in My Father's Hands] by Khadidiatou Diallo. Comic books, too, have entered the fray, for instance Patrick Theunen and El Hadji Sidy Ndiaye's *Diariatou and the Tradition*, sponsored by the DAPHNE programme of the European Commission and available in Dutch, French, German and English. Why a comic strip? Administered following a documentary on FGM in schools, a questionnaire revealed that, for many pupils, the material was too complex. Livelier and 'better adapted to a young audience,' the illustrated takes Diariatou, a typical teen in Brussels preoccupied with chatting, music, and boys, to her parents' home in Dakar and to their village where, at the command of her grandmother, the youngster is overpowered, bound, and already spread-eagled on the ground with a knife at the ready when two heroes intervene. Oddly paired, one is great Aunt Naicy, who lost urinary control (via fistula), her only child, and her mind to excision. The other is Souleymane, Diariatou's cousin, who raps against the rite:

-Sis, don't count on the cops to fix
-Don't do like the other chicks …
-Excision for life is the pits
-Your brother says: Call it quits! (36)

Popular culture's promise further informs a commercial spot for cinema designed for Terre des Femmes by students in Munich's film school in 2000. It opens on a familiar apartment hallway where three little girls are playing ball. An older woman in Somali dress appears, carrying a satchel. Handing her an envelope, the father walks away leaving his wife standing at the threshold. She beckons to their child. But just as the beribboned youngster skips into view, a razor slashes through a candle flame recalling the mother's trauma. A touching moment ensues in which first a gentle caress on the little one's cheek and then a whisper in her ear release her, unscathed, to rejoin her waiting playmates. A decisive headshake sends the message. You can say 'No' (Die Geschichte...).

Bafing Kul, singing 'c'est pas bon' [Excision isn't good] agrees. The CD, 'Africa Paris,' was produced by CAMS, Commission pour l'Abolition des Mutilations Sexuelles, a venerable association founded in 1982 by Awa Thiam and presently run by Linda Weil-Curiel, the world's foremost attorney prosecuting cases of excision in the Ile de France. Prescient for her marriage of media and law, Linda has had 'Bafing tape a couple of [her] poems,' she told me after a reception at the House of Lords (9 October 2007) to launch FORWARD's prevalence study of FGM in England and Wales. 'But to press the CD,' Linda went on, 'we need funding.' Hopefully, this will be forthcoming as a growing number of rock and pop groups are including in their repertoires texts against FGM. 'An outspoken Somali woman singer-songwriter,' Maryam Mursal, for instance, 'performing her famous anti-FGM song...brought attendees [at a 2004 training session that FORWARD offered London Metropolitan Police] to their feet in appreciation and support... [She] uses her music to advocate against FGM' (FORWARD Annual Report 7). In Berlin, as well, on 10 October 2007, SISTER FA & Band rapped in the club 'Surprise,' their programme featuring two original selections explicitly denouncing FGM (AHOI). Berlin is likewise home to BENKADI, e.V. Kultur Raum Afrika, an NGO whose aims include sponsoring activist African musicians. The non-profit's motto – 'Culture is the key to development' – unlocks a promising philosophy that links advocacy to music, and Berlin performances have financed operations for women suffering from VVF (vesico-vaginal fistula) as a result of FGM (BENKADI homepage).

In Africa, pop stars from Mali's musical firmament have also appeared in CDs and DVDs in Bambara, Pulaar, Senouofo, Dogon and Sarakole. Engaged by Sini Sanuman, Adama Yalomba and others have recorded 7 tracks against FGM and produced a music video broadcast on Africable radio to ten African nations. According to *The Somerville Journal*, 'The musicians sing, 'If we have a daughter, we'll never excise her. It hurts!' (Horton).[18] 'Anciennes Exciseuses' —former excisers—concur. Though not an exciser herself, Ténin Bomboté wrote the lyrics to 'I Abandon,' recruited former cutters including Kaniba Kanté and Hawa Ballo, and, for Sini Sanuman, produced a music video in which 18 ex-excisers bury their blades and show their pride in turning to other income-generating tasks.[19] Some hold signs that read 'Je suis fière de ne plus exciser,' 'Disons Non à l'Excision' ('I've stopped and I'm proud' 'Say 'no' to FGM') ('Help Stop' [flyer]). That these developments on the music scene extend great promise can hardly be doubted: after all, Ousmane Sembène's masterpiece *Moolaadé*, in immolating women's radios, strongly suggests the media's revolutionary edge.

Poetry, another significant genre, carries the abolition message, too. One striking instance is Maryam Sheikh Abdi's 'The Cut,' a narrative free-verse that describes not only the butchery but also the aftermath when 'hot sand' is poured on the gash from which '[her] precious blood gushes ...and foams.' Drawn by the massacre, 'scavenger birds...circle and perch...on nearby trees' well before the *malmal*, a mixture of 'dried donkey waste and many herbs,' is applied to the wound. Then, following the pasting is the tying; 'strong ropes from camel hide' bind the limbs. Provided with 'long stick[s],' the 'new women' are shown 'how to walk, sit and stand.' They then 'slide' for three hours in the heat toward home where, for the next four weeks, they 'heal,' despite lice having infested the bonds and urine trickling 'bit by bit,...no washing, no drying,' but, instead, eternal flames.

The brutal brilliance of Abdi's concrete images offers an instructive contrast to other symbols, vivid and moving but equivocal. I'm referring to painting and sculpture deployed in anti-FGM campaigns. One European effort from 2005 is 'Scarred by Tradition. Art against FGM' ('Female...'), a co-operative endeavour involving the European Parliament, the German 'Illustrators Organisation e.V.' and the Fulda-Mosocho-Project among the Kisii in Kenya.

9

An earlier, African venture, 'Through the Eyes of Nigerian Artists,' is a travelling exhibition conceived in Lagos in 1998 by advertising executive Joy Keshi Walker. The display remains unique in linking activism to water-colours, stone and oils. First circulated in Nigeria, the canvases communicate to both literate and illiterate the hardship attendant on genital attack, eluding ethnic guardedness by avoiding words. The artwork implicates; it does not alienate. And art ennobles. The exhibit is about FGM, to be sure, but also about artists, dignity, and a life free from harm.

Its history is instructive as well. After Nigeria, the paintings travelled to the Women in Africa and the African Diaspora (WAAD) conference at the University of Indiana. From there they re-crossed the Atlantic where, for six years (4 February 2000–26 February 2006), FORWARD-Germany placed the exhibit in more than 70 venues, including all major urban centres. The tour's highpoint, on November 22, 2000, was Westminster as Parliament celebrated a multi-partisan report leading to the UK Female Genital Mutilation Act of 2003. Continuing to raise awareness, the paintings moved on to the United States where they have been seen at Brandeis University, Harvard University (on 9 February 2007 in the Faculty Club), Cornell University, Bucknell University, SUNY – Fredonia, Bridgewater State College and Monmouth University.

In Europe, because NGOs continue to request the works, FORWARD – Germany approached artist Godfrey Williams-Okorodus. Would he ask his colleagues to return to their easels? A stunning new exhibit opened on 13 July 2008 in Ghent, Belgium; spent a day at the University of Frankfurt (18 August 2008) and has been displayed in Italy from November 2008 through February 2009. It differs from the first collection primarily in that now more women artists are exhibiting. (A catalogue, *Vrouwen, een Leven vol Pijn*, [Women: Lives of Pain] is available from the Forum van Vlaamse Vrouwen [Flemish Women's Forum].)

You may be surprised to learn that 80 per cent of works in the first exhibition were by men. 'It has been said again and again, the practice would cease within a generation if only men would announce their [acceptance of] uncut wives' (Afele 34). Are they increasingly willing to do this?

Creative writers, many of whom are discussed in the following pages, hold out hope. Like Ousmane Sembène, an impressive number of African male authors, intellectuals and public personalities have taken unequivocal stands for abolition. These comprise creative writers such as Ahmadou Kourouma (Ivorian), Annor Nimako (Ghanaian), Osman Conteh (Sierra Leonean), Nuruddin Farah (Somali), as well as social scientists and university dons including G.K. Nukunya (Ghanaian), Christopher Ukhun (Nigerian), and Isaac Olawole Albert (Nigerian).

Should ambivalence emerge, seemingly hesitant positions often derive from the very 'indeterminacy of art.' What Stephen Bishop calls 'oppositional' is a literary means of criticising FGM avoiding insult or anger because it is in tune with African values and traditions. Specifically, several authors who eschew direct, overt condemnation of the practice, probably fearing it as counterproductive, rely instead on incongruous stories including voices both for and against. Readers decide.

Looking more broadly at 'ambivalence, indictment and commitment' in creative writing about FGM, Augustine H. Asaah provides a helpful overview specifically attuned to authorial positionalities. After outing an equivocal early Ngugi (whose personal opposition is now forthright), Asaah also enlists Kourouma, Beyala, Barry, Nimako, Conteh and others whose outrage is clear and engagement strong. For these authors, FGM is a brutal violation of fundamental human rights and, as such, is not a private matter. In 'Community versus Individual Rights in Africa: A Viewpoint,' Rebecca Ganusah argues that cultural practices such as FGM are antithetical to dignity (18). 'Human rights issues,' she concludes, 'are ...of universal concern, as they transcend regional or personal idiosyncrasies' (19). In much the same way as Darfur, Ebola fever and Burulli ulcer are not African problems but belong to the world, so, too, does FGM. As Ngugi observes:

> In a situation of flux, our effective use of the delicate skills of navigation may well depend on whether we are swimming against or with the currents of change, or for that matter whether we are clear in what direction we are swimming – toward or away from the sea of... connection [to] humanity. Local knowledge is not an island [but] part of the main, part of the sea. (Responses 152)

For Ngugi, our 'creative potentiality as human beings' flows out to a 'boundless universal,' (152) a breadth of creativity captured in Elisabeth Beker's approach to excision. In the authors she reviews, genital assault, rarely a subject in its own right, has been enlisted to explore broader socio-cultural issues, such as colonisation, national repression, misogyny, feminism, or 'w/human's rights.' Whereas the earliest work, Bekers finds, focuses on clitoridectomy and infibulation in colonial conflicts, from the 1970s and 1980s onwards authors scrutinise with a far more critical eye the surgical procedure, the excised woman's suffering, and in particular the gender structures upheld by the rite.

A similar focus on gendered power lies at the heart of 'an activist's ... bibliographical excursion.' Pierrette Herzberger-Fofana interrogates explicit stances taken by African creative writers within the context of campaigns. How has their opposition been received? Surveying fiction and memoir mainly by cultural insiders who challenge the right to the rite, Herzberger-Fofana moves from acquiescence in Flora Nwapa and ambiguity in Ngugi to the direct opposition of authors like Alice Walker, Waris Dirie, Fatou Keita, and Khady, for whom the amputation of the clitoris or stitching of the vulva has no place in 21st century life. As Beninois Jean Pliya frames it, 'Construction of a modern nation demands the destruction of certain relics from the past. ... We must dare to shout 'STOP' (3).

Indeed, the decibel level is high in Annor Nimako's *Mutilated*, a novel approved by the Ghana Education Service as an optional literary work for secondary schools. Because of its awareness-raising promise, the Ministry of Women's Affairs and the Ghana National Commission on Children chose to distribute it for classroom use in regions where FGM is practised. Anne Adams offers an incisive analysis of the narrative's strong and weak points. A superb representation of the custom's health dangers, its threat to dignity, and its devastating effects on female sexuality, the novel accounts less well in revealing complex emotional attachments to the rite emerging from the dynamics of gender and ethnicity.

Also an emotional investment, critiques of Alice Walker emanating from the Diaspora community in the USA are analysed by Tameka Cage. Suggesting that the Georgian's genre has been misunderstood, Cage looks at Walker's 'Diasporic dreams' and uses her 'sisterhood' as a lens to address crucial issues of race, 'place,' and trauma that emerge from *Warrior Marks*. Read as Walker's attempt to heal and bring together the African and African American communities, the documentary identifies Walker's return to the coast of Senegal as a 'homegoing,' undertaken to 'remember the ancestors' and lay the narrative of enslaved Africans beside and within that of 'circumcised' women – clearly an African American mission.

Cage's ocean crossing continues in Tobe Levin's look at a 'wandering' Jew, whose trajectory pulls her from eastern Africa all the way to San Francisco. In *Bailey's Café* (1992), Gloria Naylor presents the young Ethiopian, Mariam, whose excruciating ordeal, infibulation, is mimed in the evisceration of a plum, the gesture's brutality clearly revealing the author's censure. Nonetheless, Naylor's decision to make her infibulated heroine Jewish is troubling: the character's ethnicity may have been a bad aesthetic choice. While it is true that Ethiopian Jews' scarred labia have been found during gynaecological exams in Israel, the custom never entered liturgy. Performed on women *despite* their faith, Naylor's implication that Jews, too, do it demands to be interrogated for the motive of the author. Why did she make this unusual move?

Another atypical voice on this theme, Audre Lorde is better known for celebrating the lesbian erotic than for mourning its erasure. Nonetheless, Jennifer Browdy de Hernandez rosters her into the pantheon of opposition using ''mother' as a verb.' For Lorde, sex broadly understood is a fountain of self-love and empowerment. Dam(n)ing that pleasurable stream, as clitoridectomy and infibulation do, denies women an important reservoir of confidence and can lead to self-destruction. Grave as these consequences are, however, extrapolating from Lorde's work suggests that, unlike Walker, she would not endorse even the symbolic murder of the mother-surrogate, as an effective campaign-mobilising tool. Quite the contrary: elevating the maternal, Lorde makes it sexy, names its rebellious potential, and broadens its scope. In her *oeuvre*, women mother not only children but also each other and themselves.[20] Precisely because an 'erotic mother' is, both North and South, an oxymoron, deployed in its challenging impossibility, it exhorts its audience to think and perhaps to change.

Thought unchanging by male anthropologists most often given to studying her, the Somali woman in Marianne Sarkis' hands exhibits unexpected flexibility despite traditions that deny her individuality. Supposedly a pawn exchanged between clans to further parental economic interests, she finds her sexuality excised and her activities circumscribed by codes of honour and shame. Because infibulation ensures 'chastity' and marital suitability, the surgery inducts her into the responsibilities of women to their husbands, children, and extended kin; and because women's bodies have been thus literally inscribed with social values, rejection of FGM becomes akin to dismissal of the core ideals of 'womanhood.' Three Somali-born authors, Ayaan Hirsi Ali, Waris Dirie and Fadumo Korn, contradict these conservative views denying women's agency.

Agency of a different sort emerges from Muthoni Mathai's memoir asking, 'Who's Afraid of Female Sexuality?' Despite a downward trend in clitoridectomy over the last generation, many Kikuyu today, women and men, continue to see FGM as a patriotic duty. '... it's the likes of you who abandon tradition that have weakened the Kikuyu people,' Mathai remembers being told as a child and could as easily hear today. Uncircumcised women are thought to lack docility, challenge male dominance, weaken the collective, and undermine the state. They also spread AIDS. Clitoridectomy, therefore, should revive, as even the author's male friends suggest. What is to be done?

Nura Abdi has part of the answer: face the issue. In her chapter 'I Was Bravest,' set immediately after a brutal collective cutting, sewing, and disposing of severed genitals, Abdi writes: 'To this very day I can recall my father's face [as] the door opened and he stepped inside. That is, he stood on the threshold and peered at us girls on the floor. I can still see the look in his eyes. He was close to tears and words stuck in his throat. Saying nothing, he quickly turned around and closed the door.'

Abdi's father shows empathy. She expresses rage. Together, the emotions remind me of pot-banging mourners after the murder of Theo van Gogh at Dam Square. As actress Nazmiye Oral told the crowd: "We came to make noise from the heart. If we can touch each others' hearts, then there is hope" (Sellar).

EMPATHIZERS

Elisabeth Bekers

From Women's Rite to Human Rights Issue: Literary Explorations of Female Genital Excision since 'Facing Mount Kenya' (1938)

'Cette pratique [de l'excision] n'est véritablement traitée en tant que telle.'

Awa Thiam

Heavily debated for decades, female genital excision, or female genital mutilation (FGM) as activists call it,[1] has, not surprisingly, also found its way into literature.[2] The best-known literary exploration of the topic is undoubtedly Alice Walker's *Possessing the Secret of Joy*. The novel offers a bitter critique of the practice by unfolding an African woman's life-long struggle to deal with the traumas she has suffered as a result of her infibulation.

Although the media-hype around *Possessing the Secret of Joy* suggested otherwise,[3] Walker was neither the only nor the first literary author to take up the subject. The very same year fellow African American Gloria Naylor published her novel *Bailey's Cafe*, also starring a traumatised infibulated girl. Though Walker and Naylor could hardly be accused of choosing an everyday topic, and criticism of the representation of female genital excision in literature was virtually non-existent,[4] literary interest in the practice was not a new phenomenon. In fact, female genital excision has been quite persistently addressed by creative writers, especially by authors of African descent, ever since Jomo Kenyatta addressed the subject in his ethnographic study of the Gikuyu, *Facing Mount Kenya*.[5]

The body of fiction, poetry and drama dealing with female genital excision available today is written in various languages, almost exclusively by men and women from the African continent and Diaspora.[6] It reflects the immense religious, geographic, and linguistic diversity of practicing ethnic groups[7] as well as some of the political and literary-historical

15

developments in Africa and its Diaspora in the last four decades of the twentieth century. While (written) African literatures in Europhone languages consolidate their stake in world literature, the period witnesses independence arising from the anti-colonial struggle, subsequent disenchantment with the new African states, increasing prominence of African women, their experiences both in- and outside literature, and the rise of African authors in Diaspora. Authors writing on excision and infibulation have also communicated what Ngugi wa Thiong'o calls the 'moving spirit' of their respective eras (qtd. in Thiam 68), for they rarely treat the subject 'en tant que telle [as such]' (Thiam 63). Whether it appears as a key motif or even the central theme in their works, some autobiographically-inspired, the authors generally use female genital excision to explore broader socio-cultural issues, such as colonisation, national repression, misogyny, feminism, or w/human rights. This chapter sketches the development of creative writing on female genital excision from 1938 to the present, focusing on the discursive and narrative strategies employed over the years. Notwithstanding authors' diverse temporal, geographical and social backgrounds and various genres, some diachronic trends can be observed.

In his 1938 monograph on Gikuyu culture, Kenyatta, freedom fighter and later President of Kenya, defended clitoridectomy as 'the very essence' of female initiation and 'a deciding factor in giving...a girl the status of ... womanhood in the Gikuyu community' (128). No Gikuyu worthy of the name, he insisted, would dream of marrying an uncircumcised woman as she would not be regarded as mature.[8] With his positive appraisal of excision as an indispensable female rite of passage, Kenyatta challenged the British ban on the practice that had lead to the eruption of bitter conflict over the issue in colonial Kenya around 1930.[9] A first literary response to Kenyatta's ethnographic account of excision appeared barely a year later in *Red Strangers* (1939) by the British settlers' daughter Elspeth Huxley. An example of the socio-anthropological novels about native East Africans that were popular in Britain in the 1920s and 1930s (Tucker 148–149); Huxley's fictional portrait of the Gikuyu considers not only the historical crisis over female genital excision but also the procedure itself. Notwithstanding her self-professed sympathetic standpoint vis-à-vis Gikuyu culture in the introduction, her literary appraisal of the gender ritual is far less positive than Kenyatta's.

Huxley's novel fails, however, to convey the significance of excision to the Gikuyu community that is so central in Kenyatta's account. His attention to the ceremonial framework pointing to the rite's socio-cultural meaning is in *Red Strangers* replaced with crude descriptions of the operative procedure, which bears resemblance to the slaughtering of an animal ('pinned down,' 'slashes,' 'convulsive shiver,' 'blood spurted' [Huxley 108–109]). Furthermore, Kenyatta's neutrally-phrased and minimalist cutting of the 'tip of the clitoris' (140) has in *Red Strangers* become an amputation involving the complete excision of the clitoris and the labia minora (108). Not surprisingly then, the focal point of Huxley's discussion of the ritual is not the exciser and her skill – in *Facing Mount Kenya* she is said to operate with 'the dexterity of a Harley Street surgeon' (Kenyatta 140) – but rather the female initiates and their extreme physical suffering, the 'pain that seared their nerves' (Huxley 108). By solving the conflict over female genital excision with the sudden conversion of all villagers to Christianity in a closing scene that is much more farcical than dramatic, *Red Strangers'* author presents the Gikuyu as a fickle and laughable people defending their native culture on a whim rather than an oppressed community standing up for the survival of their ethnic identity. Instead of offering a 'compassionate picture of the problems which have beset the African as a result of the Christian and Western invasion of his land,' as Martin Tucker contends in his review of the novel (149), in her portrait of female genital excision Huxley leans towards a perspective typical of colonial anti-excision campaigners.

POSTCOLONIAL CRITIQUES OF COLONISATION AND HESITANT GENDER CRITICISM IN EARLY AFRICAN LITERARY 'CIRCUM-SCRIPTIONS' OF FEMALE GENITAL EXCISION

A much more complex portrait of Gikuyu's colonial predicament is presented in three early postcolonial Kenyan novels: *The River Between* by Ngugi wa Thiong'o, *Daughter of Mumbi* by Charity Waciuma, and *They Shall Be Chastised* by Muthoni Likimani. Writing in the years shortly after and before Kenya's independence in 1963, Ngugi and his female colleagues use the practice of female genital excision to demonstrate the destructive effect of colonisation and evangelisation among their people and replace Huxley's superficial tug-of-war with 'strangers' with a highly unsettling internal struggle. In each of the Kenyan novels a colonised, rural Gikuyu community stands divided over the ritual: while the converts adopt the missionaries' negative reconstructions of excision as a savage and totally unchristian practice, the conservative villagers strongly defend its traditional gender significance as a female rite-of-passage. Ngugi even integrates this discord into his novel's structure by unfolding the clash between two neighbouring Gikuyu villages, appropriately located on opposite ridges. To *The River Between*'s traditionalists, unexcised girls are not just immature but also 'dirty and impure' and a major threat to the traditional identity and unity of the Gikuyu: 'That way, lay disintegration' (Ngugi 121; 141). Following the example of the British missionaries, the Christianised villagers, however, regard excised girls and their families as stuck in 'the dirty mud of sin' (Ngugi 32), thus offsetting the traditional Gikuyu definition of ethnic purity. Ngugi, but also Waciuma and Likimani, reveal that, as a result of this discursive conflict, the gender ritual is given a 'new [ethnic] significance' (Ngugi 31) and reinterpreted as a means to construct and uphold the traditional Gikuyu identity or to prove (by rejecting it) one's conversion to Christianity.

In the colonised communities of *The River Between, Daughter of Mumbi* and *They Shall Be Chastised*, a woman's (un)excised body is consequently no longer simply read as a gender script testifying to her maturity or immaturity, but as a political pamphlet of ethnicity, signalling the woman's (and by implication her relatives') allegiance to either the traditional Gikuyu ways or the mores and convictions recently introduced by the colonisers. Waciuma shows in her autobiographically-inspired novel *Daughter of Mumbi* how such a reading is literally performed at the mission school in the shape of a thorough medical examination, on the basis of which the wholly Christianised girls – the 'really serious Christians' as they are called at the mission school in *They Shall Be Chastised* (Likimani 179) – are set apart from the half-hearted converts. These 'circumcised [pupils] were segregated from the rest' and 'spent their three years at school in half-seclusion, where their lives were made a misery' (Waciuma 83). This reverses the situation in the village, where unexcised girls are made the laughingstock, as Waciuma's first-person narrator herself experiences. Whereas in the precolonial past the reading of African women's bodies had been indisputable to all members of the community, the three authors demonstrate that in the colonial era the interpretation and subsequent categorisation have come to depend on the interpreter's point of view.

Noteworthy is the fact that none of the three Kenyan novelists endorses British imperialist constructions of the practice as barbaric and evil. Ngugi refuses to openly take sides in the ethnic tragedy he presents in *The River Between*. Rather than conclude with a facile restoration of peace as Shakespeare does in *Romeo and Juliet*, he shows in his postcolonial translation of the Elizabethan play that a reunion of the feuding parties is less easily achieved in a historical colonial community divided by irreconcilable cultural ideas. By emphasising in his adaptation the practically irreparable 'disintegration' of Gikuyu unity, Ngugi effectively questions Shakespeare's claim at the end of his play that 'never was a story of more woe/ Than this of Juliet and her Romeo' (Bekers 308–309).[10] In Waciuma's *Daughter of Mumbi*, the first-person narrator uses the crisis over female genital excision to construct an anti-imperialist plea for her people's right to self-determination – even if she does not see excision as a prerequisite for either woman's traditional gender identity or ethnic loyalty. Although unexcised herself, she understands that, because of the ethnic significance of female genital excision in the colonial conflict, the missionaries' ban, rather than put an end to the practice, 'actually increased the people's attachment to their old customs' (Waciuma 95). A far more pronounced anti-colonial and pro-traditional standpoint is adopted by Likimani, who resolutely sides with her traditionalist characters in the various conflicts that arise over the practice in *They Shall Be Chastised* and ends the novel with an emphatically positive appraisal of tradition. The black mission school teacher Mr. Obadiah rebukes his white colleagues for failing to understand the effect of the excision ban on their pupils, 'the humiliation which the uncircumcised girls had to suffer [...] completely ostracised from their age group' (Likimani 231). He also introduces excision ceremony dances into the school curriculum and, with this triumphant defence of his people's traditions, effectively shocks Reverend Smith and Miss Green into silence in the novel's last line.

While Ngugi, Waciuma and Likimani present female genital excision as a highly problematic issue in colonial Kenya, they are careful not to undermine the practice itself. Unlike Huxley, they avoid describing the physical operation, the most heavily targeted aspect, and refrain from fictionalising, as Huxley does, extreme events such as the excision and murder of the white missionary by the Gikuyu resistance.[11] Characters who undergo the rite in *The River Between*, *Daughter of Mumbi*, and *They Shall Be Chastised* are not traumatised by it, unlike Walker's and Naylor's infibulated protagonists, and in contrast to many women in later works, they submit to it voluntarily. Even though Ngugi and Likimani readily expose the ambivalence of mission-trained male protagonists towards their own circumcisions, female converts are not allowed to voice any doubts concerning their excision. Ngugi's Muthoni, for instance, is determined to go through with the rite, despite her Christian upbringing: 'No one will understand. I say I am a Christian. ... I have not run away from that. But I also want to be initiated into the ways of the tribe' (Ngugi 43). Like Waiyaki, *The River Between*'s male protagonist, Muthoni has grown up in a culturally hybrid environment, but, unlike him, she does not experience this as confusing and simply wishes to fulfil both aspects of her composite identity. She is far from 'torn by inevitable circumstances between two diametrically opposed religions' as Charles Nama suggests (141), but eager to embrace both. Even Muthoni's fatal excision does not serve to bring the practice into disrepute, but is integrated into Ngugi's critique of the colonial interference in Kenya, as Muthoni's death widens the rift in her community.

The three Kenyan writers clearly give priority to their denunciation of the colonisers' interference in the indigenous culture and take care not to jeopardise their literary contributions to the decoloniation process with too violent a portrayal of the Gikuyu resistance, or too critical an analysis of gender roles traditionally constructed by means of excision. The latter are explored in two contemporary texts, both written by women: Rebeka Njau's play *The Scar*,[12] the first African literary text to deal with female genital excision, and Flora Nwapa's literary debut *Efuru*, the first exclusively women-centred African novel. Even if *The River Between*, *Daughter of Mumbi* and *They Shall Be Chastised* already pay more than usual attention to African women than do most contemporary works, in *Efuru* and *The Scar* the colonial conflict recedes completely into the background and the situation of women in traditional, rural communities becomes the focal point. Although the Nigerian Nwapa and the Kenyan Njau both show dissatisfaction with their societies' traditional gender requirements and even provide women with an alternative female identity – Nwapa's Efuru becomes a revered worshipper of a local goddess and Njau's Mariana establishes herself as a feminist woman leader – neither author directly attacks female genital excision. Nevertheless, the authors' discomfort with the practice is detectable in the narrative and discursive manner in which they approach it.

Nwapa avoids all analytical commentary and allows inconsistencies to arise in her literary exploration of Efuru's genital operation. Like the Kenyan novelists, she prefers not to focus on the ritual's heavily targeted physical aspect and never reveals what 'painful' procedure her protagonist's 'bath' actually involves (Nwapa 12). Instead, she calls attention to the traditional cleansing purpose of the practice through her terminology[13] and highlights the festive character the ritual has in Efuru's community. Newly excised women are pampered, and so too is Efuru, who is said to be 'feasting' (15). Although the novel's tightly knit rural female community accepts female genital excision as a prerequisite for womanhood, Nwapa's otherwise headstrong and exceptional protagonist is unusually conformist when it comes to the excision rite. Efuru – nor any other character or the narrator for that matter – does not even question the rationale of the ritual's existence when her 'bath' fails to offer the post-natal protection it promises for mother and child: Efuru's infant dies while Efuru is never granted another chance at experiencing 'the joy of motherhood' that is so highly valued in her society (221). In *Efuru* female genital excision is presented as problematical only in a round-about way, so that Nwapa clearly falls into the first category that Lloyd Brown distinguishes in his seminal study of African literature by women: '[their gender criticism] ranges from indirect statements of some writers to the direct protests of others' (13).

A more openly feminist critique of the traditional construction of female genital excision appears in *The Scar*, in which Mariana's anti-excision activism motivates her entry into the struggle for female emancipation. Still, even Njau's woman leader rhetorically constructs her rejection of female genital excision without denouncing the practice in itself. Having declared 'obsolete' the 'old' gender codes that were constructed by means of excision, Mariana simply argues that the custom has lost its purpose and become a mere 'physical operation' without any meaning (Njau 14). The 'new' gender training that she proposes has to be acquired through other means than the now 'empty' excision ritual; it requires a 'different initiation' (14). Notwithstanding the brave stance the woman leader adopts in the course of the play, in the closing lines Njau forces her main character to withdraw from her feminist campaign, so that Mariana falls short of booking the kind of victory that some of the protagonists in later works are granted.

Whether they offer a postcolonial critique of colonisation by exploring the politicisation of the female initiation rite in the (anti) colonial conflict (Ngugi, Waciuma and Likimani) or formulate, with relative circum-spection, a feminist appraisal of female gender roles traditionally constructed by female genital excision (Nwapa and Njau), these early authors remain aware of their roles as cultural ambassadors in the sensitive context of decolonisation. They carefully steer away from too negative an appraisal of their people's traditions and literally write around the more controversial aspects of the practice in their early literary 'circum-scriptions' of female genital excision.

GROWING DISSATISFACTION WITH AFRICAN WOMEN'S MUTE/ILATED PREDICAMENT AFTER INDEPENDENCE IN FEMINIST DISENCHANTMENT NOVELS

The authors who write about female genital excision in the 1970s and 1980s scrutinise with a far more critical eye the operative procedure, the victims' suffering, and in particular the gender structures upheld by the practice, and therefore even more clearly belong to Brown's second category of 'direct' gender critics than Njau does. In contrast to their predecessors, they explore the situation of African women in post-independent, mostly urban environments rather than in colonised, rural ones. However, they unanimously repeal the discursive contrast Njau constructs in *The Scar* between tradition and modernity and show how the advent of independence does not put an end to the patriarchal oppression of their female characters, whose ethnic and social backgrounds nevertheless greatly vary – as do the authors', who hail from the Western Sub-Sahara, the Mashriq and the Horn of Africa. In fact, the second generation of African writers who take up the subject demonstrate that the gender predicaments of the last pre-independent generation of women and their post-independent offspring do not differ all that much, as for example the Senegalese author Aminata Maïga Ka shows in her novella *La voie du salut* (1985). Her young protagonist Rabiatou may escape excision as a result of her family's move to the city after independence and enjoy a relatively free upbringing and financially-independent life, yet her marital relationship turns out to bear remarkable similarities to her highly conformist mother's.

Writing against the background of the United Nations International Women's Decade (1975–1985), which encouraged world-wide discussion of women's issues including female genital excision and publication of feminist explorations of the practice,[14] African authors of the 1970s and 1980s adopted an unambiguous, feminist perspective towards the surgery and its gender implications. In sharp contrast with Kenyatta, they construct the practice as a lasting corporeal and psychological mutilation. Tanga in *Tu t'appelleras Tanga* by the Cameroonian Calixthe Beyala no longer refers to the tradition as a necessary purification (Nwapa's 'bath') but speaks grievously of 'l'entaille sanglante de l'enfance mutilée [the bloody slashing of a mutilated childhood]' performed by 'l'arracheuse de clitoris (Beyala 1996a, 20) [the clitoris snatcher]' (Beyala 1996b, 12). In *Sardines*, by the male Somali author Nuruddin Farah, an embittered Medina informs the reader how in Somalia, if you happen to be born a woman, 'they mutilate you [infibulate, i.e. excise and suture your genitalia] at eight or nine [and] open you up with a rusty knife the night they marry you off' (58). This is as true for the unschooled nomad girl Ebla in Farah's debut novel *From a Crooked Rib* as for the sophisticated and Western-educated Medina in his later novel. In fact, Farah, Beyala and their contemporaries present the life-stories of their female protagonists as endless concatenations of physical and psychological pain, in which the blade or the bleeding wound appear as harrowing motifs illustrating the women's deep trauma. Salimata in *Les soleils des indépendances* by the male Ivorian writer Ahmadou Kourouma persistently relives the nightmare, which literally stains red the memories of her village youth, 'le vert de la forêt puis le jaune de l'harmattan et enfin rouge, le rouge du sang, des sacrifices (Kourouma 1970, 31) [the green of the forest, the yellow of the Harmattan, then red, blood-red, the red of sacrifice]' (Kourouma 1981, 20). 'I fear the descending knives which re-trace the scarred wound, and it hurts every instant I think about it,' Medina likewise admits, and goes on to explain that infibulated women have to deal not only with the haunting memory of their genital operations but also with its actual recurrence. To them, 'life is [...] a series of de-flowering pains, delivery pains and re-stitching pains' (Farah 58), as they are re-infibulated after each birth.[15]

To emphasise women's suffering, the second generation writers aggravate their protagonists' excision or infibulation traumas by also burdening them with psychological disturbance resulting from more readily recognised acts of phallocratic violence, such as forceful defloration and rape. In *Les soleils des indépendances* flashbacks to Salimata's excision continue to interrupt her description of a day in her life, a day marked by grief over her inability to conceive and the attempted rape assault by the marabout she consults to remedy her infertility. Nawal El Saadawi also underscores the ceaselessness of women's pain in *The Circling Song*. In this novel the perpetual suffering of Hamida, who is excised and repeatedly violated in the course of her young life, is not just symbolised by the tragic fate of her namesake in the children's circling song referred to in the narrative frame and title. The vicious circle of pain in which the female protagonist is caught is also rendered visible in the repetitive style and circular structure of the narrative, of which 'the beginning and the end are joined together in a single, looping strand' (8; 84), as the narrator notes at the novel's opening and close.

The female gender identity constructed via the blade is by all authors of this generation dismissed as utterly repressive, but nowhere is the imagery as poignant as in *The Circling Song*. El Saadawi creates an aura of death around the recently excised Hamida, who is lying 'on the cement floor, surrounded by four cement walls, her arms and legs rigid and bound together into a single bundle.' The girl's surroundings are reminiscent of a tomb, while her restricted movements closely resemble those of a prisoner or a living mummy. Significant in this regard is also 'the iron padlock of a hard metal belt' that the narrator visualises between Hamida's legs and his/her parenthetical addition: '(This has entered history as the chastity belt.)' (67).[16] Excision here unmistakably appears as an instrument in the patriarchal repression of women, a mechanism designed to confine female sexuality within the frame of (legitimate) reproduction. Looking back on her own excision, the schooled Liberian protagonist Martha in *Renaître a Dendé* by Roger Dorsinville (Haitian-born but at the time of writing the novel resident in Africa) refers to the gender training she received in her mother's home village as an 'endoctrinement [indoctrination]' designed to transform her into a 'femme sans désir, et fidèle [woman without desire, and loyal]' (18–19, my translation). By further comparing the genital operation to the butchering of animals, El Saadawi and her contemporaries dismiss the custom as utterly dehumanising. In 'Who Will Be the Man?' by El Saadawi's fellow countrywoman Alifa Rifaat, the excised Bahiya recalls how her terrified screams resembled 'the shrieks of a slaughtered baby rabbit' (75), while in *The Circling Song* Hamida sees her own fear of the razor mirrored in the eyes of a sacrificial ewe. In a rather enigmatic passage two scenes are blurred, the killing of the female sheep and Hamida's clitoridectomy, and the pronoun 'she' that initially referred to the ewe also comes to indicate the young girl, 'her wide black eyes open in terror' at the sight of the approaching knife (46–47). This continued connection between female genital excision and women's subjugated status in the post-independent era – or as it is said in *Sardines*, the perpetuation of 'a tradition where women were commodities, bought and sold, and were sexually mutilated [and] synonymous with subjugation and oppression' (58) – is exposed in all second-generation texts.

Elaine Scarry's scepticism regarding the expressibility of pain notwithstanding, the authors writing on female genital excision from the 1970s onwards are surprisingly successful in rendering their protagonists' subjective experience of agony, even when they are literally silenced during the procedure. Nevertheless, victims in works by the second generation do not always denounce it as an act of patriarchal violence. In fact, the protagonists of *Les soleils des indépendances*, *From a Crooked Rib*, *The Circling Song* and *La voie du salut* either acquiesce in their lot or are completely disabled by their grief. Since in these novels the most tragic fate is bestowed on the most liberated protagonist – Ka's unexcised and independent Rabiatou ends up committing suicide – the authors use their narratives primarily to demonstrate that for their heroines there is no (permanent) liberation from the shackles of tradition. In short, the life histories presented here by Kourouma, Farah, El Saadawi and Ka are all tragically failed *Bildung* tales.

More encouraging are contemporary narratives in which female protag-onists, like the earlier-cited Medina and Tanga, openly dismiss female genital excision as a misogynist strategy of repression. Building upon initiatives in *Efuru* and *The Scar*, these characters, moreover, actively seek to improve their own and other women's situation. In *Sardines* Farah's Medina stands up to her traditional mother-in-law and leaves her home to prevent her daughter's infibulation, while the protagonist of Beyala's *Tu t'appelleras Tanga* refuses to prostitute herself any longer or to 'alimenter les statistiques [feed the statistics]' with another hungry child forced to loiter in the slums (Beyala 1996a: 166; Beyala 1996b: 120). While Tanga constructs a new identity for herself by adopting a street child and joining a group of counterfeiters, Bahiah in El Saadawi's *Two Women in One* resolutely opts for her 'stronger' self, a much more confident and independent female identity than the 'obedient and well-behaved' one prescribed by her patriarchal society (57). As a result, she is hardly recognised as a woman: 'Had it not been for the two small breasts showing through the blouse, they would have sworn she was a man,' the narrator explains (120). Similarly, Firdaus in El Saadawi's best-known novel *Woman at Point Zero* surprises her male aggressor by stabbing him to death, an unexpected reaction in a society in which women are forced into passivity. Her mutilating assault on his body is reminiscent of her own excision, the repeated thrusts of her knife mimicking the countless unwanted penetrations she has suffered in her life: 'I raised the knife and buried it deep in his neck, pulled it out of his neck and then thrust it deep into his chest, pulled it out and plunged it deep into his belly. I stuck the knife into almost every part of his body' (95).

Rifaat's young protagonist as well, in 'Who Will Be the Man?' learns that subjugation is what womanhood holds in store for her when she is brutally abducted from her bed to be excised one morning and later that same day is raped by an unidentified midnight intruder. Though still a child, she confronts her relatives with protestations no less piercing than those uttered by the old woman in another short-story by Rifaat. The protagonist of 'Bahiyya's Eyes' refuses to regard her waning eye-sight as a medical condition but blames it on the tears she has shed as a result of her womanhood, on her unhappiness over her arranged marriage and her bitterness over the excision she unequivocally labels 'a wrong that could never be undone' (9). In Rifaat's stories the women may not respond as drastically as Firdaus does in *Woman at Point Zero*, but they do leave their family and the reader little doubt about their utter dissatisfaction with their female lot.

The agency attributed to women in some of the second generation's works – in 'Bahiyya's Eyes,' 'Who Will Be the Man?' *Tu t'appelleras Tanga* and *Woman at Point Zero* – is also reflected in the narrative structure. In these texts the women take control of their lives by becoming the captivating first-person narrators of their own life histories. More than simply asserting their identity through communication, they explicitly enlist their fictional and real audiences to join in protest against women's repression and female genital excision, and this from within the confinement of their prison cells or their own homes. Especially in *Tu t'appelleras Tanga* and *Woman at Point Zero* the connection between the imprisoned protagonist and the woman to whom she communicates her story surpasses an ordinary interactive link between (an active) narrator and (a passive) listener.[17] In fact, Tanga's and Beyala's acts of narration become a stark mode of survival and forceful acts of rebellion when Tanga's fellow inmate Anne-Claude and Beyala's unnamed psychiatrist become important 'mediator[s] of discourse' (Malti-Douglas 131). While Firdaus's words continue to resound in the doctor's head after the latter has left the prison and the former has been put to death, Tanga's story even becomes her listener's own when the dying Tanga commands Anne-Claude to take on her identity, an instruction repeated in the novel's title, and to spread her story for the benefit of other women. In the course of the 1970s and 1980s the authors dealing with female genital excision gradually come to illustrate the view of Floya Anthias and Nira Yuval-Davis in *Woman-Nation-State* that women need not limit themselves to reproducing the gender roles imposed on them by society, but can actually take part in modifying them, discursively and practically. Their mut(ilat)ed protagonists adopt an increasingly defiant attitude, as a result of which, like El Saadawi's Firdaus and Beyala's Tanga, they are labelled 'savage and dangerous' (Saadawi 1983: 100) and regarded as 'élément[s] subversive[s] et incontrollable[s] [subversive and uncontrollable element[s]' (Beyala 12) in their urban, post-independent communities.

In various second-generation works, the female protagonists' rebellion is targeted against society's patriarchal gender structures as well as against reactionary national politics.[18] In fact, in one way or another, all the authors of this generation integrate their literary explorations of female genital excision into a larger debate on the condition of African women after independence. With this marked gender interest, the authors present a feminist critique of the male bias displayed in the so-called disenchantment novels (e.g. Chinua Achebe's *A Man of the People* and Ayi Kwei Armah's *The Beautyful [sic] Ones Are Not Yet Born.*) They demonstrate in their works the inextricability of gender and national oppression, by showing that not only are the repressive strategies remarkably similar, but also strategies of resistance against patriarchy that strike the government and vice-versa.

Bahiah, in *Two Women In One*, regards the authority of her father at home, which on important occasions is supported by 'all the men of the family' (94), as an extension of the police forces that strike down the labourers and students demonstrating in the streets of Cairo for the liberation of Egypt from its repressive government. Detained by the police for her political protest but bailed out by her father and her uncle, Bahiah feels 'she had been arrested again, but this time by another kind of police [. . .], taking her to [another kind of] guillotine or a prison cell' (94).

In *Sardines*, set against the background of Siad Barre's corrupt totalitarian regime, Farah shows how strategies of repression employed by Somalia's military government cannot be separated from those used by patriarchy. Medina sees no difference between the General's treatment of his subjects and her patriarchal grandfather's management of the women in his household. Her grandfather's claim, 'A woman, like any other inferior being, must be kept guessing, she mustn't be given reason to believe she is certain of anything', is for Medina 'precisely the same concept as the General's. The masses must be kept guessing. The masses are inferior...' (140). Hence Medina's struggle for her uninfibulated daughter's intactness, and against the suffering of women in general, is inextricably connected with her fight as a journalist against the General's doctrine, just like Bahiah's protest actions aim to break both the governmental and patriarchal 'chains coiled around [the] necks' of 'the people of Egypt,' men and women alike (116).

The feminism of the second-generation authors thus closely corresponds to Alice Walker's womanist concern for the 'survival and wholeness of entire people [sic], male and female' (xi), and – when the texts are read together – even transcends traditional class divisions, as the protagonists in this cohort stem from all layers of society.

GROWING GLOBALISATION OF DEBATE ON EXCISION IN RECENT AFRICAN AND AFRICAN AMERICAN LITERATURES

The next generation of authors continues to attack the instrumental role of female genital excision in the phallocratic domination over women and even use the same imagery as the preceding generation to describe the destructive and dehumanising effect of their protagonists' operations. Rahma in the short-story 'Against the Pleasure Principle' by Somali-born Hagi-Dirie Herzi, for example, distinctly remembers how the 'explosion of pain in her crotch, hot searing pain [had] made her scream like a rabbit when the steel trap snapped its legs' (779). The horrified protagonist E. in *L'excisée* by the Egypto-Lebanese author Evelyne Accad – despite its early date the novel belongs to the third generation, as will become clear – likens the shrieks of the excised girls without reservation to 'ceux d'un chien qu'on égorge (Accad 1982: 122) [those of a dog whose throat is being slit]' (Accad 1994: 59). In the novel *La Petite Peule* by the Senegalese-born Mariama Barry the first-person narrator, a six-year-old Fulani girl, recalls not only the pain of the procedure but also the terrifying experience of being 'asphyxiée par [le] poids [suffocated by the weight]' bearing down on her and unmistakably labels herself as a 'sacrificiée [sacrificial victim]' brought to the 'abattoir [slaughter house]' (13; 23: my translation).

Female genital excision is an equally degrading experience in Alice Walker's contemporary novel *Possessing the Secret of Joy*. The doll-like characteristics attributed to the post-operative Tashi heavily contrast with her energetic temperament before infibulation: 'Her eyes no longer sparkled with anticipation. They were as flat as eyes that have been painted in, and with dull paint.' Even some time after her mutilation it still feels to Tashi 'as if my self is hiding behind an iron door. [...] I am like a chicken bound for market' (43–44).

However, while Farah, El Saadawi and their contemporaries discuss women's oppression within the context of national political repression, which affects both men and women, and present female genital excision as an intra-cultural affair, their successors explore the practice in a much wider, inter-cultural context, in response to the globalisation of the debate on female genital excision in the aftermath of the United Nations Decade for Women. Walker, for instance, draws an explicit parallel

29

between her protagonist and oppressed women across the world and throughout time, situating them on one 'continuum of [female] pain' (159). On this continuum Tashi has her place alongside the colonial Victorian women parading in the White Ladies Lane whose task it was to '[reproduce] the master of the house,' the Chinese women whose feet were bound so that they could not run away from their husbands, but also the American women suffering from frigidity because '[their] husband, man, lover, is or was unfaithful to [them]' (85; 159). Walker moreover confronts her incredulous African protagonist with the fact that even in her country of exile there are women such as Amy, a white woman from New Orleans, who are forced to share Tashi's genitally excised existence.[19] Walker here follows the example of hattie gosset[20] who, in her poem 'is it true what they say about coloured pussy,' lists traditional body modification practices such as 'clitoridectomy' among modern ones such as 'forced sterilisation and experimental surgery' and muses about a global revolution of all 'pussies' (gosset 412).

Such a globalisation is also noticeable in the extremely diffuse geographic distribution of the authors. Though of African descent, most of the writers – the majority of whom are women – reside in various corners of the African Diaspora rather than on the African continent. The broader perspective of the third-generation writers, however, is not always unproblematic, and neither are their detailed descriptions of the operations, often more harrowing than those penned by their predecessors.

While in *The Color Purple* Walker's terminology still endorses the traditional discourse of female genital excision when she briefly refers to the 'female initiation ceremony' of Adam's wife Tashi (202; 235), a decade later she devotes a whole book to the mental and physical suffering of the infibulated Tashi, in which she unmistakably labels the same rite a 'mutilation' and the infibulated 'gelded women' (235; 215). Much more explicitly than any of the preceding authors, Walker demonstrates in *Possessing the Secret of Joy* how her once passionate protagonist's sexual life and chances at a natural birth are irrevocably destroyed. Tashi's extremely difficult delivery contrasts sharply with the orgasmic birthing experience of her husband's mistress: 'The obstetrician broke two instruments trying to make an opening large enough for Benny's head. Then he used a scalpel. Then a pair of scissors used ordinarily to sever cartilage from bone' (55). Although research confirms that Tashi's peri-natal problems are, regrettably, not exceptional,[21] Walker's description of Benny's birth smacks of melodrama – especially the breaking of the instruments.

Not just *Possessing the Secret of Joy*, but most of the recent works tend to present what actually occurs in graphic detail. Naylor also allows one of her characters in *Bailey's Cafe* to perform a rather repulsive re-enactment of an infibulation by gutting a succulent plum. Although Eve plays the devil's advocate in another scene in the book – she helps Jesse Belle kick the habit by providing her with drugs – her plum-excision does not improve the fate of the infibulated Mariam. It merely reproduces the destructivity of the ritual[22] and verges on sensationalism. Similarly, the narrator's satirical *laudatio* of the Somali infibulator figuring in Moses Isegawa's *Abessijnse Kronieken* (*Abyssinian Chronicles*) – she is 'a natural talent, one in a thousand,' 'an artist' even, who 'could cut a little girl with a machete without doing any damage' – may be in keeping with the novel's cynical style; the inconsequentiality of the character in the narrative and the author's lack of interest in the cultural context in which the infibulator is said to be practising her skills render Isegawa's over-stated references to female genital excision rather gratuitous and suspect.[23]

Equally problematic is the discussion of female genital excision in *Re/membering Aunt Jemima: A Menstrual Show*. The African American playwrights Breena Clarke and Glenda Dickerson may successfully deconstruct the racist stereotype of Aunt Jemima, marketing icon of a brand of pancake mixes highly popular in the United States, and rehabilitate her as 'the most famous coloured woman in the world' with a long string of noteworthy female descendants (35); they nevertheless reinforce the Western stereotypical conception of the silenced, excised African woman, victimised by the patriarchal African male. She is represented in the play by Aminata, the only one of Aunt Jemima's many daughters to return to Africa after Emancipation. While her twin sister enters 'Yarvard Law School' (38), Aminata is threatened with excision, imposed by the same authoritarian father who took her back with him to Africa in the first place. With their general reference to 'Africa' as Aminata's new place of residence, Clarke and Dickerson, moreover, inaccurately implicate the whole continent, as the practice is unknown in large parts of Africa. Not just these African American authors, but also the Somali Herzi sketches a rather black-and-white picture of her home country versus the United States, to which I return presently.

The stereotyping of female genital excision in the third-generation narratives is aggravated by a lack of genuine interest in the cultural context of the practice. While not all authors go about it as drastically as Clarke and Dickerson, who never clearly reveal the motive for Aminata's excision, the cultural significance of the rite is subsidiary to the feminist and/or human rights agenda of the third-generation writers. For instance, Rahma in 'Against the Pleasure Principle' ignores her mother's (justified) traditionalist concerns that she (Rahma) will abandon her culture's traditions in the United States and instead focuses on the positive health implications of her emigration: not only will she benefit from 'the best medical care in the world' when delivering her first child, but her new-born daughter will also be saved from infibulation (778; 782). Similarly, in *Possessing the Secret of Joy* Tashi's anti-colonial constructions of the rite cannot hold in Walker's feminist discursive frame. Like Muthoni in Ngugi's *The River Between*, Tashi chooses genital surgery to affirm her affinity with her culture's traditions, which are threatened by colonisation and evangelisation: 'Because when I disobey you, the outsider, even if it is wrong, I am being what is left of myself. And that sliver of myself is all I now have left' (238). Walker, however, undermines Tashi's construction of infibulation as an embodiment of her community's culture by showing how her protagonist's intended contribution to the struggle against the colonial oppressors is in fact a serious blow to her own fighting spirit and by having the African American characters in the novel condemn Tashi's action. In contrast with Ngugi's novel, Walker's feminist denunciation of the practice takes priority over an exploration of its cultural significance (whether as an instrument for the construction of gender or ethnicity). Contrary to the opinion of Walker's critics,[24] the author of *Possessing the Secret of Joy*, as the references to Clarke and Dickerson's play and Herzi's short story show, does not differ much in this respect from her contemporaries, whether they are African American or African, outsiders or insiders.[25]

Still, by bringing the issue of culture into their gender debate and even introducing the West as a positive point of comparison, the third-generation authors render their condemnation of the practice more complex than their predecessors' intra-cultural approach. When in *L'excisée* E. denounces the exciseuse as a 'sorcière [witch]' (repeated three times on the same page) and the operation the woman is performing on the girls in the compound as a 'massacre' (122), the unexcised Lebanese protagonist, unlike Tanga and Bahiya in *Tu t'appelleras Tanga* and 'Who Will Be the Man?' is commenting not on her own people's traditions, but on those upheld in her (Palestinian) husband's desert community in Egypt.

Similarly, in *Bailey's Cafe* Eve and Nadine's criticism of the Ethiopian Mariam's infibulation is complicated by the fact that the American women are both outsiders. Moreover, rather than find out about Mariam's own view on the practice, the reader has to make do with a displaced reaction, the reaction of an outsider, i.e. Nadine's anger: 'I was so angry I wanted to break something. Blame somebody. I told Eve to shut up' (152). In fact, excised women have little or no voice in *L'excisée* or *Bailey's Cafe*. Also in 'Re/membering Aunt Jemima,' the audience learns only indirectly about Aminata's protest against her impending excision, when *Time* magazine telephones to tell Aunt Jemima that 'Aminata has fled Africa and thrown herself on the mercy of the World Court. She says she ain't having no clitoridictomy [*sic*]' (41).[26] Although she manages to prevent her own excision, Clarke and Dickerson do not focus on Aminata's resistance to the practice, and the girl's own voice, in contrast with some of her sisters, is never heard in the play.

Exile (to the West) rather than direct confrontation is presented as a solution not only in *Re/membering Aunt Jemima*. E. too flees from her husband's compound together with her little protégée Nour, whom she sends to Switzerland, and the run-away Mariam joins the marginal people who have gathered at Bailey's American diner.

The excised protagonist of the Dutch-language novel *Idil: Een meisje* (*Idil: A Girl*), by the Somali-born Yasmine Allas also looks for a better life by trying to escape to Europe with her Belgian lover and reminds her daughter that in Somalia 'you'll never be able to be who you want to be. Look at what they have done to me. [...] They have slaughtered me' (127). Allas and her contemporaries, however, do run the risk of offending traditionalist Africans' sensibilities with their characters' rather superficial embrace of the West.

Nonetheless, it must be added that the widely publicised, patronising interventionist stance Walker displays in interviews and documentaries appears to have affected the critical reception of her novel; for in *Possessing the Secret of Joy* the author is not only more positive about excised women's agency than some of her reviewers make out, she is also more positive than most of her contemporaries. While in *Bailey's Cafe*, 'Re/membering Aunt Jemima', *L'excisée*, 'Against the Pleasure Principle' and *Idil*, women's agency is more or less limited to their (attempted) exile, only the protagonists of Walker's *Possessing the Secret of Joy* and *Rebelle* by the Ivorian Fatou Keïta continue the example of their sisters in some of the second-generation works by directly confronting their African societies, as Mariana did in *The Scar*. Unlike the lone rebels in the second-generation texts, who called in the help of a sympathetic listener to spread their stories only after their deaths, the women in *Possessing the Secret of Joy* and *Rebelle* are united in a feminist struggle against repression and female genital excision. Malimouna in *Rebelle* becomes a champion of women's rights in the city and although her campaign against excision destroys her marriage, at the end of the novel she triumphs with the support of other women, as Tashi does in the last pages of Walker's novel. Tashi's rebellious murder of M'Lissa, a national icon, is presented as a victory over the repressive gender and national political structures of her society as well as over her own trauma. At the very moment of her execution Walker's protagonist takes full possession of the fact that the secret of joy lies precisely in this resistance against one's oppression: 'There is a roar as if the world cracked open and I flew inside. I am no more. And satisfied' (264).

Walker and Keïta, moreover, acknowledge the discursive agency of excised women, and in contrast to *Bailey's Café*, *Re/membering Aunt Jemima* and *L'excisée*, they even raise to a thematic level the issue of African women's speaking out against female genital excision. While Keïta makes Malimouna the mouthpiece of a women's group battling against excision, Walker relates how Tashi finally succeeds in 'exploding the boulder' in her throat that had prevented her from speaking about her own and her sister's victimisation (15). Despite her mental instability, the infibulated Tashi (even different *personae* of the latter) is included among *Possessing the Secret of Joy*'s many first-person narrators, and her consciousness occupies the largest space in the novel. By emphasising women's right to mental health and physical integrity and presenting female genital excision as a human right's issue, the authors of the third-generation have come a long way from the earliest authors and their emphasis on the cultural significance of this traditional female rite of passage.

LITERARY CONTRIBUTIONS TO THE EXCISION DEBATE THROUGH TIME AND ACROSS THE DIASPORA

As this overview reveals, different approaches to female genital excision do not depend on the author's sex, ethnicity or nationality, as for example the works of male and female writers from the same generation differ less from one another than texts by women from different generations. Moreover, works by authors from different ethnic backgrounds within one generation bear more similarities than those of authors of the same ethnicity belonging to different generations. Since the publication of Rebeka Njau's play *The Scar* in 1963, the first African literary text to deal with the practice, three consecutive generations of authors of African descent have explored the subject in their writing. Whereas in the 1960s and early 1970s African authors are carefully writing around the topic of female genital excision, and either focus on the political/ethnic significance of this traditional gender ritual in the struggle for independence or formulate an indirect feminist critique, in the 1970s African writers gradually start to speak out against the practice as an instrument of a particular society's phallocratic gender politics, and in the 1990s authors of African descent sharply denounce excision as an example of the global oppression of women.

The slowly increasing attention to creative writing on female genital excision in African literary criticism – the publication of this volume of essays two decades after the conclusion of the United Nations Women's decade is a notable case in point – and in discussion of female genital excision in general suggest that (critical analyses of) literary explorations of the practice may add to this debate. This hypothesis is supported by the growing number of internet sites on the subject that in the last couple of years have added lists of creative writing. Although in her scholarly study with the evocative title *Woman, Why Do You Weep? Circumcision and Its Consequences* the Sudanese doctor Asma El Dareer does not explicitly mention creative writing for adults, she emphatically declares that awareness education for abolition should not limit itself to one particular medium: 'All channels of communication should be involved, for example: 1) Public lectures, in schools and social clubs; 2) Articles in newspapers and journals; 3) Interviews and talks on radio and television; 4) Discussion groups; 5) Publication of Pamphlets; 6) Children's Books; 7) Plays, either in theatres, on radio and television and performed in rural communities' (106).

Since El Dareer's statement in 1982 many of these, and other, channels have been chosen by activists and artists wishing to discuss female genital excision. For instance, an example of a lecture held in 1987 by Zainaba to the midwives of Touil can be found in Margot Badran and Miriam Cooke's volume of Arab women's writing, while internet sites list various documentaries on the subject, including Alice Walker and Prathiba Parmar's controversial *Warrior Marks*. Four years earlier Mali film-maker Cheick Oumar Sissoko produced a Bambara-spoken (fictional) motion picture, entitled *Finzan, a Dance for the Heroes*, in which the practice is not presented as the subject of an outsider's surprisingly egocentric investigation but integrated into a broader critique of women's social position. The Somali Soraya Mire in her film *Fire Eyes* (1993) presents the perspective of excised women, while Stephanie Welsh's picture story on a female genital excision ritual in Kenya was awarded the Pulitzer Prize for Feature Photography in 1996. In 1999 Enda-Tiers-Monde in Dakar published, with Belgian support, an educational comic strip entitled *Le choix de Bintou* (*Bintou's Choice*) to promote public awareness of Senegal's brand-new law against excision. Female genital excision in a changing society is also the subject of a Malian musical play *Fura* (meaning ritual), written by Habib Dembele Guimba and directed by Abdoulaye Diarra, which the theatre group Opera Bambara had performed in Mali prior to coming on tour to Europe in 1999.[27] In 2004 the renowned Senegalese filmmaker Ousmane Sembène devoted what sadly was to be his last film to the subject. In *Moolaadé*, as in *Fura*, the central event is a girl's refusal to undergo excision.

Nigerian painters and sculptors have also lent their support to an anti-female genital excision project set up by their local NGO, Women Issues Communication Services Agency, with an impressive art exhibition in 1998.[28]

All these examples illustrate how various activists and artists of African descent have taken El Dareer's suggestion to heart and explored different ways to express themselves on the subject of female genital excision. As the Yoruba proverbial saying 'ònà kan kò wo ojà' has it, there are many different roads that lead to market.[29] Literature may be only one among a range of media that address the issue, but I am convinced that, for those wishing to participate in the debate, the literary explorations of female genital excision, especially when taken together, can profoundly enhance understanding of the practice's complexity.

Stephen Bishop

Oppositional Approaches to Female Genital Mutilation (FGM) in African Literature

Female Genital Mutilation or FGM has increasingly become a popular axis of discussion for debating and identifying a wide variety of topics, such as feminism, human rights, Africa, and religious/political fundamentalism. It rose to new prominence in Western academia and arguably even general Western media discourse in the 1990's when Western legal systems began recognising FGM as grounds for asylum,[1] and international organisations and conferences on Human Rights and on Women's Rights began routinely addressing it.[2] This observation is not meant to suggest, however, that the issue is new or discussed solely in Western circles. Alongside the work of indigenous African activists, African literature has treated the subject with a certain degree of regularity since the mid-1960's, with many of the novels and essays presenting didactic condemnations of the practice. Such negative attention and criticism, however, has been met with strong counterattacks supporting FGM on the basis of respect for tradition and a refusal of 'Western feminist neo-colonisation.' While some changes in social practices and national laws have occurred in Africa over the last forty years despite such defences of FGM, this anti-colonial, maintenance-of-tradition discourse remains a powerful, unwavering force of resistance to change that cannot be dismissed lightly.

This chapter therefore addresses some attempts to circumvent the common sharp binary that splits the FGM debate into two mutually unintelligible discourses with room for only one victor. More specifically, the current dominant discursive clash sees one side that types itself as a progressive, pro-woman movement fighting against a retrograde, misogynistic practice and another side that sees itself as protecting time-honoured, traditional African and/or Islamic society against invasive foreign propaganda. Such categorisation leaves little room for compromise and leads to a hardening of ideological positions.

That said, this chapter does not advocate a solution of compromise in which both sides agree that just a little less cutting would represent the happy medium. I want to see FGM disappear, sooner rather than later. Yet, while the efforts of those who roundly condemn excision and infibulation are to be applauded, such direct, aggressive, and critical assaults on a long-standing custom can backfire as often as they succeed. Uneven results are due to the split effect of such criticism's shock value – an effect that can produce the desired result of countering complacency and emotionally moving others to action, but also the undesired effect of offending the target group's traditional society and leading to a defensive retrenchment of the maligned procedures.[3] This understandable reaction of outrage to and distrustfulness of 'cultural neocolonialism' is the point Jomo Kenyatta forcibly made in *Facing Mount Kenya: The Tribal Life of Gikuyu* over forty years ago, and which shows no sign of having abated since then.[4]

For example, replacing the previously widespread term 'female circumcision' with a label such as FGM – Female Genital Mutilation – represents precisely the kind of discourse that will not easily persuade all parties concerned. Certainly 'mutilation' is a word that elicits more negative reactions than 'circumcision,' and that is precisely what its coiners want. But consider calling common male circumcision Male Genital Mutilation, or 'MGM.' Most Westerners, especially circumcised men, would object to or at least find strange such a description.[5] While it is certainly true that the two practices differ in important ways,[6] the fact remains that defenders of excision frequently accuse anti-FGM activists of hypocrisy because few of them are also against 'MGM.' The argument goes that Westerners, who so arrogantly and vehemently accuse Africans of barbarism and cruelty in performing female mutilation, or circumcision, blithely continue the wide-spread practice of male circumcision/mutilation. Just as most Westerners are likely to dismiss accusations that they are cruelly and unnecessarily mutilating their sons, so too are FGM proponents likely to reject calls to suppress what they understand as religious, social, and medical obligations involving their daughters.

Accordingly, this chapter features a manner of criticising FGM in literature that holds out special promise. Without insult or anger, it undermines arguments for FGM as an important African practice precisely because not to cut is more in tune with African values and traditions. Specifically, we will consider several authors who eschew direct, overt condemnation of the practice, probably because they fear it as counterproductive, and rely instead on what can be called *oppositional narratives* – presenting incongruous stories, which may be both for and against the practice – that challenge the reader to reconsider traditions such as FGM without delivering their own ultimatum of rejection. Works such as Ngugi wa Thiong'o's *The River Between*, Ahmadou Kourouma's *Les soleils des indépendances*, and Awa Thiam's *La parole aux négresses* started this process of *seductive persuasion rather than polemical attack*, which has been continued and supported in different ways in later works such as Calixthe Beyala's *Tu t'appelleras Tanga* and *Lettre d'une Africaine à ses soeurs occidentales*, Nuruddin Farah's *Sardines*, and Waris Dirie's *Desert Flower*. While several of these writers, most notably Dirie and Thiam, have made express condemnations of the practice elsewhere, we will consider some of the more indirect, literary discussions of FGM and how they leave the interpretive responsibility in the hands (or minds) of the reader. We will consider how and why these indirect literary approaches achieve greater success in engaging with certain opposing viewpoints through avoiding binaries of modernity versus tradition and a rhetoric of superiority that characterise so much of the non-literary campaigns against FGM. Finally, we will examine Cheick Oumar Sissoko's film *Finzan* (1990), the first cinematic treatment of the subject, as well as Ousmane Sembène's *Moolaadé* (2004), a counter example of rhetorical strategies that oppositional narrative strives to avoid.

Many justifications for FGM are offered by its proponents, and while most can be readily dismissed as superstition and all can be attacked on the basis of statistical, medical, and/or scriptural (in the case of the Koran) evidence by anti-FGM activists, their reality and relevancy to FGM practitioners is not to be readily dismissed. Although Islamic-based justifications are hotly contested by activists, Islam, the dominant religion in some regions where FGM is practiced, is still unjustifiably thought to support it to control women's unhealthy sexual appetites and keep them from straying. It is also thought to prevent madness and certain physical diseases, to clean and/or purify a woman in a spiritual and/or physical sense, and to protect men and newborns, as contact with the clitoris can kill or harm them. In some cases, the rite also literally or metaphorically ushers a young girl into womanhood. While this list of justifications may appear questionable or even ludicrous to those who oppose FGM, it illustrates the procedure's gravity in the eyes of those who perform it.

Such legitimating reasons join the simple but powerful force of tradition, of doing as one's ancestors have done. Tradition is by definition part of a deeply held belief system essential for maintaining a sense of social identity and coherence that all human beings desire. Accordingly, this *chapter posits a shift in desire*, from wanting to see FGM as normal, admirable, and integral to certain African societies, to an openness to see it as unusual, objectionable, and even detrimental to these same societies. The goal is to diminish FGM's power in a given society by weakening its perceived ties to that same society's traditions. To accomplish this, oppositional narrative comes into play.

Oppositional narrative is therefore about shifting desire rather than forcing change. It holds as a key tenet that social transformation endures when people actively desire it rather than when they merely follow orders or react to coercion. Not seeking to destroy the dominant paradigm in play, oppositional narrative aims rather to influence it through the mediation of desire. Such a goal is accomplished through 'a (mis-)reading of the discourse of power,' rather than through the attempted erasure of such discourse (Chambers xvi). Accordingly, the practitioner of oppositional narrative seeks to deploy the same discourse of power she contests, both as a disguise and as a tool of her motives for change. In one sense then, oppositional narrative is always complicit with the discourse it is trying to affect. It mimics that discourse so as to remain invisible and avoid becoming the always already doomed resistance. This is mimicry in the sense of 'camouflage,' described by Bhabha (in turn borrowing from Lacan) as the act of becoming speckled before a speckled background rather than harmonising oneself with that background ('Mimicry' 126). Through this mimicry, a narrator gains at least initial access to a reluctant or suspicious audience.

The narrator can thereby project a story of seduction, one which will not force the reader to change her mind, but rather encourage her to desire a change on her own. This process of writing and reading is what

Chambers describes as oppositionality's power to shift the reader's identity from that of the textual narratee to that of an 'interpretating subject' (26). The reader is encouraged to interpret the narrator's situation from the reader's own point of view, as opposed to acting either as a stand-in for the narrator or accepting the traditional role of passive narratee. In this way the reader, while certainly being influenced by the narrator's story, is making her own personal decision about what she believes to be proper and acceptable. Such a choice always carries greater conviction than an enforced one in the long run, and is therefore the basis for oppositional narrative's unique capacity to engender positive change in a discourse of power in a stable, long-term manner.

In the context of the FGM debate, this philosophy means that success at changing the dominant socio-religious order is not confined to bold attacks on FGM aimed simply at outlawing it (since such an approach fails to alter the underlying reasoning and desire for FGM) nor in emotionally and vibrantly positive representations of victory over injustice and suffering (since they often only serve to 'blow off steam'). Instead, oppositional narrative can modify readers' desires for the regulation of society, or in this particular case, the regulation of women's genitalia and sexuality. By presenting FGM in ways that reveal a disconnect and/or failing of the tradition without necessarily requiring readers to identify with specific narrative subject positions, oppositional narrative 'forces' the audience to draw its own conclusions, thus following Pascal's adage that, 'People are generally better persuaded by the reasons which they have themselves discovered than by those which have come into the mind of others' (*Pensées* I: 10).

We begin to investigate this approach with an example that does not directly address FGM in any way – Mariama Bâ's classic short novel of African feminism, *Une si longue lettre*. While concentrating on the negative effects of polygamy in African culture, and never once mentioning FGM, the widely read book exemplifies oppositional writing in an African context. Ostensibly a letter written by Ramatoulaye to her friend Aïssatou after the death of the former's husband, Ramatoulaye's discourse recalls the uncomfortable, embarrassing, and sometimes painful events that each woman went through when their husbands both took second, younger wives after years of seemingly idyllic marriages. Aïssatou reacts to the second wife by immediately leaving her husband, taking the kids, getting a great job, and leaving the country. Ramatoulaye, on the other hand, though sharing Aïssatou's education, aspirations, and pain, chooses to stay with her husband and largely maintain her lifestyle. For these reasons, many Western readers mistakenly type-cast Aïssatou as the accomplished feminist and Ramatoulaye as the proto-feminist. The error here is that while Aïssatou may be the accomplished feminist in a Western context, she is largely invisible in Senegal and more importantly can be easily dismissed as a shockingly unconventional bad wife and mother. In an African social context, she is the exception that proves the rule.

The character of Ramatoulaye, however, by demonstrating the more or less proper behavior of a good Senegalese Muslim wife, mother, and member of society, avoids the label of outcast. By not aggressively criticising Senegalese society on all fronts, her later 'social indiscretions' – driving a car, going to the movies alone, not disowning her pregnant unwed daughter, refusing her brother-in-law's offer of marriage, etc. – are much more powerful statements that are less easy for the reader to dismiss as abnormal. More to the point, a great deal of responsibility is placed on readers to decide for themselves what is and is not proper behavior and custom in Senegalese society. The novel is short on direct criticism and Ramatoulaye resolutely refuses to revolt completely against all Senegalese social practices. Instead, Bâ consistently sets up situations where an unquestionably strong, admirable *traditional* Senegalese woman suffers and struggles under equally traditional practices. The reader, rather than being told how bad certain Senegalese social customs are and that they must be eliminated, is faced with the need to form her own opinion on this disconnect of traditions, and hopefully to desire social change to rectify the inconsistency. This is the type of narrative approach that is important in the struggle against FGM.

One of the first examples of such an approach addressing FGM is found in Ngugi's *The River Between* from 1965. The river in question is between two villages that have separated themselves along the lines of religion and social mores. One village has become strongly Christian while the other maintains traditional religious beliefs. While there are other issues at play, the main symbolic conflict arises over the practice of excision, which is thought integral to the traditional village's identity and beliefs and an anathema to the Christian villages. This clash initially comes to a head when Muthoni, the daughter of a prominent Christian leader, goes against her father's wishes and undergoes the ceremony, only to die from complications. The rift is then played out by the increasingly difficult romance between Muthoni's sister, Nyambura, and Waiyaki, an up-and-coming leader of the traditional village.

Throughout the rest of the novel, multiple points of view on FGM – positive, negative, and somewhat ambiguous – are displayed for the reader's consideration through different characters' comments. However, the issue of FGM, though one of the central axes of dispute between the two villages, is never vilified at the authoritative narrative level. In fact, the reader is witness to a back and forth series of arguments that is imbricated in a larger struggle encompassing other social practices. Both sides have good arguments and bad arguments, and both sides take improper and rash actions that undermine their claims of behaving in society's best interests. Anti-FGM opinions are therefore neither dominant nor unquestioned. There are even positive observations from the unidentified omniscient narrator such as the following:

> Circumcision was an important ritual to the tribe. It kept people together, bound the tribe. It was at the core of the social structure, and...something that gave meaning to a man's life. End the custom and the spiritual basis of the tribe's cohesion and integration would be no more. (68)

This moderate attitude towards FGM is not meant to suggest that the book is pro-FGM either, however, as later on the central character, Waiyaki, comes to realise that

> Circumcision of women was not important as a physical operation. It was what it did inside a person. It could not be stopped overnight. Patience and, above all, education, were needed. If the white man's religion made you abandon a custom and then did not give you something of equal value, you became lost. An attempt at resolution of the conflict would only kill you. (142)

While the overall picture of FGM in the novel is accordingly ambiguous on the surface, Ngugi is encouraging a change in attitudes toward the practice. He has merely recognised that long-held customs cannot simply be eliminated with no negative consequences, and that people must have something to look forward to if traditions are to be left behind, to desire the change rather than be forced into it.

Awa Thiam, in her sociological study *La parole aux négresses*, represents a more aggressive opposition to FGM. Nonetheless, she also adopted this oppositional approach in some of her writing. Thiam does indeed devote parts of her book to direct attacks on problems African women encounter such as FGM, polygamy, and arranged marriage. For example, she states that

> This polygamy is imposed on [women] from the outside. Some women are, still today, considered as objects, as sub-humans. Everything happens as if they were denied a human conscience. The most convincing example is that of young girls married or fiancéd as soon as they are born. (73)

Nonetheless, most of the chapter devoted to FGM (entitled 'La Clitoridectomie et l'Infibulation') consists of historical facts, representative regional statistics and practices, and testimonies by women who have experienced FGM, none of which contains polemical attacks on the subject of the chapter. Thiam is true to her work's title ('African Women Speak') in that the critical words – meaning both those that are important and those that criticise – come largely from the African women directly concerned with the issue. By interviewing women who have undergone FGM procedures in their countries, she accomplishes two things. First, she allows for a diversity of opinions on FGM to be heard, so that readers need to draw their own interpretations from the text. Second, she avoids accusations of presenting authoritative 'outsider opinions' on an African cultural topic.

The diversity of opinion is represented by women who denounce FGM, those who defend it, and those who offer mixed messages. One woman, 'P.K.,'[7] recounts the painful and terrifying details of her excision at age 12, although she does not editorialise the event to directly condemn it (81–4). Another woman, a 26-year-old divorced Malian with a child and degree in economics, actually defends the procedure:

> I was, during my childhood, excised. I speak according to my personal experience. Today, I consider myself satisfied with this operation that I

was made to undergo: excision. In effect, if I maintain such a position, it is because it fulfiled its function for me. […] it permits a woman to be the master of her body. That is why I do not at all perceive it as a mutilation. (88)

Still another, a thirty-five-year-old professional Malian with an advanced degree who is both excised and infibulated, relates how, though recognising that both practices are important aspects of her culture, she had nonetheless decided not to have her three girls undergo either one. Her mother, however, had other ideas. One day Thiam's interviewee returned home to find three tear-stained faces: the grandmother had had her daughters excised while she was at work – without her permission (84–5).

Through these and other stories, Thiam reveals why some individuals approve of FGM. She shows that it is a strongly-held custom, especially for the older generation, and that some women appreciate its function while others are not ashamed of having undergone it. And yet, her message remains easily readable as anti-FGM since these very women who are ambivalent or even receptive to cutting present stories that expose FGM's inconsistency as a positive custom. The fact that a grandmother would secretly have her grandchildren excised against their mother's will is extremely disturbing and immediately reveals a disconnection between the two generations. The pain and suffering P.K. describes as having undergone is unavoidably recognised as thoroughly unpleasant even by an FGM supporter. And the twenty six-year-old Malian who praises excision's effect on her 'body control' does so because, as she states, she has had no sexual urges for the past four years (88). If women who are not anti-FGM campaigners offer such damning praise of this procedure, a reader is led to question its real value to traditional society.[8]

Because Thiam herself clearly questions it, we might suppose she risks accusations of complicity as a 'Western feminist coloniser'. Perhaps to evade being called on the carpet, she warns 'those who expect feminist discourse [to] avoid reading this study' (22) and consistently demonstrates suspicion of and even hostility towards too much Western intervention in Africa. To illustrate her point, she quotes an old article by a French feminist, Annie de Villeneuve, critical of FGM who states, 'In this abominably venal race, such a barbarous custom could very well have been born and can still perpetuate itself by means of a love for money' (105).

Thiam comments: 'What makes for the venality of this race? Is it more venal than any other race? Is it more venal than a race that is rapacious to the point that it does not hesitate to pillage other races by murdering them and deporting them? Is it possible to compare indigenous Somalis with indigenous French of capitalist France? Assuredly not' (105).

What Thiam is not forgetting is that blanket, direct criticisms of African customs can be just as much about establishing or maintaining a sense of Western superiority as about helping Africans.

In her conclusion, Thiam casts doubt on the benefits of some Western-inspired feminist ideas coming to the aid of African women on a variety of issues, including FGM. Commenting on what African women should strive for, she queries,

> 'A society in the image of European society in full disaggregation? Must Africa marry this model? If there is something to do to save a State newly freed from colonials or residing there still, it is certainly not to imitate a society where the family is torn apart, where individualism reigns. [...] The struggle of African women can certainly be conceived of other than [as] a pure and simple copy of the struggles of European women' (182).

Thiam is not rejecting all intercultural discourse and insight in favour of resurrecting an infallible African cultural past. While some writers have had recourse to this overly fantastic response, such as Oyèrónké Oyewùmí in her study *The Invention of Women*, placing all blame for modern gender differences on colonialism, Thiam is simply being guarded about the source of solutions to FGM. Thiam recognises the complaint later voiced by critic Juliana Makuchi Nfah-Abbenyi:

> What I find negative is the fact that a good majority of ... feminists who address this issue often *do not* delve into the reasons why it happens, nor do they propose any solutions that can be helpful in the lives of these women. We are told that circumcision takes away the pleasure for life. This is sometimes followed by a plethora of examples that depict African men as inherently savage and violent. What ends up happening is unfortunate, given that in the bid to match African women's (sexual) victimisation with African men's brutal nature/patriarchy, the women seem forgotten or remain in the shadow of the discussion that is (supposedly) about them and their sexuality. (26)

Another, more literary early example of oppositional narrative is the celebrated novel *Les Soleils des indépendances* by Ahmadou Kourouma. Kourouma's masterpiece was a breakthrough for several reasons, not only for its 'Africanised French' prose and for turning its critical eye from the degradations of the coloniser to those perpetuated by the formerly colonised, but also for its broaching the subject of FGM. The protagonist's wife, Salimata, relives the horror of her coming-of-age ceremony involving FGM and the subsequent physical and emotional problems she has experienced due to it. Salimata's recollection of an excruciating excision is symbolically linked, both in her own mind and in Kourouma's writing, to her memory of rape by Tiékoura, the traditional healer, entrusted with caring for her wounds (36–9): 'Excision! Its scenes, colours, smells. And rape! Its own colours, pain, revulsion' (31). The whole story is narratively framed and interrupted by Salimata being jolted from her reveries in bed by biting lice and her rude husband's poking and turning, further underscoring the assault on her body by a despoiled, patriarchal society (31–9).

Yet, again, there are no overt authorial condemnations of FGM, and Salimata represents a dutiful, respectful wife that all can admire. In fact, as she works her daily job selling food in the market, she fields compliments and marriage proposals from men proclaiming her the ideal wife (59–60). However, precisely because she is strong, admirable, and traditional yet routinely mistreated by her conservative husband and occasionally by other men, her presence in the novel strongly suggests a society gone astray. At the same time, Kourouma avoids reducing this implicit call for change to either a return to a glorious past or a turn towards liberating modernity. Salimata's husband Fama is as (superficially) traditional as any member of society, and yet his selfishness and unwillingness to accept change leave him bitter, useless, and ultimately dead. Salimata, on the other hand, who is beyond reproach as a traditional Malinké woman, perseveres and survives by showing a willingness to adapt without losing her traditional identity. Just as Kourouma indirectly condemns many practices maintained by a traditional society that is as morally bankrupt as the postcolonial regime due to its unwillingness to adapt to new social conditions, he is presenting the dangers of holding on to FGM without addressing the negative aspects of it. There is no diatribe against FGM; simply another presentation of its inconsistent values within traditional

African society, which inconsistency pushes the reader to reconsider its status as automatically valid in the face of encroaching Western standards of acceptability.

This practice of challenging FGM through oppositional narrative has continued across the African continent through various periods and genres. Written works demonstrating varying degrees of oppositional narrative technique include Calixthe Beyala's novel *Tu t'appelleras Tanga* and her long essay *Lettre d'une Africaine à ses souers occidentales*, Nuruddin Farah's feminist political novel *Sardines*, Nawal El Saadawi's autobiographical sociological study *The Hidden Face of Eve*, and Waris Dirie's autobiographical *Desert Flower* among others. Instead of examining these additional written texts, however, we will turn to a different genre of creative social commentary exemplified in a pair of films that address FGM in West Africa. In 1990, Cheick Oumar Sissoko directed a film called *Finzan* that looked at two young women who resist traditional practices – forced marriage and excision – in Mali, and in 2004 Ousmane Sembène released his film *Moolaadé*, which deals with excision in a Burkina Faso village.

While film is a genre distinct from the novel, these two movies are nonetheless pertinent to this chapter for two reasons. First, in the African context, cinema often performs the function literature professors like to think literature does in societies with higher literacy rates; these are very low in almost all of Africa, and even if a person can read, books are far more expensive in relative terms, so that literary culture is more focused on oral rather than written storytelling. Films therefore are more likely to reach a much broader segment of society.[9] Second, *Finzan* and *Moolaadé* are specifically relevant because both admirably demonstrate certain oppositional principles discussed, although in very different ways. *Finzan*, a rather depressing and pessimistic film, enacts some of the tactics of oppositional narrative and successfully confronts FGM according to those principles. Meanwhile, an overly optimistic *Moolaadé*, because its attack on FGM is so aggressive, stands in sharp contrast with the tactics of oppositional narrative and thereby allows us to recognise them more clearly in our discussion.

The part of *Finzan* that concentrates on excision follows the story of a young woman named Fili who was never excised as a child. When she is sent from the city to a rural village by her father in order to learn proper respect and behaviour, she is targeted as an uncircumcised girl and eventually forcibly circumcised. The arguments for and against the procedure are fairly standard – it is a question of Fili's individual rights versus the village's traditional communal practices - but the rhetoric is not particularly sharp on either side. The actual circumcision scene, however, is brutal and difficult to watch, as Fili goes under the knife kicking and screaming at the hands of the *exciseuses*. In the end, it is unclear whether Fili even survives the ordeal. The audience is therefore left with a very disturbing dissociation between the arguments calling for the continuation of the tradition and the actual event. The hypocrisy of the pro-FGM message – that 'it is for her own good' – is readily readable, but it is not put forth in a one-sided, didactic manner. There is no question that *Finzan* is an anti-FGM film, but its full message requires some degree of viewer participation, or interpretation in recognising the lack of consistency in FGM's own discourse of authority. This involvement in the assessment process is what makes for a shift in the desire of the reader, or viewer in this case, more likely and can thus result in a conviction that FGM is undesirable rather than simply 'legally proscribed' by the government or looked down upon by others, namely 'outsiders.'

Moolaadé, on the other hand, mixes messages to a sharp degree, and ends up destroying its oppositional nature with a resolutely revolutionary ending. This oppositional failure is not apparent from the beginning, however, as Sembène appears to be crafting an oppositional cinematic narrative. For much of the first half of the film, Sembène presents conflicting ideas on the issue of FGM. The protagonist, Collé Ardo, resolutely stands against it, harboring four young girls who have fled the ceremony, having already refused to circumcise her daughter Amsatou seven years earlier, and displaying her badly scarred belly as proof of the resultant dangers of FGM. Yet within her own family, she is met with half-hearted, uneven support and even criticism. Amsatou at first expresses conflicting emotions as to her *bilakoro* (uncircumcised) status and attendant poor marriage prospects; Alima, her husband's third wife, finds Collé Ardo's resistance troubling and wants no part of it; and Khadjatou, the first wife, is a cipher in her alternately supportive and critical attitudes towards Collé Ardo's decision. Just as important, the depiction of village life, including the power and formal garb of the excising women of the Salindana and the respectful demeanour of women to men and of all people to figures of authority, reinforces a general sense of esteem for and deference to tradition on the film's part. Although reviews (and the director's reputation) certainly make any question as to the film's ultimate position moot, the first half itself could just as easily be leading to a pro-FGM message as an anti-FGM one.[10]

All this ambiguity changes drastically in the second half of the film, however, as the women and even some of the men band together to overtly denounce FGM. The ruling Kémos (elder men) are openly defied, and the Salindana are publicly disgraced – their excision knives are confiscated and burned, their leader's staff is trampled on, and they are referred to as 'child killers.' In the penultimate scene, the chief's son and Amsatou strike a dramatic pose indicating that he will take her, defiant *bilakoro* that she is, as his wife after all. This successful cinematic revolution makes for a satisfying happy ending for those already convinced of FGM's negative and unnecessary consequences, but it is equally likely to insult and enrage FGM proponents, and convince them of the need to retrench their positions against such blasphemous modern attitudes.

Moolaadé is a very good film in many ways – it has excellent cinematography, powerful performances and several instances of good humour in bringing the subject of FGM to the forefront of current African cinematic discussions. Not surprisingly, it has received exceptionally positive commentary and reviews from the Western media. Much of this laudatory response is certainly well deserved, but in a certain context. That context is generally from within the debate conducted in Western society on how to eliminate FGM immediately and specifically lies within the community of those who are already resolutely opposed to FGM or are easily convinced to oppose it due to its status as a barbarously 'Other' practice. Such current and future conviction is not to be dismissed, but the argument here has been that firm believers in the value and necessity of FGM will not only be least swayed by such didactic anti-FGM discourse, but potentially even reinforced in their pro-FGM convictions by it. For those who cherish custom, oppositional narrative can better influence their own desire to reconceptualise traditional African society, and thereby provide a necessary complement to the more overt, vigorous fight to end FGM in Africa and the Diaspora.

Tameka L. Cage

Going Home Again: Diaspora, Female Genital Mutilation (FGM) and Kingship in 'Warrior Marks'

'Middle Passage': the WORD means blues to me.
Look at it front or backside, it still means BLUES to me.
If I'da been a sailor on the Seven Seas
I'da sailed the seven ENDS and let the MIDDLES be...
But if I'da been a sailor, I'da still been black.
THAT'S why the blues keeps sailin' back.
The blues keeps sailin' back....
James A. Emanuel, 'The Middle Passage Blues'[1]

I...rely on the inspiration I get from glimpsing the possibilities that
bridging our differences as women of colour hold. We cannot permit
separatism or fear to deny those possibilities or crush that future.
Barbara Smith. *Homegirls: a Black Feminist Anthology*

NAVIGATING THE 'BLACK ATLANTIC'

The dispersal of peoples from the African continent to the US, Europe,
and the Caribbean to form the African Diaspora has enabled varying
creative and critical representations of Blackness, frequently at odds over
what, in fact, defines Blackness and whose Blackness is privileged over the
'Other.' As Angeletta Gourdine poignantly asserts in *The Difference Place
Makes*, her study of sexuality, gender, and Diaspora identity, the 'cultural
identity of Blackness has become contentious intellectual property'.[1]
Although this contention is informed, in part, by post modernity, which
calls for decentring socio-political representation from the majority to
the subaltern, one must look to the history of people of African descent

to find the core of our representational woes. When Africans were forcefully migrated from the continent via the villainous character of slavery, what resulted was 'the presence of African bodies in non-African places' (Gourdine ix). This 'presence' resulted in multiple, hybridised identities, where Blackness no longer denoted 'Africanness' alone, producing a meta-narrative of Blackness across the Atlantic. Though persons of African descent may share 'cultural patterns of behaviour' (Gourdine 7), have an ancestry, even perhaps a global, socio-economic struggle in common, we lack a mutual social identity. Yet, as diasporic citizens, we fall under the 'unfinished identity' (Gilroy 1) of being 'Black' people. The implications for this homogenising ambiguity are vast, particularly when considering the boundaries that are so easily blurred, unjustly crossed, or potentially violated when members of the Diaspora misrepresent an/other, and specifically, in this case, denounce and demonise what to some is ennobling and good. What is the subject here? We're talking about FGM, one pièce de résistance in any narrative of Black Atlantic ties.

In his classic *The Black Atlantic: Modernity and Double Consciousness*, Paul Gilroy offers a triumphant, provocative exploration of the Diaspora that captures the plight of its people who, since the Middle Passage and the slavery that ensued, have been resilient, yet fragmented as an undone jigsaw puzzle, trying to locate its 'self.' He exposes the social, geographical, and intellectual difficulty in breaching the gap between the African homeland and the lands to which Black people have been 'shipped.' I centralise his interest in the relationship between transatlantic difference and gender struggle as a facet of Diaspora disconnectedness. Though Gilroy does not explore this relationship in depth, I position it as critical to my argument. I locate the 'place' where Black feminist discourse engages the discourse of the Diaspora, forming a transglobal body of intellectual and political work that considers, first, how to remap the Diaspora's traumatic history and then how to represent its 'sisterhood' relations in the context of 'the kinship that Diaspora implies' (Gourdine ix). Gilroy explains,

> The precise weight we should attach to the conspicuous differences of language, culture, and identity which divide the blacks of the Diaspora from one another, let alone from Africans, are unresolved within the

political culture that promises to bring the disparate peoples of the black Atlantic world together one day. ...The themes of nationality, exile, and cultural affiliation accentuate the inescapable fragmentation and differentiation of the black subject. This fragmentation has recently been compounded further by the questions of gender, sexuality, and male domination, which have been made unavoidable by the struggles of black women. (34)

These 'struggles' beckon to West African shores, to the Black female slave's journey over uncertain seas, her hope to cultivate a spirit of resistance, whether boisterous or subtle, in her female descendants. Feminist activists like Barbara Smith, a US-based foremother of Black women's intellectual thought, received the baton of hope from their enslaved ancestor with confidence that solidarity would help secure freedom from racial discrimination, patriarchal injustices, and economic disparities. By lobbying for race-gender equality, Smith, together with Gloria T. Hull, Patricia Bell Scott, Michelle Wallace, bell hooks, Audre Lorde, and Alice Walker, all US residents, envisioned a Black feminism, or 'womanism,' that would enable Black women to represent themselves in the social, political, and intellectual spheres. Their claims to kinship with African women, however, elicited distrust.

Typical of wide-spread critique, specifically of Walker's 'womanist' standpoint, is the following:

An unpublished statement released on November 19, 1993, by 'a group of African women who have ... worked ... to abolish the ... practice' [of FGM] deplores Walker's portrait of 'an African village, where the women and children are without personality, shadows ... dancing and gazing blankly through some stranger's script of their lives. The respected elder women of the Secret Society in the Gambian village turn into slit-eyed murderers adorned with blood money and wielding rusted weapons with which to butcher children' (Allan 2 in Levin 243).

Similarly, a 1993 *New York Times* editorial penned by African residents in the United States charges Walker with acting out of wholly egotistical motives rather than genuine concern for an issue that is really foreign to her. *Warrior Marks*, they fear, is 'emblematic of the Western feminist tendency to see female genital mutilation as the gender oppression to end all oppressions...a gauge by which to measure distance between the West and the rest of humanity' (Dawit and Merkuria A-27). Walker's 'effort to stand with the mutilated women, not beyond them' (Warrior 13) hasn't worked for African readers in the USA.

Attempting to address this failure, I look at Walker's 'diasporic dreams' and use her 'sisterhood' as a lens to clarify such crucial issues in *Warrior Marks*, primarily the politics of race, 'place,' and trauma. As Walker's attempt to heal and reconcile the gap between the African and African American communities, *Warrior Marks*, generally discussed as though it were 'only' about FGM, becomes the visual representation of Walker's 'homegoing,' as she returns to the coast of Senegal to 'remember the ancestors' by setting the narrative of enslaved Africans beside and within the narrative of 'circumcised' women. Moreover, *Warrior Marks* operates in tandem with *Possessing the Secret of Joy* as part of Walker's effort to remap her personal history as a daughter of 'Africa.' If *Warrior Marks* is Walker's 'travelogue' and campaign against FGM, it is also an effort to heal her disjointed relationship with Africa and the 'slave past.'

For Walker, female 'circumcision' is part of the 'untold' discourse of the Diaspora. She argues that any 'Western' heritage is debunked by her familial connections to the African continent, thus enabling creative space (and 'speaking' privilege) to protest excision and infibulation as harmful practices damaging to women.[2] Though Walker would agree that American slavery, a dire institution, crippled the lives of millions over centuries, she asserts that slavery 'intervened' as the vehicle that connects her to her ancestral 'home.' She deliberately recounts traumatic images of the Middle Passage to remember the female ancestor, who may have crossed the Atlantic without intact genitalia, placing that narrative alongside the widely historicised narrative of the trauma Black bodies incurred in the bowels of slave ships, wounded – and often dying – in its limited space.

However, as the politics surrounding Walker's attention to FGM illustrate, representing the Diaspora, no matter how sincere the effort, can rarely – if ever – be accomplished devoid of controversy and potential confusion for the author and/or her audience. Walker writes that her ancestor '*might* have been genitally mutilated' (Giddings 2). Questions arise: from which West African country can Walker trace her heritage?

Did the country practice female 'circumcision'? If so, was the form clitoridectomy or infibulation? Walker's lack of knowledge (but deep concern) about this forebear who may or may not have been genitally mutilated brings us back to the 'inescapable fragmentation' Gilroy attempts to negotiate in *The Black Atlantic* (34).

Since Nettie's journey to Africa in *The Color Purple*, and Celie's vicarious travels via Nettie's letters, Walker has clearly been fascinated with the 'homeland,' and therefore sought to negotiate its space by journeying her female characters into its depth. As US-based African feminist Oyèrónké Oyewùmí explains, 'It is perhaps not surprising that the search for Africa continues to structure questions of black identity in the United Sates. This quest for Africa, often articulated as a theme of 'paradise lost,' is an idea whose resonance partially rests on the infinite plasticity and malleability of Africa in the black American imagination' (14). The following section investigates Walker's personal fragmentation concerning the African continent, a private longing made public through her writings.

WARRIOR MARKS AND DIASPORIC REPRESENTATION
In *On the Winds and Waves of Imagination: Transnational Feminism and Literature*, Constance Richards observes:

The 'invention' of Africa in the political and literary imaginings of African peoples, continental and diasporic, represents a contested space divided along the lines of culture and nationality upon which location, positionality, and identity construction determine political practices that extend to the acts of writing and reading texts (103, 104).

Critics frustrated with Walker's reading of African women's and girl children's bodies, then, might look to the author's history and ethnic origins. As Walker addresses her readers, 'I do not know from what part of Africa my African ancestors came, and so I claim the continent. I suppose I have created Olinka as my village and the Olinkas as one of my ancient, ancestral tribal peoples' (285). Walker's 'claim' to 'the continent' invites multiple interpretations, but, perhaps most earnestly, it can be accepted as a desperate yearning to understand the place from which her foremothers and fathers came, a hope lodged not only in Walker's heart and imagination, but perhaps, too, in the collective souls of African America. To Walker, Africa is more than 'place'; it is her birthright and inheritance.

Warrior Marks: Female Genital Mutilation and the Sexual Blinding of Women is a documentary film and book Walker co-created with Indian-British film director Pratibha Parmar, featuring interviews with activists against FGM, all of whom are African; women and girls who have been 'circumcised'; mothers who have had or will have their daughters cut; women who assert they will never take a razor to their offspring; and village circumcisers.[3] Yet, *Warrior Marks* is as much Walker's personal journey 'back to Africa' as it is a documentary to spread awareness about FGM in hopes of ending it. Set in various parts of West Africa, including Senegal and the Gambia, footage also shows London, where Walker interviewed Efua Dorkenoo and Aminata Diop, a young woman who fled her home in Mali to avoid being cut. To date, the book and film have been understudied in the United States as crucial texts in arguments about women's global empowerment and sisterhood relations.[4]

The screen version opens with Walker reading from a letter she had written to Parmar as African women dance to the sound of a drum. Adolescent girls wrapped in colourful fabrics from head-to-toe, and accompanied by one four-year-old 'initiate', sit nearby, their faces blank. The girls have just spent two weeks healing after the circumcision rite and have 'come out'. In celebration, the women stomp and swing. Walker reads,

> Dear Prathiba, I am sending you the little script that I hope will be part of the film. I don't know just how you'll do it, but I think it can be worked in throughout the discussions about genital mutilation so that *I'm a part of the subject, and not just an observer. I've done this in a deliberate effort to stand with the mutilated women not beyond them. I know how painful exposure is* [emphasis mine]; it is something I've had to face every day of my life, beginning with my own first look in the mirror in the morning. (13)

Writing herself into the documentary script as 'part of the subject' is Walker's attempt to negotiate her history and also to stand in solidarity with women who have been 'circumcised.' As Gourdine explains, Walker is 'searching for [her] kin, looking for the social, cultural, and political space into which [she] can insert [herself]' (15). From Walker's perspective, the 'first look in the mirror' is the adhesive that binds her with genitally injured women: the phrase explains Walker's 'visual mutilation' at age eight. Clearly, Walker intimately associates her 'blackwoman's' (Gourdine 15) body with the mutilated woman's. Yet, these bodies, though 'Black' and female, are not the same.

After reading the excerpt, Walker recounts how, when a child, she had lost an eye to her older brother's B.B. gun, a Christmas present, which she, a girl, had not received. The mature Alice notes, 'What I had, I realised only as a consciously feminist adult, was a patriarchal wound. . . . It is true I am marked forever, like the woman who is robbed of her clitoris. . . . It was my visual mutilation that helped me 'see' the subject of genital mutilation' (17, 18).[5] Walker concludes that her blinding is actually a 'warrior mark' because from the ashes of her childhood devastation, including her parents' lack of protection and emotional support, she has become 'someone who loves life and knows pleasure and joy in spite of it' (17, 18).

Once so named, this 'warrior mark', from Walker's perspective, becomes a sign of resistance against patriarchy, and represents her decision to live full and free, in direct opposition to the life of subjugation intended for her as a girl and woman. Walker identifies her injury as deriving from patriarchal systems that support male violence while simultaneously blaming women for their own victimisation.[6] She then equates the wound incurred from her brother's gun with the surgical pain of excised women and girls, claiming that as a 'maimed' woman, she, too, can insist 'that mutilation of any part of the body is unnecessary and causes suffering almost beyond imagining' (19).[7]

Here, Walker assumes solidarity with all women who have suffered the razor, an attitude challenged by some who resent Walker's speaking for them, for even if they acknowledge the operation's sting, they persist in claiming it as part of their culture. And it is true: while many African women abhor the practice, the majority favour it (logical, of course, for otherwise no international movement would be needed).[8] Ignoring this uncomfortable fact, Walker explains to Parmar the interconnection she feels with the 'initiated' girl, her emotions derived from the sense of abandonment that overwhelmed her after her brother's assault, an incident her family called 'Alice's accident' (Walker 16):

My own visual mutilation...led me to a place of great isolation in my family and in my community and a great feeling of being oppressed. And also, there wasn't a sufficient reason given for it, nor was there sufficient comfort given to me as a child. And I see this mirrored in the rather callous way that people assume, 'Why, yes, you take a little child off, you know, and tell her she's going to visit her grandmother. On the way, you divert her attention from the trip to the grandmother's and you instead hold her down and relieve her of her clitoris and other parts of her, you know, genitalia.' And basically you leave her to heal from this as best she can. Everybody else is making merry, you know; she is the only one crying. But somehow you don't care, you don't show sensitivity to this child's pain. I made a very strong connection with that.

Walker's memory of physical and emotional injury experienced during childhood drives her choice to identify with the girl whom she describes as having been tricked into 'circumcision,' uncomforted, left to mend her own wounds and, ultimately, to recover, alone.[9] She assumes that both her hurt and theirs occur under the auspices of patriarchal oppression.

Walker, however, does not appear to have considered alternative ideals about the body in various socio-cultural contexts, strong beliefs that, if abolition is our aim, deserve to be aired and taken seriously. As Nako asserts, '[Walker's] representation of the African woman's body...does not account for [its] meanings [in] different cultures. ...Her reading of African women's bodies is informed by her Western...privileging of the body' (191). In Nako's view, Walker neglects to interpret female 'circumcision' as part of a complex social system of identity and therefore underestimates the strength of its role as a cultural marker.

Yet, the 'connection' Walker feels with excised and infibulated women and girls extends beyond the body politic to the 'significance of place.' From Walker's perspective, she and the women she chooses to 'stand with' share a common heritage, and though they were reared on either side of the Atlantic, are nonetheless 'kin.' As part of their respective journeys, Parmar and Walker film some of Walker's commentary on FGM at the House of Slaves on Gorée Island in Senegal. The House of Slaves is one of many 'slave houses' that remain along the coast of Africa, though one might more appropriately think of these towering edifices as 'dungeons.' The 'houses' now exist in memoriam to thousands of African men and women who, once transported to the 'house' from their various villages, would experience their 'last bit of Africa before being shipped to America' (Walker 74). And even this 'last bit' of 'home' was experienced in chains, which indicates the extent to which 'home' had already been lost.

In her remembrance of the day, Parmar observes, 'On the twenty-minute ferry trip to Gorée, we shot some beautiful reflective shots of Alice' (Walker 214). Perhaps the decision to film Walker's Black, female body crossing the waters en route to Gorée is intended to tap into our collective consciousness, and thereby, evoke the Middle Passage. Clearly, Walker's 'homegoing' is pivotal to the film; her body functions as the centre of the production.[10] Even as spectators witness several interviews and protests against FGM, as well as a powerful, interpretive dance by Richelle, to demonstrate 'the removal of...pleasure...via genital mutilation' (Walker 227), the lens of the camera coaxes viewers to study Walker's frame as it moves from water to landscape.

When the crew arrived at the House of Slaves in 1993, Joseph Ndiaya was its administrator and curator. Ndiaya is an important figure in my consideration of Walker's transatlantic journey. Like the West African griot, he escorts Walker into her past to help negotiate her present. He offers her a sculpture of a Black man in chains and remarks to both Walker and her assistant, also African American, 'I know you have come here on a pilgrimage, and it is good that you are here. You are very welcome. You could be my distant cousins or my long-lost relatives. We, each of us, are related' (Walker 214). Ndiaya not only confirms the case of kinship I have attempted to make here, he also affirms Walker's need to find her 'kin' while on this voyage. He hints, too, that like the African American, the African is also searching for her/his lost relatives, carried across an ocean, never to return, except for the possibility that their descendants might migrate to the continent as Walker does.

Walker notes that Ndiaya looked 'just like my mother's brothers' (74) and 'the fatherly kindness of his voice and his look of being a relative completely undid me, and I started to weep, completely without intending to or even thinking that I might' (74). Perhaps Walker's tears are triggered by her need to reconcile personal issues of family. After all, she had incurred a 'patriarchal wound' in America, but was now in the presence of a man who made her weep out of kindness rather than pain.[11] Further, while Ndiaya's presence comforts Walker, it also reminds her, perhaps, of what she has lost in the way of ancestral, familial ties to the continent. She adds, 'I suddenly realised that this is probably the response of many African Americans who come to Gorée Island...' (Walker 74). Here, Walker attempts to explain, through her own emotions, the African American experience of 'going home,' when travellers' bodies return to the site from which their ancestors may have begun, if not on Gorée, then perhaps another 'slave dungeon' on the African coast. Before departing the House, Walker writes in the guest book: 'My ancestors, mother and father, sister and brother. I feel you so strongly here in this place. I weep without intending to; I will continue to remember and pray for your rest in my soul' (Walker 75).

Earlier, I highlighted Walker's purpose to tell the 'untold' story of the female slave who may have been 'mutilated.' Research indicates that female 'circumcision' has been practiced for thousands of years though the origins of the practice are unknown. Many West African countries that perform the procedure were conduits for captives of the slave trade, not limited to but including Benin, Burkina Faso, Ghana, Sierra Leone, and Senegal. Feasibly, a female slave from any of the ethnic groups currently known to practice FGM would have undergone some form of 'circumcision' before her forced journey to the West.[12] As Parmar and Walker stand on the grounds of the House of Slaves, Walker contends,

> Well, nowhere have I seen any mention of the fact that women who were enslaved along the coast of Africa here (on Gorée Island) and who came out through this particular house, for instance, there's no record to show that they were probably mutilated and infibulated, so we have to think about what that was like for those women who were not only subjected to all of the cruelties that everyone else was subjected to, but they in addition had been stitched shut so that every bodily function through the vulva had to be horrendous.

While Walker's concern may have implications for the African slave woman's experience as a displaced body in the West, questions arise. Would a circumcised female slave have attempted to continue 'circumcising' her descendants, using the miniscule power she might possess? Would female 'circumcision,' then, have become endemic in antebellum African America? Would slave owners have banished the practice from fear that the cut might affect fertility and in line with their obsession with breeding/mass producing Black bodies? I raise these questions not only to interrogate Walker's consideration of this aspect of the slave woman's story, but also to situate its significance in her anti-FGM campaign. Walker's attempt to map the Diasporic history of the excised woman's body overlaps with her hope to locate and contextualise her own history and diasporic identity. Because this section engages 'place,' I am interested in the locale of Walker's discourse of the genitally mutilated body 'in transit' as she stands on Gorée Island, the 'other' side of the Atlantic, the 'other' side of her history.

As Walker concludes oration on the plausibility of genitally wounded woman's 'middle passage,' the camera zooms on her image standing at the infamous 'Door of No Return,' the slaves' final destination on African soil before boarding the nearby ship. The pose is striking: a darkened silhouette of Walker's body in contrast with the open door, illuminated by sunlight and the ocean.[13] Arguably, hundreds of years later, Walker, too, is in a place of uncertainty, not about where she will be taken against her will, but about her African ancestry before slavery. As she slowly walks from the door, Walker's voice-over begins: 'The House of Slaves on Gorée Island in Senegal was the beginning of the [end] for many of our captured and enslaved ancestors bound for the Americas.' The image and Walker's commentary call on the audience to remember that though Walker is free, her ancestors were not. Yet, she chooses to identify with their painful voyage.

Walker's 'personal journey' in the book *Warrior Marks* ends with a shot of her standing beside a group of African women. She explains the portrait below:

While Pratibha and I had discussed making the film back home in California ... I'd told her my vision for the end of the film. I want to be walking down a road with African women, I'd said; I want it to be clear that we are going on with life, and I want the audience to feel it should rise up and go on into life with us ... [And then, coincidentally] what should we see coming down the road toward us but a group of colourfully dressed, fast-stepping women. ... So there we all were, on a dusty, middle-of-nowhere road in the far outback of the Gambia, walking with a steady if hasty beat. The women were beautiful and full of humour. Even though we didn't speak each other's languages, we managed to laugh a lot. ... It was like a dream, really. I knew them so well, I felt; indeed, I felt I knew the very road we were walking on. And somehow I also knew that, together, we'd get to the end of it. (Walker 85, 86)

There is a tone not only of kinship, but perhaps most earnestly, of friendship in Walker's analysis of this moment, as she stands with African women on a solitary dirt road. Yet, at the same time, the solipsistic, self-referential emphasis on Walker's own feelings gives the passage an aura of distance from its subjects, for whom the track is not celestial but everyday.

Few would dispute that Walker's search for Africa materialises also as a search for self and Diaspora kinship. Whether she achieves it pales in contrast to what her efforts opened in terms of trans-global discussion and transnational communication. As a result of Walker's initiative – and she was, after all, the first truly famous voice to critique FGM as a gross violation of human rights—, feminists invested in social change have begun to participate in *zakhor*, 'translated into English as both an imperative and an obligation: remember' (Simon *et al.* 10). For Walker conveys how critical it is to choose appropriate alliances, break taboo, and recall the probably 'circumcised' captives, in empathy with their pain.

Jennifer Browdy de Hernandez
'Mother' as a Verb: the Erotic, Audre Lorde and Female Genital Mutilation (FGM)

When African American feminist Audre Lorde theorises female sexuality and eroticism, she provides an original frame through which to view the many injurious practices known as female genital mutilation (FGM). In her celebration of the feminine erotic, she joins activists such as Alice Walker and the signers of the Bamako Declaration in opposing a social custom whose end is the opposite of Lorde's. For Lorde, erotic potential is a fountain of self-love and empowerment. Dam(n)ing that pleasurable stream, as clitoridectomy and infibulation aim to do, denies women an important reservoir of confidence and can lead to self-destruction. Grave as these consequences are, however, extrapolating from Lorde's work suggests that, unlike Walker, she would not endorse even the symbolic murder of the mother-surrogate, as an effective campaign-mobilising tool. Quite the contrary: elevating the maternal, she imbues it with renewed sexual energy, names its rebellious potential, and broadens its scope. In Lorde's *oeuvre*, women mother not only children but each other and themselves. Precisely because an 'erotic mother' is, both North and South, an oxymoron, deployed in its challenging impossibility, it exhorts its audience to change.

QUESTIONING CULTURE
To what extent is it permissible for one culture to pass judgement on another? This question arises whenever distinct societies mingle, and with increasing urgency in these times of globalisation. In the context of a worldwide feminist movement, the issue becomes one of moral positioning: can recourse to a hypothesised 'universal sisterhood' justify

condemning social practices embedded in other traditions? Along with many like-minded individuals who have taken a stand on this in recent years,[1] I think the answer is a guarded and contingent 'yes': certain discriminatory behaviors are indeed legitimate targets. What is important is to work across ethnic and state borders toward shared aims. As Chandra Talpade Mohanty scripts it, solidarity is a child of understanding 'the historical and experiential specificities and differences of women's lives as well as the... [links] between women from different national, racial and cultural communities,' taking care to chronicle not only divisive litanies of domination but also mirrored moments of 'struggle and resistance' (243).

Nowhere has the need for effective global coalitions been more evident than in addressing female genital mutilation (FGM),[2] a set of entrenched procedures decried as a human rights violation of women and girls.[3] Practiced for centuries in Africa, the Middle East and their Diasporas, FGM is a surgical intrusion that can range from a largely symbolic 'nicking' of the clitoris that allegedly leaves no lasting damage (Shell-Duncan and Hernlund 5),[4] to clitoridectomy (in 85 per cent of cases) and infibulation (in nearly the totality of the female population in the Horn of Africa), where, after the clitoris and labia are removed, the vagina is sewn or pinned shut, leaving a miniscule opening for urine and menses. Obviously, these 'rites' carry serious health risks, especially since they are most often performed in unsanitary conditions, using razors or knives, with no anaesthesia or modern means of haemorrhage prevention.[5] 'It is pain,' notes one critic, 'that leads to accusations [by advocates for abolition who call] genital operations... 'torture'' (Walley 37). While there are small but significant movements in each of the twenty-six practicing African countries, with many NGOs under the aegis of the militant IAC (Inter-African Committee), FGM remains widespread, affecting millions of girls each year with its unequivocal genital assault.[6]

Read against this grim imprint, no one has been more outspoken about the value of sexuality as a font of pleasure and liberation for women than African American feminist Audre Lorde (1934–1992). Celebrating the power of the erotic, Lorde beautifully defined it as 'self-connection shared' (1984, 57), a 'profoundly creative source' which could 'give us the energy to pursue genuine change within our world' (1984, 59). Although Lorde's published writings often reach back through her ancestors to African traditions, and sexuality consistently appears as a force for the empowerment of women, she addresses female genital mutilation directly in only one passage, in her 'Open Letter to Mary Daly,' a response to Daly's controversial book *Gyn/Ecology: The Metaethics of Radical Feminism.*

In her letter, published in the 1984 collection *Sister Outsider*, Lorde chastises Daly for treating 'noneuropean [*sic*] women…only as victims' and, in Daly's words, as "token torturers" of each other. While granting that inclusion of 'African genital mutilation was an important and necessary piece in any consideration of female ecology, and [that] too little has been written about it,' Lorde questions exclusive attention to the issue while ignoring 'the old traditions of power and strength and nurturance found in the female bonding of African women.' This, she says, appears to 'deny the fountain of noneuropean [*sic*] female strength' (1984, 68–69).

Ironically, FGM proponents often cite the value of 'female bonding' when they defend the practice. Apologists, for whom the cutting is worthy of retention because it promotes group solidarity and celebrates female strength, have labelled international feminist and human rights efforts to stop the practice 'imperialistic intervention from meddling Westerners of privilege'[7] (Shell-Duncan and Hernlund 25), with humanitarian efforts reviled as smacking of arrogant racism and ethnocentrism.[8]

Lorde criticises Daly's deployment of FGM precisely along these lines, arguing that *Gyn/Ecology* is racist and ethnocentric for its insistence on African women's debility. But in the same breath, Lorde recognises FGM as one of patriarchy's 'many varied tools' often 'used by women without awareness against each other' (1984, 67). FGM may be, in anthropologist Gerry Mackie's words, 'women's business' (279), but the purpose of the genital cutting has everything to do with men. The women who bring their daughters to the circumciser believe the procedure to be physically necessary to render girls fit for marriage.[9] Practicing cultures attach a strong stigma to uncircumcised women, who will not be accepted as brides but instead mocked and harassed for their deviance. Thus, in submitting daughters to the practice, mothers accept short-term pain thinking it results in long-term benefit,[10] and derive their own advantages from conformity, thus enjoying their culture's 'virtual deification of mothers' (Ahmadu 306). For these upholders of tradition, the very idea of abandoning the cut 'would constitute a most unfathomable 'insult' against their [own] mothers and grandmothers' (Ahmadu 307).

Women hurting women out of a purported respect for women—this is a conundrum that few feminists have written about more eloquently than Audre Lorde, who perceived that women, like other oppressed minorities, are often manipulated into wounding each other unwittingly in obeisance to patriarchal norms. Lorde also wrote often about pain, and the way Black women the world over have risen above it to survive despite the odds. To clarify, she drew an important distinction between *pain* and *suffering*:

> Pain is an event, an experience that must be recognised, named, and then used in some way in order for the experience to change, to be transformed into... strength or knowledge or action. Suffering, on the other hand, is the nightmare reliving of unscrutinised and unmetabolised pain. When I live through pain without recognising it ... I rob myself of the power that can come from *using* that pain... to fuel some movement beyond it (171–72).

One of the most outspoken Western critics of FGM, Alice Walker, employed this distinction in her novel *Possessing the Secret of Joy*, whose protagonist, Tashi, endures for years the psychic and physical trauma that follows her infibulation, until she finally finds the strength to convert her suffering into pain by going back to Africa and assassinating the old woman who had destroyed her genitalia and those of so many others. Though Tashi is executed for her crime, she dies satisfied, believing that the killing has launched a new national dialogue, which may result in changed public opinion and official policy on FGM. In Lorde's terms, Tashi has transformed her extended silence into language and action, just as Alice Walker has done by writing this widely read novel and making the accompanying film, 'Warrior Marks.' Would Lorde have agreed with Walker, however, that the solution to the problem of FGM is to resist the practice unequivocally – to, in effect, kill the circumcisers, metaphorically of course, no matter what the cost?

Lorde is certainly no stranger to the kind of rage that fuels Walker's activism. 'Every woman has a well-stocked arsenal of anger potentially useful against those oppressions, personal and institutional' that elicited her wrath, she says. 'Focused with precision it can become a powerful source of energy serving progress and change' (1984, 127). Concerning FGM, the question becomes, where and how should indignation be applied?[11] As Mackie notes, '[outsiders'] bullying...breeds defiance or sham abandonment. ...Threats to outlaw FGC have often been met with increases in FGC' (277–78), the result of a psychological mechanism Mackie identifies as 'reactance' in which 'the greater the pressure to comply, the more one wants to defy' (277).

Given this resistance, some critics deploy a more nuanced approach. They advocate keeping certain aspects of the rite while abandoning others. Sierra Leonean Fuambai Ahmadu, in a vivid account of her own circumcision, rationalises that initiation, though 'physically excruciating,' also 'celebrat[es] women's pre-eminent roles in history and society.' She tells us, 'I felt that I was participating in a fear-inspiring world, controlled and dominated by women, which nonetheless fascinated me because I was becoming a part of it' (Ahmadu 306). Ahmadu advocates a 'ritual-without-cutting model' to 'replace the physical act' of amputation with 'an equally dynamic symbolic performance...retain[ing] the same fluidity in associated meanings – eschewal of masculinity, womanhood, fertility, equality, hierarchy, motherhood, and sexual restraint' (308–09).[12] Ahmadu admits, however, that for her tribe at least, excision remains an 'all-important' part of the procedure.[13]

This opens up the contested question of just how damaging to women's sexuality excision actually is, often argued heatedly in the absence of hard evidence, due to an appalling history of under-funding for research. It wasn't until June 2006 that the first call for papers for wide-scale study of the sexual response of mutilated women was issued by the World Health Organisation ('Call for Proposals: Research on Female Genital Mutilation and Female Sexuality'), with the investigations themselves starting only in January 2007. Reviewing the understandably wide disparities in ideological and anecdotal studies of this topic, the editors of *Female Circumcision in Africa* conclude that 'a reliable evaluation of the effect of FGC on sexual response is often difficult to obtain, since in many cases the procedure takes place at such a young age that the woman has no prior sexual experience with which to compare post-FGC sensitivity' (Shell-Duncan and Hernlund 17). Nonetheless, since 'the external clitoris constitutes [only] a small fraction of the total nerve endings that produce [the entire appendage's] sensations,' Ahmadu argues that, even after excision, '... sensitivity [can] remain for the most part undiminished.' After all, she asserts, most women of her tribe, the Kono, 'do not perceive [themselves] as inhibit[ed] in any way' by their clitoral loss (305).

Nonetheless, documented cases reveal women severely affected in their subsequent sex life. For instance, to be deflowered, a bride who has undergone 'pharaonic' infibulation must be ruptured, an excruciating event often requiring that the groom rip her open with a knife; and with each birth, she must again be defibulated, increasing the danger of labour (Balk, 56; World Health Organisation *Lancet* study).[14] An on-going problem for infibulated women is the 'chronic retention of urine and menstrual fluids, or the development of fistulae that may produce foul odors' (Balk 60), disheartening conditions distressing to victims and their husbands alike.[15]

FGM AND EMPOWERMENT EROTICS?

It is hard to imagine Audre Lorde, who celebrated female sexuality with an almost religious fervour, supporting a practice that makes sex into such a trial. Where would she have laid the blame? On tradition-conscious African women? On the men who insist on circumcised wives? No doubt she would have looked more deeply into the issue before passing judgement, and in doing so would have uncovered the *pierre de résistance*, the fact that the practice is all the more entrenched where it is anchored in cosmological beliefs, still cited today, namely that the clitoris is an 'unnatural' male part of the female whose removal is mandatory if proper gender harmony and order are to prevail. Among the Kono people in Sierra Leone, for example, Ahmadu explains, 'children must be 'made' into either 'male' or 'female' depending on the appearance of their genitalia at birth, in order for them to be able to reproduce and [enter into] 'culture'.' Reminiscent of Simone de Beauvoir's famous pronouncement that 'women are made, not born,' in Sierra Leone and elsewhere in Africa initiation marks 'the social and cultural construction of [exclusively] 'male' and 'female' beings, [with] genital cutting the key' (Ahmadu, 297).

To get a sense of what Lorde's response to this cultural rejection of androgyny might have been, we need look no further than the Prologue of her 'biomythography' *Zami*, where she candidly admits, 'I have always wanted to be both man and woman, to incorporate the strong[est] and richest part of my mother and father within/into me – to share valleys and mountains upon my body the way the earth does in hills and peaks' (1982, 7). Celebrating the 'deep inside...of [her],' she talks of imagining 'the core of it, my pearl – a protruding part of me, hard and sensitive and vulnerable in a different way' (Ibid). Given Lorde's *avant-la-lettre* queer sensibilities, she is unlikely to have accepted the traditional African idea that a clitoris must be excised in order to render a girl female.

Other justifications for the practice are more related to married women's status as the property of their husbands. As one Kenyan man puts it, 'Circumcision is [like] a [cattle] brand. If a girl is not circumcised, she can stay with her family, and can have sex with boyfriends. We get a brand to show that she is mine, and can only be with me, and will bear my children. ...Branding makes her mine' (Shell-Duncan, Obiero and Muruli, 118). A woman from the same Kenyan tribe, the Rendille, puts it slightly differently: 'When a man has married, he takes control of you. You must follow his rules. ...If you make a mistake...he can leave you without animals, and without food and water, and he can beat you' (Ibid 119). A woman is respected only if she marries and bears children; but in order to wed she must accept the brand of circumcision as well as her husband's 'control' over her.

Obviously 'circumcision' is tightly bound up with the patriarchal nature of the cultures that practice it, and, regarding women's oppression under patriarchy, Audre Lorde had much to say. 'Only within a patriarchal structure is maternity the [sole] social power open to women,' she comments in her famous essay 'The Master's Tools Will Never Dismantle the Master's House,' in which she urges women to defy the patriarchal strategy of 'keep[ing] the oppressed occupied with the master's concerns' (1984, 111), in this case policing the cutting of their daughters. Women should look to each other, instead, for support and validation, to defy 'the [tyrant]...deep within us' (1984, 123).

While Lorde is firm that 'no woman is responsible for altering the psyche of her [tormenter],' (1984, 133) even when the bully's mind wears a woman's shape (1984, 133), she does insist that 'self-empowerment [of women]...is the most deeply political work there is, and the most difficult' (1984, 170). Women, and especially Black women, 'must establish authority over [their] own definition,' (1984, 173), resisting and transcending the 'old blueprints of expectation and response, old structures of oppression, [which] must be altered at the same time as... the living conditions [that] result [from them]' (1984, 123).

Lorde identified a primal patriarchal 'structure of oppression' in the containment and regulation of women's sexuality by a variety of means, one of which would certainly be FGM. Female sexuality should not exist just to satisfy male desire, Lorde declares in her important essay, 'Uses of the Erotic: The Erotic as Power,' and yet it has been systematically 'vilified, abused and devalued' (1984, 53) by men for fear of its deployment other than 'in [their] service.' Women, having become themselves metonymies for sex, are distanced, kept in an 'inferior position to be psychically milked, much the same way ants maintain colonies of aphids to provide a life-giving substance for their masters.' And yet, the feminine erotic, a source of strength 'ris[ing] from our deepest... non-rational knowledge' (1984, 53) should be re-deployed for women's good, for it offers 'a well of replenishing and provocative force to the woman who does not fear its revelation, nor succumb to the belief that sensation is enough' (1984, 54).

Distinguishing between the erotic and the pornographic, Lorde argues that 'pornography emphasises sensation without feeling,' while the erotic provides 'an internal sense of satisfaction and completion' (1984, 54). Such plenitude goes beyond the merely sexual – suggesting a seditious possibility if the erotic is indeed 'creative energy empowered' (1984, 55) or 'self-connection shared' (1984, 57).

This utopian vision of empowerment may pale against the massive line-up of excisers' razors but in fact movements are growing to resist FGM, one of the most successful run by Tostan, an NGO largely sponsored by UNICEF and the government of Senegal.[16] Tostan offers an ambitious six-month programme to rural villages that includes training in literacy, problem-solving skills, health and hygiene, preventing child mortality, financial management, strategising for innovative village projects, leadership and group dynamics. According to Gerry Mackie, 'the pedagogy uses local cultural traditions and learner-generated materials, including proverbs, stories, songs, games, poetry, and plays,' and the trainers and facilitators are all indigenous (259). It was women in a Tostan programme in Malicounda who in 1997 persuaded their neighbours to become the first in Senegal to publicly outlaw FGM. The example of their public declaration was soon adopted elsewhere in the region, leading to national legislation banning FGM in that nation in 1999.[17]

For Mackie, it is crucial that the drive to end FGM originated with the women of Malicounda themselves, convinced to take action not by browbeating or propaganda, but credible information. The Tostan programme, he stresses, 'is nondirective. People are *never told what to do*' (259), but encouraged to apply new skills in responsible, innovative ways.

Lorde would surely have supported this kind of self-empowerment – giving women tools other than 'the master's' in order to 'pursue genuine change within our world' (1984, 59). She would also have approved of Tostan's refusal to cast blame or pass judgement, and applauded its choice to present information, especially on human rights, that led participants to reject FGM on their own. The programme exemplifies the kind of communitarian nurturing that Lorde always supported—not seeking to eliminate disparities, but rather to work through them, 'learning how to take our differences and make them strengths' (1984, 112). As Molly Melching, Tostan's founder puts it:

> You know, some words that never come up in development jargon or academic papers are love and respect. But the truth is that one of the main reasons our programme works is because of the mutual love and respect between the villagers and Tostan. When people have another agenda – let's end FGC – it often boomerangs because it implies that all you care about is changing people, which means you don't accept them the way they are. Whereas when one loves and respects and trusts others to make the right decision it happens quite naturally (qtd. in Mackie, 278).

Love, respect and trust – these are human emotions that Lorde often wrote about. In *Zami*, she describes her route through a series of damaging relationships until she finally encounters Afrekete, the semi-mythic African mother-lover-goddess, with whom she enjoys erotic fulfilment. And if role models like Afrekete are hard to find, Lorde says, women can nonetheless 'learn to mother ourselves,' by which she means affirming our self worth, 'laying to rest [without resentment]...what is weak, timid and damaged...protect[ing] and support[ing] what is useful, and...jointly explor[ing]' differences we share (1984, 174).

WALKER AND LORDE

An example of such 'joint exploration' enriches Alice Walker's *Possessing the Secret of Joy*. When Tashi returns to Africa to confront M'Lissa, the old woman who circumcised her, both Tashi and M'Lissa emerge changed and enlightened as a result of their dialogue.[17] In M'Lissa's tribe,[18] the position of circumciser is hereditary, and while M'Lissa's grandmother is completely unfeeling in her work, having become 'so callous [that]...she would circumcise the children and demand food immediately after; even if the child still screamed' (Walker 221), M'Lissa's mother is more sensitive. When circumcising the girls in her own daughter's age group, 'she tried to get away with cutting lightly.... But the other women saw. What my mother started,' M'Lissa tells Tashi, 'the witchdoctor finished,' and he was merciless:

> In fright and unbearable pain my body bucked under the razor-sharp stone he was cutting me with. ...I could never again see myself, for the child that finally rose from the mat three months later, and dragged herself out of the initiation hut and finally home, was not the child who had been taken there. I was never to see that child again (Walker 221–222).

Later, engaged in 'joint exploration' with Tashi, M'Lissa does in fact reconnect with the young girl she had been, excavating memories that revise her professional image and in a sense permitting her to 'mother herself anew'. 'I finally see her,' she tells Tashi with excitement:

> The child who went into the initiation hut...I left her bleeding there on the floor, and I came out. She was crying. She felt so betrayed. By everyone. They'd severely beaten her mother as well, and she blamed herself for this. M'Lssa sighed. I couldn't think about her anymore. I would have died. So I walked away, limped away, and just left her there. (Walker 225)

When Melissa resumes her narration, a shift has occurred, from chronicle to myth. The real little girl left crying on the floor, M'Lissa, now whispers, has never stopped. Having nested below the surface of the cutter's mind, she went right on weeping and hasn't ceased since. 'No wonder I haven't been able to [cry],' the soon-to-be murdered mid-wife exclaims. 'She's been crying all our tears' (Walker 225).

After this revelation, M'Lissa is able to identify for herself more critically what Lorde has called the 'structures of oppression' that have shaped her: 'I have been strong,' M'Lissa says. 'Dragging my half-body wherever half a body was needed. In service to tradition, to what makes us a people. ... But who are we but torturers of children?' (Walker 226).

Like Walker, whose portrait of the circumciser as an endlessly wounded, crying child gives us a sense of compassion for the aged M'Lissa that we might not otherwise have had, Lorde also evokes the image of 'the brave bruised girlchild within each of us,' to whom we should 'be tender,' 'lov[ing] her in the light as well as in the darkness, quiet[ing] her frenzy toward perfection, and encourage[ing] her attentions toward fulfilment' (1984, 175). By being 'gentle with ourselves,' Lorde suggests, we can learn how to 'be gentle with each other,' and then to 'stand toe to toe within that rigorous loving and begin to speak the impossible – or what has always seemed like the impossible – to one another. The first step toward genuine change' (Ibid).

In Walker's novel, however, Tashi is far from gentle with M'Lissa, and it is her ability to access her own anger that gives her the strength to rescue herself from depression and despair. Audre Lorde has argued strongly that anger is a valuable source of power and change for women. 'When we turn from anger we turn from insight, saying we will accept only the designs already known, deadly and safely familiar. ... The angers of women can transform difference through insight into power. For anger between peers births change, not destruction, and the discomfort and sense of loss it often causes is not fatal, but a sign of growth' (1984, 131).

As cultural outsiders moved to act by conscience against child abuse and violation of human rights, our anger is an understandable response that Lorde would not have us suppress. She would remind us, however, that if we are committed to changing this reality, we must stand alongside courageous and embattled activists grappling with FGM at home, and support *their* efforts rather than imposing our own pre-defined agendas.[20] As Lorde insists; 'You do not have to be me in order for us to fight alongside each other. I do not have to be you to recognise that our wars are the same. What we must do is to commit ourselves to [a] future that can include each other and to work toward that future with [each of our] particular strengths' (1984, 142). What better credo than this for a global feminist coalition to accelerate the end of FGM?

ENRAGED

Augustine H. Asaah

Female Genital Mutilation (FGM): Ambivalence, Indictment and Commitment in Sub-Saharan African Fiction[1]

What better bettering can there be, I ask myself, than engaging literature to put an end to torture? (Levin 1)

INTRODUCTION

Long a muted topic, Female Genital Mutilation (FGM) has failed to receive the consistent attention from Sub-Saharan artists it deserves.[2] I share the view of Awa Thiam, Dennis Hickey and Waris Dirie who contend that FGM, although a sensitive and emotional issue, merits sustained scrutiny and debate until it is abolished worldwide. This does not imply that literary circles have been completely silent on the subject. Indeed, African creative writers such as Ngugi wa Thiong'o, Ahmadou Kourouma, Nuruddin Farah, Calixthe Beyala, Mariama Barry, Fatou Keïta, Nura Abdi and Khady have represented FGM in fiction. Similarly, in their critical works, Rangira Béatrice Gallimore, Pierrette Herzberger-Fofana, Béatrice N'guessan-Larroux and Cilas Kemedjio have visited the topic. Joining them in bringing FGM out into the open, this chapter discusses the theme in African narratives written by both established and emergent authors. Like Chantal Patterson and Tobe Levin, I employ the term FGM to cover all forms of ablation, notably excision, clitoridectomy and infibulation, to which the sexual organs of female infants, girls and women are subjected.

Underpinning my perspective is a female-centred political discourse that seeks to improve the lot of women and society by deleting outmoded

75

cultural practices. Like Herzberger-Fofana, I, too, see FGM as a violent infringement and a major obstacle to societal development. It is at variance with the African Charter on Human Rights as much as it is with the UN Universal Declaration on Human Rights. If we are now witnessing an international effort by concerned citizens of both sexes to ban FGM, it is borne out of the fact, as Hickey emphasises, that 'there can be no significant social transformation if the rights of women are not pursued with the same conviction and vigour as are those celebrated, if often neglected, 'rights of man'.' (244).

Gender myths that assign specific social roles to males and females as well as encourage cults of violence are constitutive of all cultures. Across time and space, hegemonic ideologies have flourished on the wings of literature, not least in parables, proverbs and exempla. In the case of FGM, myths and other imaginative genres that legitimate the practice also sustain it. Yet a radically different meaning emerges from myth when contemporary writers use it to contest the ideological and ritualised bases of genital ablation and re-deploy it in innovative ways, thereby birthing a new ethos and a new socio-political pact. As iconoclastic wordsmiths dismantle retardant legend and replace it with new fables based on inclusive ethics, bonding and human rights, they illustrate Simon Gikandi's argument that myth can serve a reconstructive function in realising new social dreams and expressing shared ideals (150). The discussion will later show that this contestatory strand is a marked feature of FGM discourse in contemporary Africa.

CULTURAL IDENTITY, INTERPENETRATION OF LIVES, AND COMMITMENT

In the Confucian *Weltanschauung*, human nature is the same; only customs distinguish one group from the next (Kodjo 94). If then humans are identical by nature, it is their culturally nurtured traits, their traditions, which account for differences in fortune and mentality. Culture, in this light, appears as a site of reciprocal exclusiveness, and its stranglehold may explain deviation: why certain nations or ethnic groups pride themselves on consuming the meat of the whale, an endangered species; why others view criminalising widows and perpetuating slavery as their unique cultural heritage, while still others see in FGM a mark of proud distinctiveness.

The notion of shared experience and interrelationship, however, that sustains modern epistemologies such as peace, postcolonial and postmodern studies, stresses that identity is a project in process to which endogenous and exogenous groups necessarily contribute. Embedded in this model is the modern configuration of human destiny as one of interpenetration, not mutual exclusion. Rejecting the idea of cocooned cultural identities, Arjun Appadurai notes: 'Recent work in anthropology has done much to free us of the shackles of highly localised, boundary-oriented, holistic, primordialist images of cultural formation and substance' (336). For his part, Jean-Loup Amselle asserts that, like all deterritorialised entities such as the Americas and Europe, Africa also represents a dynamic concept whose semantic logic frees it of territorial entrenchment, thus making it possible for those who so desire to connect with it (15). These views resonate with Achille Mbembe's position: 'African identity does not exist as a substance or as an essence . . . Neither the forms of this identity nor its idioms are always self-identical. And these forms and idioms are mobile, reversible, and unstable' (16). Mbembe concludes that manifestations of identity cannot be reduced to custom, precisely because the latter is perpetually being reinvented and reconstructed (16).

Coincidentally, the Confucian notion of common human nature articulates, over and above cultural differences, the intersection of lives and unity of destinies. Confucius could, however, imply as well a need for customs that stand the test of time, constitute a source of well-deserved pride, and especially, by their sheer visionary quality, elicit envy and inspire imitation. As we shall later observe, most African novelists who write on FGM consider this cultural practice to be inconsistent with modern statehood, and still less apt to satisfy the criteria of respectability or emulation.

Even if to a certain degree, Confucius' axiom can be thought to uphold the uniqueness of cultural practice, because peculiar landmarks and local ecology necessarily influence it, we should note that humans are prone to mutation. To the extent that geographic and ecological conditions themselves are modified, they force people to change. Diverse nations and, therefore, diverse cultural groups, including citizens, tourists, diplomatic staffers, visiting athletes, traders or politicians, may be directly affected by natural disasters (the Sahelian drought, tsunamis, etc.) that not only trigger migration but also involve displacement of international crisis managers. Additionally, although cultural hybridisation is not new, it is iconic of modernity as populations experience an unprecedented scale of intermarriages, migration, communication, education, demands of modern statehood (with constitutions invariably *for* human rights and *against* discrimination), international conventions, pressure from civil society organisations and global cultural exchanges. As a result, cultures open up to one another, share artefacts, and define themselves anew. Clearly, certain core values remain whether in a group's or individual's country of origin, their adopted nation or their travels. Nonetheless, identity itself is mutable because susceptible to challenge from within and without.

From the foregoing, it becomes clear that FGM, rather than being the province of afflicted local communities or the hallowed ground of peculiar cultures, assumes an international dimension. By the same token, the surgeries concern not only victims – female neonates, girls and women – but also all citizens of the world irrespective of sex, creed, nationality or socio-economic station. As Thiam observes, focusing public attention on the mutilation of any human being in order to correct it, is a constructive act.[3]

In effect, FGM intersects with emergent disciplines such as gender, motherhood, violence, victimisation and peace studies, all of which challenge the stereotypic profiling that underpins obnoxious cultural norms, practices and attitudes. Such an interface of generally value-laden disciplines makes it possible to better appreciate Daniela Roventa-Frumasani's thesis that the modern idea of the subject subsumes three indispensable elements: one, resistance to domination (be it the colonisation of 'savages' or the phallocentric ghettoisation of women); two, freedom as a key precondition for life and happiness; and three, recognition of the other as subject (134). These elements emerge from the fiction of genital wounds.

AMBIVALENCE

The Kenyan writer Ngugi wa Thiong'o deserves credit for the first elaborate problematising of FGM in Sub-Saharan African fiction. In his novel *The River Between* (1965), Ngugi recounts the tribulations of two hostile but neighbouring Gikuyu communities in conflict, one side adhering to ancient customs, the other responding to the pull of an imported creed. Although a secondary plot in this complex tension between tradition and modernity, clitoridectomy (called female circumcision in the novel, and rightly so before the UN adopted the better term FGM) throws into sharp focus first, the antinomy between opponents and supporters of socio-cultural change and, second, efforts by moderates to reconcile both camps.

Abolitionists are the first group painted by Ngugi in the novel. As if parroting imperialistic opponents of cutting, they (are made by Ngugi to) appear bereft of any convincing arguments against the practice. Their intransigence stands only on the unacceptability of 'female circumcision' in the sight of the Christian God. For Christian missionaries, colonial administrators and zealous converts – also revealingly called 'Christian soldiers' – clitoral ablation is an accursed habit for which reason Joshua, the local Kenyan catechist and a prominent member of the godsquad, often 'devoted a prayer to asking God to forgive him for marrying a woman who had been circumcised' (31). He and his wife Miriamu inevitably underwent Gikuyu initiation rites, involving circumcision for boys and excision for girls, long before they converted to Christianity.[4]

Joshua's oppositional stance on FGM is further devalued by the fact that, for all his firebrand rhetoric, he has been unable to win his family over to the cause. Even worse, his second daughter Muthoni attempts to don the syncretistic garb by choosing to be cut. Why? She wants as her birthright insider access to the secrecy of earth-bound mores from which she, as a Christian, was exiled.

Traditionalists constitute the second faction Ngugi portrays. For Kabonyi and the advocates of FGM, surgery as a *rite de passage* moves initiates from childhood to adulthood. Victims are passed off as an inevitable sacrifice to the greater good of social harmony, and the shedding of blood that unites the community spiritually with the earth is ideologically packaged as a precondition for communal renewal. Thus conceived, clitoridectomy is deemed central to the community's cohesion and survival. Such is the importance of excision to the group, as Kenyatta also stresses in *Facing Mount Kenya*, that an intact girl becomes a pariah, impure, and a source of *thahu* or abomination. Therefore, traditional purists consider it their sacred duty to eliminate the uninitiated or force them to be cut in order that the land will become free of filth and curse.

Between these polarised fundamentalisms – Christian and traditional – stand the moderates or reformists, much like the symbolic river between the two ridges that gives its generic name to the novel. Called Honia, it means 'reconciliation,' and its durability as a feature of the landscape is stressed. Major characters, however, who urge compromise, are expendable: Joshua's two daughters – Nyambura and Muthoni – and Waiyaki. That is, prominent reformists either die or are condemned to death.

Muthoni's bold attempt at syncretism or socio-cultural synthesis comes to a tragic end when she loses her life during initiation, disowned by an unforgiving father. Neither the traditional healer nor the colonial hospital can save her. Like Samba Diallo who was futilely dispatched by the Grande Royale in Cheikh Hamidou Kane's *L'Aventure ambiguë*, Waiyaki, the boy sent by his father to the colonial school to learn the conqueror's secrets and to blend them with local wisdom, also fails to reconcile the two positions. Unlike Kenyatta and his followers who show scant interest in modifying clitoridectomy, Waiyaki wants a symbolic replacement for it. This is unacceptable to fundamentalists.

For all his stature in the village as a teacher, a social engineer and a builder of the future, Waiyaki is accused by the council of elders, the *Kiama,* of conspiracy. By associating with an uninitiated and therefore 'filthy' girl, Joshua's elder daughter, he has compromised the purity of the tribe. The death of the two 'deviants,' though not actualised in the novel, is captured in Kinuthia's nightmarish vision: a 'momentary glimpse of Waiyaki and Nyambura caught in those flames' (145) of ritual cleansing.

It is worth emphasising that Ngugi does not provide any clear sign of support for one position or the other that is neither condemnation nor defence. *The River Between* is thus ambivalent on the issue of clitoridectomy. To some extent, equivocality also undergirds Flora Nwapa's depiction of ablation, called 'the bath' by the traditional Igbo community to symbolise personal cleansing and societal purification. In her first novel *Efuru*, published a year after Ngugi's narrative, the rite is presented from the point of view of the community without the Nigerian author offering any evaluative commentary.

INDICTMENTS AND COMMITMENT

If Ngugi is the first African novelist to bring FGM fully into the public domain, Kourouma, the late Ivorian writer, is, to a large extent, the most consistent. For, in all four novels published before his death – *Les Soleils des indépendances; Monnè, outrages et defies; En attendant le vote des bêtes suavages* and *Allah n'est pas obligé*, he systematically invokes the subject and dilates on its harmful effects. For this reason, N'guessan-Larroux contends that the motifs of pain, blood, the colour red, frustration and disfigurement that run through Kourouma's depictions of FGM invest his narratives with cohesion, consistency and immediacy (7).

In *Les Soleils des indépendances*, first published in 1968, three years after Ngugi's novel, Kourouma dwells on the woes of a charming young lady, Salimata, after a botched excision. In striking contrast to Ngugi, Kourouma leaves the reader in no doubt of his sympathies – with the victim and the cause of abolitionists.

Salimata's sterility, physical brutalisation and psychological trauma –nightmares, hallucinations, dashed hopes, near frigidity—, all occasioned by excision, arguably single her out as the most authentic victim of FGM in Sub-Saharan African fiction. So intricately, so delicately is her portrait drawn that one can hardly believe she is the creation of a male writer. The convincing depiction of her anguish has contributed to making Kourouma's first novel the most widely read and discussed work in Sub-Saharan Francophone African literature. Touched by the graphic quality of Salimata's ordeal, gender activist Patterson, bringing home to the public the deleterious effects of FGM, cites a paragraph on the heroine's traumatic excision cum rape. A veritable incarnation of phallocentric oppression, Salimata is violated by the traditional healer Tiécoura, who has been summoned to heal her. Kourouma's close association of FGM with rape is no accident as both acts are forms of Gender-based Violence (GBV) visited upon women. In many respects, excision resembles rape, for as a violent act, it also defiles and maims for life.

In Kourouma's first novel, then, the heroine's ill-treatment and subsequent community demand that she procreate, when FGM has already rendered her barren, satirically places such cynical expectations and backward traditional practices in an extremely negative light. The story also shows how women are reified in patriarchy, mythical justifications of female circumcision from traditionalists notwithstanding.

The acute pain that Salimata experiences is furthermore at variance with the myths of Spartan discipline that all girls supposedly exhibit when cut:

Salimata had surrendered herself to [the traditional exciser], [and with] eyes shut...the pain had flooded up from between her legs to her back, her neck, her head, and back down to her knees. She had wanted to rise and sing, but could not, her breath failed her, the burning pain stiffened her limbs, the earth seemed to end beneath her feet, and all those present, the matrons, and the other girls, the hills and forest seemed to topple over and float away in the misty dawn; a great weight dragged at her eyelids and knees, and she broke and collapsed lifeless to the ground...(22–23).[5]

For Kouassi, the objectification and therefore victimisation of females – which Salimata's ordeals represent – show that woman, while bearing most of the hardship and torments of society, foregrounds the self-destructive nature of humanity and the sickness of the world (191). Answerable for Salimata's failure to consummate her first marriages with Baffi and Tiémoko are the excision and rape. The only person that somehow moves her is the equally sterile Fama, her first and only love, and that is because she met him before the blade. If her wounds also explain why she cannot tolerate Abdoulaye's advances, two tragic events help to unlock her sexuality and exorcise her partial frigidity. By bringing a second wife, an ambitious and spiteful widow, to Salimata's home to form a *ménage à trois*, Fama renders himself a distasteful man, a stranger, unworthy of the heroine's love. But before that, Salimata had shed Abdoulaye's blood during his attempted rape. The pent-up vengeful rage unleashed on Abdoulaye simultaneously exorcises several phobias: fear of the traditional; fear of Tiécoura the rapist; and fear of the two former violent husbands to whom she had been married by force. Her numerous and very intimate ordeals clearly show that ablation of the clitoris, the seat of female sexuality and deep hidden emotions, necessarily engenders psychological trauma, neurotic confusion and a profound sense of loss.

The narrative's apologists, like their real world counterparts, hold that since the clitoris represents impurity, sexual confusion and imperfection, only excision can confer on the initiate cleanliness, certainty and womanhood. The undue pressure of mothers on girls, including Salimata's, in spite of their own maternal premonitions, emanates from the fear that intact daughters will be ostracised. Simply put, in groups that amputate, like the Somali, Mende, Dogon, and Gikuyu, virtually no one escapes being ritually 'cleansed.'[6] Yet not all Malinke initiates, the novel reveals, are as 'lucky' as Salimata. Moussogbe, the legendary beauty whose charms are still celebrated in the village, and Nouna, she of the finely cast nose, bleed to death, and because the village redefines their loss as a warrant for communal happiness, it is taboo to mourn them and, thus, forbidden to bring their bodies home for burial.

Despite the annual sacrifice of FGM victims, the village becomes increasingly impoverished, materially and spiritually, to the extent of rendering its inhabitants a society of famished people (60) and incurable liars (72), a depiction from which Kourouma's sarcasm emerges. Similarly, in *Allah n'est pas obligé*, Kourouma divulges, with a satiric touch, that every year several excised girls, usually the most beautiful, lose their lives, while those who 'survive' the mutilating operation are coerced into other forms of subjugation (forced marriages or 'wife inheritance') which are by no means less violent. Indeed, for Kourouma, excision fits into a fixed patriarchal chain: mutilation, forced marriage, rape, levirate/sororate, diseased life, demonisation of childless women, the cult of violence and neocolonial tyranny.

If Bafitini, the mother of the child-soldier Birahima, eludes death during the excision, Kourouma reveals that surgery leaves her infested with a life-threatening and horrible ulcer. Paradoxically, only by dying does the ulcer patient find relief. Remarkably, Birahima himself defines excision in terms that evoke debilitation: 'c'est amputer les jeunes filles du clitoris'/ 'To excise is to sever the young girl's clitoris' (186). By calling excision amputation, Kourouma demonstrates support for its suppression.

An allied critique aims to defend against the stigmatising of intact girls in Kourouma's *En attendant le vote des bêtes sauvages*. In a similar vein, in *Monnè, outrages et défis*, Djigui, the patriarchal king of Soba, explains to Héraud, the French Commandant, that marital union with a non-excised girl only brings misfortune. Therefore, if Mariam, intact, can make a name for herself as a nationalist, a charismatic community leader and a mother figure, her successes serve to underline Kourouma's iconoclastic and abolitionist intent. This comes as little surprise from a committed writer whose avowed aim, as he stresses in his interview with Sennen Andriamirado and Renaud de Rochebrune (1990), is to use his writing to restore the lost dignity of Africans. The author's commitment to the defence of human rights explains in part the many prizes that his books have won.

The irony of severing girls' genitalia and yet expecting them to procreate comes out strongly in Kourouma's indictment of FGM. Each horrifying image of excision paints women as receptacles of devouring pain even while they remain a source of life. Female suffering, in no way obviating the feminine task of ensuring group survival, makes woman an archetypal victim and quintessential martyr, symbolizing, as Kouassi notes, societal deliquescence (194).

Systemic degeneration and the fetish of violence are also satirised by the Malian writer Yambo Ouologuem in *Le Devoir de violence*, first issued in 1968. Before marrying a fellow slave, Tambira is subjected to excision and stitching to appear more 'wholesome' and 'tight' for Emperor Saïf's sexual gratification and *droit de cuissage*. For Ouologuem, excision and infibulation, which have been instituted by men for their sadistic pleasure, are tantamount to sexual enslavement (88). Shorn of its religious and mythical strictures in this novel's representation of unparalleled cruelty, infibulation becomes the ultimate means of procuring morbid pleasure for men and a tool of dehumanising women. That the author should place FGM within the context of feudalism and slavery and also contemporise horrendous events in the precolonial and colonial eras by linking them to the present neocolonial system speaks volumes for his deconstructive and abolitionist agenda. For both Kourouma and Ouologuem, and indeed all anti-FGM artists, the current violent dispensation ought to cede to a new social order that respects women's rights and therefore holistic human values.

Well-known for his feminist views and people-centred discourse, the Somali novelist Nuruddin Farah also paints a disturbing picture of FGM in his first novel, *From a Crooked Rib*. Excised and infibulated at the tender age of eight, Ebla, the heroine, so much fears the repercussions of her trauma on pregnancy and delivery that she decides not to give birth at all. She has good cause for apprehension, having been witness to the child-bearing torment of her hostess, Aowralla, who had also undergone infibulation. There is no doubt in Ebla's mind that excision and infibulation are hideous, mutilating rituals which have outlived whatever usefulness may have been assigned them by ancient patriarchs. For good reason, FGM and brutal defloration by her first husband constitute the two most harrowing experiences in her life. There is every indication that the excruciating rite will be pathologically etched on her memory and her life forever.

In Farah's *Sardines*, recurrent recollections of FGM-induced trauma inform Samater's resolve to shield her daughter Ubax and to fight Idil, her iron-willed mother-in-law, advocate of violence. In Samater's words,

'If they mutilate you at eight or nine, they open you up with a rusty knife the night they marry you off; then you are cut open and re-stitched. Life for a circumcised woman is a series of de-flowering pains, delivery pains and re-stitching pains. I want to spare my daughter these and many other pains. She will not be circumcised. Over my dead body. Ubax is my daughter, not Idil's.' (62–63)

Jeylan W. Hussein submits that infibulation, long practised in Somali society, increases women's commercial value in marriage transactions as patriarchy, via its fathers, prospective husbands and feminine agents, places a high premium on a bride's minute vaginal orifice (65). Hussein's thesis echoes Thiam for whom infibulation 'constitutes the most eloquent expression of...control exercised by the phallocratic system over female sexuality' (Thiam 60).[7] While acknowledging infibulation in Mali, among the Afars and the Issas as well as in other parts of the world, Thiam argues that the more extensive performance of the operation in Somalia has earned for Somali women the unenviable moniker, 'sewn-up women' (72).

Now, the representation of FGM in fiction is by no means limited to men. Although most African women writers have turned their back on the ritualised genital mutilation of girls and babies, Beyala, Cameroonian; Aminata Maiga Kâ, Senegalese; Khady, Senegalese; and Barry, Guinean/Senegalese have not. Along with these authors, Waris Dirie, Somali/Austrian; Nura Abdi, Somali/German; Fatou Keïta, Ivorian; and Fatou Fanny Cissé, Ivorian, have taken seriously Thiam's challenge, enunciated in the ground-breaking *La Parole aux négresses*, to expose their ordeals despite patriarchal – mandated silence.

In *Tu t'appelleras Tanga*, for instance, Beyala, like other militants, mordantly condemns FGM. According to Tanga's mother, however, clitoridectomy has been instituted to make it easier for her daughter to have sex with men, her attitude therefore marking the path towards Tanga's prostitution. And until lucidity liberates the protagonist from her alienation, Tanga will serve the interest of her phallic mother and phallocentrism. Clearly Gallimore is right when, in the manner of Thiam, Hussein, Kourouma and Ouologuem, she equates excision not only with sexual murder (53–54; 72) but also with patriarchal theft of women's body and pleasure (73). Appositely, Tanga herself declares that genital violence has impounded her zones of erotic delight, and she therefore reveals a defiance emblematic of the author's contestatory posture, underlined as well in her *Lettre d'une Africaine à ses soeurs occidentales*.

In the autobiographical *La Petite Peule*, Barry, even more than Beyala, gives unequivocal legitimacy to the call for abolition, speaking as she does from experience. The novel takes a heart-wrenching look at FGM. Girls rarely hold back on the terrifying pain they undergo as all cry out the instant the blade bites. For Barry, children are hurled before an executioner. Without anesthesia or sterilisation, clitoridectomy is nothing less than torture and the venue an 'abattoir'/ 'a slaughter house' (13). Traditionalists would want Barry to believe that this horrible genital deformation prefaces a life of bliss and purity by conditioning the initiate to adequately master the pains of womanhood. Her own experience of genital amputation and those to which she bears witness make her believe otherwise.

Barry's fears and traumatic experiences parallel those of Nura Abdi during infibulation:

> ...the one thing you knew for sure was that they were going to do something with a piece of you down there between your legs...only when your turn came would you find out what they really meant... Sweat poured out of me. I was nauseous and felt like throwing up while between my legs someone was busy with a needle in an open wound. It was as if with all my senses, wholly conscious, I was being slaughtered (in Levin 1–2).

Without doubt, these testimonies, like those of Dirie and Khady, are meant to drive the tempo of anti-FGM campaigns. In fact, victims' contestation validates Thiam's appeal. The wounded are to tell the world they want the torture stopped. They are also encouraged to act (85).

From N'guessan-Larroux's point of view, the novels, too, do this; they act. For despite their status as fiction, they inform and instruct through evocative documentary and art (9). Consider Cisse's frightful images of FGM in *La Blessure*, for instance. Readers discover with the protagonist

Mariéta that, for all its pristine shroud of mystery, excision is nothing but a form of maiming, an unqualified physiological and psychological injury. In the same vein, Kâ's *La Voie du salut* gives a harrowing account of the needless death of a three-month old baby lost to FGM. The infant's parents may believe that cutting is endorsed by Islam, but the practice has no religious anchor. Nor can it be an initiation into womanhood when a neonate is harmed.

And *Mutilated* the victim certainly is, the stark title of Ghanaian Annor Nimako's novel for youth providing yet another frank and powerful indictment (See Anne Adams' chaper in this collection.) A 'faction' (blend of facts and fiction), *Mutilated* propels the reader from conferences to workshops to sensitisation campaigns; and from seminars to counselling sessions to field work. Accordingly, the narrative provides explicit strategies, efficacious approaches abolitionists use: film-triggered discussions, school health programmes, coalitions of like-minded local and international stakeholders, recourse to the intervention of victims to give eradication drives greater authenticity and appreciation of the motives of apologists in order to better neutralise them.

Rich in facts if sometimes thin on plot and aesthetics, *Mutilated,* built around the activism of Dr Ebow Blankson and Dr Yvonne Alhassan, shows precisely why the author calls the rite FGM. Sourced from the 1987 speech of Edna Adan Ismaïl, First Vice-President of the Inter-African Committee, the novel's epigraph supports Nimako's intentions. For both Ismaïl and Nimako,

FGM is a dangerous practice with dire consequences: After all the tragedies in developing countries have taken their toll on the lives of our youngsters, we ourselves continue to catch and kill, with our own hands, those who miraculously survived all these catastrophes. Enough is enough. The killing must stop! (Epigraph).

As the narrative makes clear, the fight against FGM is difficult. Uninitiated girls, who want the glamour of the ceremony, are confused; they are subject to psychological and social pressure as they are taught that religion and cultural identity hinge on the cut. Their desires notwithstanding, narrative collaboration between local non-governmental and civil society organisations and victims on the one hand, and foreign partners on the other, illustrates Alice Walker's vision: 'We know that women and children who suffer genital mutilation will have to stand up for themselves, and, together put an end to it. But that they need our help is indisputable' (63).

Not unlike Nimako, *Unanswered Cries,* winner of the 2002 Macmillan Writer's Prize for the Sierra Leonean novelist Conteh, through the adventures of Olabisi Jones, sets out to depict FGM's morbidity. As in *Mutilated,* Conteh prefers the term FGM to female circumcision. In the professional view of Dr Asiatu Koroma, a major character, the surgery leads to excessive bleeding, possibly HIV/AIDS, childbirth complications and, occasionally, death.

For both Dr Koroma and Lawyer Oyah, who underwent FGM during pre-adolescence, the operation remains a harrowing memory. Even if Olabisi's mother, Makalay, for fear of the secret society and curse of the traditional healer, wants to amputate her daughter's clitoris, the girl, ably supported by her father, wins in court the right to corporeal integrity and is thus freed from FGM. In Sierra Leonean Temne society, as in Somalia, among Kenya's Gikuyu and in various West African Mande communities, the clitoris is perceived as 'filthy, ugly' (Conteh 68). It is therefore removed. Elsewhere in Africa, Dr Koroma explains, 'the lips of the vagina are scraped with either a blade or knife, and then sewn together [leaving] a small opening...for urination' (69). Such measures are needed, traditionalists hold, if the sexual appetite of women is to be reduced and morality assured. Scandalised by this gynophobic ideology, Ade Jones, Olabisi's father, Lawyer Oyah and Dr Koroma successfully challenge the surgery's alleged benefits. Another source of worry to the medical doctor is that most *soweys,* traditional cutters, know nothing about germs. Also, should a girl die of excessive bleeding, Dr Koroma explains, 'the death is attributed to witchcraft...[or to] *bondo* spirit, the god of female circumcision' (70). The judge concludes as he indicts: 'reasons [given] for the practice of female genital mutilation are medically without basis' (86).

Life-threatening issues associated with FGM raised in Conteh's narrative mirror those thematised by Mambou in *La Gazelle et les exciseuses* set, however, in the imaginary sites of Yanga (a village) and Djanbraz (a city). Parental support, this time from the mother, is central to the protagonist's liberation from the mutilating rite. A metaphor to capture the grace of the heroine Ayite, 'gazelle' also encodes the desperate but purposeful running that the designated victim, as prey, is obliged to undertake, across time – period of initiation, re-actualisation of the past in the present, current fetishism of ancient violent norms – and space – excision camps, savannah, forest, inimical human settlements—, in order to escape from fierce hunters in the form of FGM apologists. Safety comes from sustained pressure mounted by a coalition of progressive forces and changed mentalities in both rural and urban areas. Contending that excision is nothing more than the undue sanctification of violence and female inferiority, militants, including Ayite, her mother, her friends Jeannine and Keïta as well as law enforcement agents, finally triumph, in this saga, over tradition's unconditional defenders.

The subversive gesture is visible as well in Fatou Keïta's *Rebelle*. Having made her transgressive project transparently clear in the title, the artist invites readers into the razor's cruel sites. Appropriately, as the omniscient narrator shows, there have always been instances of subtle and staunch resistance. Progressive subjects deride the unhealthy perception of time and venerated custom as fossilised entities instead of as malleable phenomena in the local and universal forward march towards individual and collective well being. To her credit, Keïta is one of the rare African creative writers to depict the prevalence of FGM, with its attendant hazards, in migrant communities in the West. In the main, she achieves this by setting her narrative in France and involving non-Africans in the plot.

That the woman charged with excising girls in *Rebelle* bears the ominous name Dimikèla which, as N'guessan-Larroux informs us, signifies suffering and pain (5), underlines the emotional and physio-logical hurt that practising societies, through their agents, inflict on victims. Systematically maimed, girls who undergo the practice often grow to become the torturers of other feminine subjects, thus perpetuat-ing the mutilation chain. In Paris, Noura, the eleven-year daughter coerced by her migrant Fulani parents Barou and Fanta, dies from excision, for which reason her mother and father are arrested, tried and imprisoned in France. Recounted by grieving mothers, the countless casualties lend credence to Thiam's assertion that in practising communities, five to six per cent of annual female fatalities (78) can be charged to FGM. For Thiam, deplorable hygiene and ablation as such are responsible for these needless deaths (78).

Driven by heightened awareness, *Rebel's* Malimouna revolts, sustaining the tempo of Keita's bold denunciation. At age five, from her city friend Sanita then on holiday in Boritouni village, the heroine learns to protect that delicate part of her body targeted by FGM. Sanita, whose name means health ('sanitas') in Latin, symbolises the intact state. At age six, Malimouna also learns that in rural communities, the cravings of the body matter, even for so-called custodians of custom. Having stumbled upon the sexual revels the venerable Dimikèla is enjoying with a young hunter in the forest, Malimouna later makes a deal. Threatening to reveal what she has seen, she could endanger the elder woman's social standing. Dimikèla therefore feigns excision, allowing Malimouna to remain intact and thus sealing her own secret.

Keïta's satire is equally hard on polygamists, wife-beaters and Casanovas intent on marrying virgins. Illustrating this indictment, the author has the protagonist, a virgin, escape during a crucial nocturnal battle from the clutches of Old Sanou, a well-known philanderer and insecure pervert to whom Malimouna has been forcefully betrothed. Consequent upon her triumph over Old Sanou, Malimouna first leaves for the fictional city of Salouma, then departs for France, and later returns to Salouma, where she marries the seemingly politically enlightened ICT expert, Karim.

In the demystifying world of *Rebelle*, courage, vigilance, advocacy, joint women-men collaboration, consciousness raising, broken silences and mothers grieving for excision-killed daughters become the ideological and aesthetic tools advocating against Gender-based Violence: forced marriage, rape, spousal sequestration, wife battery and FGM. For Gikandi (150) as much as for Aimé Sègla and Adékin E. Boko, a myth is a social charter subject to revision as and when the need arises. The subversive but reconstructive fiction on and of FGM produced by African writers coheres with this creative vision. In *Rebelle,* for instance, at a political gathering in Salouma, women speak openly for the first time about their woes and hope for positive forms of bonding. Their model is equality. Why, they ask, must women lose their clitoris, considered 'masculine,' if men can keep their mammary glands?

Thus liberated from shame and fear of clitoral impurity, urban women are emboldened to speak about their bodies and defend them. In their view, if God had endowed them with a clitoris, which ordinary mortal, and in the name of what principles, could decide that the Almighty's work was imperfect and that all the world's women were malformed? 'Comment pouvait-on croire à la fois en Dieu et en de telles absurdités?' /'How could one claim devotion to God and yet believe these absurdities?' Inevitably, justifying amputation as securing female whole-someness cedes to a new paradigm of corporeal integrity.

Logically, then, when, some twenty-six years after she has escaped from the village, her callous husband Karim hires miscreants to abduct Malimouna and force her to be cut, enlightened women and men join forces to free her. Her dramatic liberation, carried out by the Association d'Aide à la Femme en Difficulté (AAFD) or Aid Association for Women in Difficulty, closes the novel on a forward-looking note: the prospect of a new mentality and the dawn of a renewed humanity.

In *Rebelle* as in *Unanswered Cries* and *La Gazelle et les exciseuses*, suspense, adventure, salutary civil society and state intervention are infused into the narrative structure. Additionally, in all three novels, a consciousness of self and awareness of new human realities drive the impulse to deconstruct centuries-old stereotypes, misogynic myths and backward norms. If in the past, communal harmony was precariously and erroneously predicated on obliterating individual interests and reifying women, enduring national development is now a function of respect for and satisfaction of individual needs. For if unique desires and personal aspirations make tolerance indispensable, and if durable social progress requires an inclusive paradigm, its ethos abhors the violation, ritual or otherwise, of human/woman rights, precisely because such travesty negates the supreme interest of the individual and the social whole.

Underscoring global commitment to abolition is the narrative valorisation of international dimensions to anti-FGM campaigns by Keïta, Nimako, Abdi and Dirie, and their non-African collaborators (Cathleen Miller and Marie-Thérèse Cuny respectively) in Dirie's *Fleurs du desert* and Khady's *Mutilée*. Beyond this, it is worth stressing the public's appreciation of these works. The fame of writers such as Kourouma, Farah, Keïta, Dirie and Abdi, the many international prizes won by Kourouma and Conteh, the reissuing of novels, the adaptation of *Les Soleils des indépendances* for the stage, and above all their trans-lation into different languages and adoption as prescribed texts in the curricula of pre-tertiary and tertiary institutions testify to a remarkable reception.[8] The positive response of readers worldwide to these trans-gressive but creative works validates their relevance to contemporary discourse on violence.

CONCLUSION

An avoidable blot on the conscience of humankind, FGM is a global problem requiring greater exposure and citizen support for eradication movements. As these narratives show, it endangers health and inflicts trauma, and while most African fiction ignores or condones it, those writers who treat the subject opt for a counter-discursive project stressing the need for a new myth and a new social charter.

The ambivalent Ngugi and Nwapa excepted, works like Kourouma's *Les Soleils des indépendances*, Farah's *From a Crooked Rib*, Barry's *La Petite Peule*, Nimako's *Mutilated*, Cissé's *La Blessure*, Dirie's *Desert Flower*, Keïta's *La Rebelle* and Conteh's *Unanswered Cries*, issue a credible call – implicit and explicit – to abolish FGM. This investment in eradication is grounded in imperatives of health, development, human rights and gender rights which, as themes in critical fiction, re-position tradition, bringing it in line with modernity. Similarly, Thiam's clarion appeal to African women holds out a promise of success – by breaking the culture of silence of their pain.

Anne V. Adams

The Anti-Female Genital Mutilation (FGM) Novel in Public Education: An Example from Ghana

A group of about 20 students at Accra Girls' Secondary School, when asked if they personally knew of any girl or woman who had been 'circumcised,' all answered that they knew no one who had experienced this ritual. Specifically, the response from these poised, articulate teenagers was a collective 'No,' which also reflects the consensus in the capital city as in other parts of Ghana outside of the northern regions, where various versions of genital cutting are practiced. The girls had been asked to come together because they had all read the novel by Annor Nimako, *Mutilated*,[1] borrowed from their school library.

One of a growing number of African-authored literary works – Nuruddin Farah's *From a Crooked Rib*, Fatou Keita's *Rebelle*, Osman Conteh's *Unanswered Cries*, Christian Mambou's *La Gazelle et l'exciseuse* and Khady's *Mutilée* – that condemn female genital mutilation, Annor Nimako's *Mutilated* is fiction written specifically on this topic, expressly for an audience that would, hopefully, in the near future, become agents of change.[2] The author, a former secondary-school geography teacher, who has also worked in an NGO for course development, was motivated to effect social change through literary texts in education. The geography training in his professional background afforded him knowledge of community practices in Northern Ghana, although he has no conscious acquaintance with any circumcised women. From his work developing instructional materials for Ghanaian schools, Nimako had experience in producing texts for a youthful readership and therefore embraced the genre of the novel for secondary-school students, analysing the social and medical facts around the issue of FGM in the hope that youth in the culturally distinct northern regions of Ghana, as future adults and parents, would endeavour to eliminate the practice. This book, then, belongs to the category of propaganda literature, as it pointedly dramatises the detrimental physical and psychological consequences of this tradition-based practice. Indeed, the work sacrifices the literary feature of a substantive conflict as it drives home its message about the criminality of FGM.

Its simplistic conflict notwithstanding, *Mutilated* dramatically sets the issue of FGM in unexpected contexts, thus amplifying the gravity and complexity of tradition that has preserved it. The primary setting is Accra, Ghana's capital city, where most people are unfamiliar with the practice of female 'circumcision' at all, not to mention its existence in Ghana. The drama which heightens the complexity of the problem lies in the fact that the girls and women at the centre of the narrative, though born in the North, were each taken to Accra and raised there by relatives who wanted specifically to shield them from those traditional practices. Hence, the surgery, though assumed to be limited to northern communities, is actually shown through this novel to be present any-where in the country.

The secondary setting of the novel is London. Female genital mutilation as performed by Ghanaian and numerous other African communities has been carried, along with other cultural baggage, by immigrants, thus making the 'rite' an issue challenging British health, social, and legal structures. Extending the case even further, the text makes reference to the analogous situation in France. Thus, through this novel, the issue of FGM in Ghana is brought out from its northern Ghanaian base into the entire nation and to its European Diaspora. In the process, the larger African context of FGM is similarly presented, as the practice exists in other African countries and among their emigrants abroad.

CENTRAL FOCUS: the BLANKSON FAMILY

Ebow Hansen, gynaecologist and passionate critic of FGM, works in the Korle Bu Teaching Hospital in Accra. He is married to Sarah Blankson, an entrepreneur, originally from the North, who was brought to Accra as a child by her aunt to escape FGM. The Blanksons are Catholics with two adolescent children. Two other characters critical to the action are Dr Yvonne Alhassan, the classic 'attractive widow,' who is a gynaecologist of international repute, famous for her statistical research on FGM in Africa, and who works in a hospital in the North; and Alhaji Nuhu, big (literally and figuratively) Muslim businessman, homeboy and longtime friend of Sarah's family.

Obviously, these dramatis personae by their very constitution reveal the match-ups in the drama. Briefly, the narrative takes off from Dr Blankson's frustration and strengthened anti-FGM resolve following the death of a 10-year-old schoolmate of his daughter Sheila's on the operating table from complications of 'circumcision' performed by a practitioner brought down to Accra by her grandmother. Soon thereafter, through a several-weeks-long professional seminar in London, Dr Blankson becomes a close associate of Dr Alhassan's, with both becoming campaigners against FGM in Ghana as well as in Britain among Ghanaian and other African immigrants. Meanwhile, Sarah Blankson, on a trip to her hometown at the invitation of fellow northerner Alhaji Nuhu, allows herself to be persuaded, by her mother and sisters and the Alhaji, to be circumcised (in her mid-thirties!), so that she can be fully respected and 'counted among women.' When wife and husband are back at home together, Ebow is outraged at Sarah's 'transgression,' divorces her (in the interim married to Alhaji as his third wife), and wins custody of the two children. In the end, the two doctors, not surprisingly, pair up, professionally and domestically. Sarah, chastened by her physical and mental ordeal, regrets her 'circumcision,' divorces Alhaji and joins in the crusade against FGM.

Thus the author focuses on FGM's extension to women geographically and, more significantly, *socially* removed from the base of the practice, to demonstrate how forcefully tradition maintains its hold. Its cultural tentacles reach beyond Western education including medical understanding, bourgeois class standing, and international boundaries separating 'developing' from 'developed' societies. As a result, African audiences of urban, schooled, 'Westernised,' 'been-to' milieus cannot assume a stance of unaffected superciliousness, or of smug ignorance of the phenomenon as a fact of life in their societies. Indeed, Sarah is not the only such 'modern' woman who, because of enculturation, is an advocate of the tradition (at least up until the time she herself suffers from it). Another character of similar socio-economic standing is effectively inserted into the narrative to challenge Sarah's contradiction between belief in the practice and failure to have it herself.

That contradiction within Sarah Blankson, London-educated and a seemingly otherwise 'liberated' woman (as evidenced by her freedom of movement and of association), plagues her and her marriage throughout most of the narrative. At age five, Sarah was brought by her well-off Aunt Dora from Mongasi, their village in the Upper Eastern Region, to be raised in Accra, specifically to save the child from being subjected to 'circumcision.' Herself, the victim of botched cutting, Aunt Dora had discovered, upon marrying, that she was unable to bear children due to the resulting chronic pelvic infection, and was summarily divorced by her husband. As a consequence of her experience Aunt Dora repudiated the 'ancient and obnoxious practice' (18) and vowed to protect her informally adopted daughter from the same fate.

Nevertheless, in spite of Aunt Dora's influence, the Accra upbringing and schooling, not to mention a London post-secondary education, Sarah, as a mature, married mother, is still subject to the weight of tradition. The oppression comes in several forms. The most constant is ostracism by local acquaintances from her home region or ethnicity: 'Our people know about me. They know that I was taken away by you to avoid 'circumcision', Sarah tells her husband.[3] 'I never visit friends and relations at Mataheko and Nima without someone alluding to it. They keep embarrassing me, especially Alhaji Nuhu. I'm sure it will be worse when I visit home during the Damba festival' (18). And, further, from Alhaji Nuhu, as mentioned, who, in a Big Brother role, embodies the culture of their people, comes counsel of moral support for the ethnic sister who is married to a man from a different tribe which does not hold to, and, more importantly, is unsympathetic to, their shared traditions. And then there is the litany nagging by her mother and sisters at home in Mongasi whenever Sarah visits. Her 'persistent refusal' 'to yield to pressure and be circumcised' (87) disgraces them before their community.

This constant heckling from several directions ultimately brings Sarah to capitulate; this, in spite of the fact that she was only five years old at the time she left the village. Even though she was undoubtedly exposed to the approval – and perhaps even the reality, for some of her age-mates – of 'circumcision' during those first years of her life, it would seem unlikely that such first-hand influence would sustain her adherence to the tradition after being removed from the locus as a young child. On the other hand, no information is given as to the amount of contact she was able to maintain with her home and family after settling in Accra. We do know that she enjoys participating in the traditional *Damba* festival, from which we must assume that she was in frequent enough contact, at least until travelling abroad for education. Hence, Sarah's loyalty to the practice is driven less by having grown up around it than by accumulated socio-cultural pressure *in adulthood*. Thus, it is the power of the tradition *in its psychological representation rather than in its actual practice* that overpowers this otherwise urbane, independent, self-conscious woman. Even though Sarah favours the tradition for girls, generally, as a part of ethnic identity, she feels that she herself, as a married mother in her thirties, has passed the age where it matters.

But Sarah's decision to submit to the surgery was greatly influenced by the persistent urging of her respected, trusted friend, the Alhaji, skilfully playing up the sentiments of ethnic identity in the context of Sarah's mixed marriage. In effect, the self-assured, successfully wedded, 30-something-year-old Sarah *dares* Alhaji to try to get her to submit to 'circumcision' when she agrees to travel with him to their home for the nostalgic annual *Damba* festival. So, upon learning that Alhaji, who had a manner that made it 'hard for somebody to say no to his requests,' had anticipated and allayed her logistical reservations, she acquiesced. 'But,' she confidently admonished him, 'don't think you can make a Muslim and a traditionalist out of me' (67). Ultimately, he would succeed in doing exactly that.

The Alhaji employs a double-barreled strategy in pursuing this end. Recognising that Sarah is a sophisticated, urbanised woman, he arranges for her to meet a social counterpart, also from their area, also an Accra-transplanted 'circumcision' escapee, also a Christian, *but* circumcised after marrying and bearing children. This new acquaintance, Mary, is able to debate the issue with her from Sarah's own perspective, and thus manages to put a wedge into Sarah's resistance by puncturing the basis of her seeming rationalisations. The other 'barrel' of Alhaji's strategy finishes off the job of 'gentle persuasion' by breaking down the last barrier of rationalising resistance: 'What happens to me if [my husband] divorces me precisely because of such indiscretion?' 'I'll marry you, Sarah. I'll make you a Muslim. I'll send you to Mecca. I'll have children with you. You'll be counted among women. Your children will be respected' (92). And, so, with only a 'token protest' from her 'inner voice' Sarah capitulates.

In invoking the spectre of her husband and the prospect of his divorcing her for the 'indiscretion' of voluntarily undergoing 'circumcision,' Sarah is referring to a far more crucial objection than just that 'my husband is not from the same ethnic group as us.' Even adding, 'And you know his views on female genital mutilation,' is a gross understatement. Not only has the subject of female 'circumcision' been a constant source of contention in their marriage, as she defends her people's practice, but, furthermore, as a gynaecologist he finds it abhorrent and is therefore professionally committed to its eradication.

That commitment is announced from the first page, with Dr Blankson's frustration over his helplessness to save the life of his daughter's friend. Immediately following the child's funeral begins Dr Blankson's engagement with the local professional seminar on FGM.

A DOUBLE IRONY

So, Sarah's decision to undergo FGM – or rather, her *acquiescence* – produces double irony in this narrative. First, the timing coincides with her husband's trip to London for an intensive course, from which he emerges a crusader for the eradication of FGM. Second, her decision to travel home with her family friend Alhaji (whom Ebow has barely met) is made without prior consultation with her husband, whose plans to travel to the UK had already been mutually agreed upon. So, her matter-of-fact announcement to him of her simultaneous voyage stands as an act of independence and self-direction, with which her husband, by his agreement, is obviously comfortable. Therefore, the capitulation of this woman to the persuasion of Alhaji and the guilt-trip imposed by her mother is ironic, at the very least (if not altogether unmotivated in the plot). This double irony highlights the fact that the fight against FGM is indeed the object of the narrative for which the character of Sarah is merely the vehicle. Hence, situated right at the crosshairs of her family's and the Alhaji's gun sights, Sarah succumbs to group pressure from home that overpowers her reason, the sanctity of her marriage, and her self-consciousness, an understanding of self shown to be dominated, ultimately, by her ethnic identity.

Lest it appear from the discussion to this point that Sarah Blankson is, or should logically be, the central character in the book, that is, that her personal dilemma is the major conflict – that is definitely not the case.

Mutilated is not about Sarah; it is about Sarah's *husband*: the central character in this tale of female genital mutilation is Dr Ebow Blankson. It is a novel about this man whose professional and personal life become consumed by his abhorrence of what he sees. And, in the true style of young people's literature, Dr Blankson is a genuine 'hero,' with the virtues and deeds to match. Females in this novel, with the somewhat contradictory exception of Dr Yvonne Alhassan, are the supporting characters for *his* story. In fact, Dr Blankson's stature is so elevated that he is consistently referred to as 'Dr Blankson,' regardless of situational context, as for example, at home with his wife, who is consistently referred to by her first name: 'By eight o'clock Sarah and Dr Blankson were up, going through the morning routine and dressing themselves' (155). More incomprehensible, even, is the fact that in contexts with his colleague and, later, companion, Dr Yvonne Alhassan, our 'hero' is consistently referred to as 'Dr' while his 'girlfriend,' Dr Alhassan, is primarily referred to by her first name, which is the discursive feature that confers 'girlfriend' status on this highly respected fellow physician. In fact, all other professional counterparts are referred to with professional titles except Dr Alhassan in spite of the high esteem in which she is held by the whole professional community. For the reader, however, the almost exclusive use of the first name – opposite the titled male counterpart – reduces her from the status of a respected clinician and researcher on FGM to the inferior status of the 'hero's girlfriend.' For example, in preparation for a major talk at a seminar in London hosted by the Royal College of Obstetrics and Gynaecology, '*Yvonne* walked to the podium, placed her handbag on the floor near her seat and her folder on the table. She rejoined *Dr Blankson* and they both checked the transparencies on the table where the projector had been fixed. Satisfied, *Yvonne* walked to *Professor Keith Jones* at the podium while *Dr Blankson* took a seat in the front row' (98, italics added). Or, when Dr Blankson is speaking on behalf of his colleague, Dr Alhassan, in magnanimously committing them to return to London to lend their expertise in a worthy project initiated by a local gynaecologist:

'We'll be at the hospital in full force to assist in the examination of the girls and help you decide what action to take – the form of surgery, that is. ... Just send us return tickets and Yvonne and I will be back to assist at no cost to the patients' (136).

Or, when the couple is having dinner together at a restaurant: 'The maitre d' seated Yvonne while Dr Blankson pulled a chair and sat down at the table' (110). Thus, in this novel about female genital mutilation all females – whether they are mutilated patients, Sarah Blankson, or Dr Alhassan – are depicted as subordinate to the 'hero.'

Always an opponent of FGM, Ebow Blankson is passionately stirred when he encounters actual victims or discusses it within his family. His attitude results from a combination of the procedure's remoteness from his own culture and his medical knowledge and experience. Consequently he has zero tolerance for his wife's defence of her people's custom. 'They had argued about [FGM] not once, not twice; it had been an ongoing and unrelenting argument about the merits and demerits of the practice…' The death of the schoolmate of their daughter Sheila provokes him to lash out at Sarah: 'When will your people stop this stupid, harmful and needless practice? When will they stop killing these innocent children?' Her defence, though adamant, is awkward: "My people are not stupid and they won't be insulted just because a few unfortunate deaths have occurred as a result of the practice.'

THE CULTURAL IMPERATIVE

Thus Dr Blankson's professional zeal, flamed by the immediate example of its object, causes him to lose his composure and insult his wife, whom he otherwise treats with gentle respect. Later in that same argument he calls her 'You ignorant defiant idiot,' which evokes her threat to walk out should he insult her people in that manner one more time (8–9). Here again, we see the salience of ethnic identification – and, hence, the defence of the practice—over material evidence, in the form of the child's death and the threat to her marriage. In the heat of this argument, then, the *principle* of the FGM issue as a cultural imperative threatens to destroy the union.

And ultimately, it does destroy the marriage. For, when an unsuspecting Ebow discovers, upon the couple's first (and last) effort to have intercourse after their respective trips, that his wife has been circumcised, he recoils in offended wrath, never to go near her sexually again. Using accusatory language, the husband regards it as a willful transgression and takes it as a personal affront:

'How could she betray me with such cheeky defiance? He thought. *That bastard of an Alhaji must have put her through it. What was the motive? To ruin my marriage?* He regretted very much for trusting her, for loving her, for allowing himself to be so despicably humiliated by her. She knew his views on female genital mutilation; she knew he was working to help eradicate it. So why did she do it? To spite him? To ridicule his efforts?' (150, italics in original)

The husband's sense of outrage is understandable, given his personal and professional abhorrence of the practice, and given that his wife did not tell him. Nevertheless, his reaction is that of a master 'defied' by a 'cheeky' subordinate. And, correctly inferring the collusion of the Alhaji, imputes motives *directed against him as her husband.* Viewing her act as a form of devious infidelity and betrayal, Ebow rebukes himself for having *ever* trusted and loved her, as though she had been plotting this move throughout their fourteen-year marriage and was waiting only for the opportunity of his extended absence to carry it out. In other words, Ebow Blankson's reaction to his wife's 'circumcision' revolves totally around *him*, as though *he* had been 'cut' by his own scalpel wielded by his wife.

Ebow Blankson's subsequent decision to divorce Sarah can certainly be understood on grounds of sexual incompatibility, now that he can no longer become emotionally and, hence, sexually intimate with her. Sarah, for her part, makes no effort to defend her action. Instead, she is reduced to tears at the court hearing and follows her attorney's advice not to contest the divorce, even though she had adamantly assured Ebow during their confrontation that she would fight the divorce suit. Further, his legal justification for seeking custody of their children is reasonable, on the grounds of fear that their mother would subject the daughter illegally to 'circumcision.'

However, the tack taken by Ebow's lawyer is to vilify Sarah as the perpetrator of a crime against society. The attorney, in both cases, portrays Sarah's betrayal of the marriage and potential harm to her daughter as heinous and especially criminal 'in spite of her education' which should have obviated any need for 'the applicant [to] subject... herself to that disgraceful, humiliating, obnoxious and harmful traditional practice of female genital mutilation...' (228). Although Sarah's counsel successfully objects to the tirade, it makes its point.

Yet prosecution of this case goes beyond a lawyer's aggressive tactics, criminalising the 'educated' wife and mother for having submitted herself to 'circumcision.' His position is shared by other representatives of society's professional caretakers. The judge, for example, in denying Sarah custody of the children, calls Sarah's 'conduct... in subjecting herself to the harmful and totally unnecessary practice of female genital mutilation ... most reprehensible ... [and] prejudicial to the welfare of the children, especially Sheila...' (236). Inexcusably unprofessional is the behaviour of a gynaecologist whom Sarah consults, after her marriage to Alhaji, about her failure to become pregnant, who goes as far as drawing an analogy between FGM and 'other criminal acts': 'I don't want to know why you did it. That should be a private matter. Don't doctors treat armed robbers who sustain serious gunshot wounds in exchange of fire with the police? We don't leave them to die, do we?' (242). While the physician's professional ethics would appear to respect the privacy of the patient's decision, his analogy, especially in its sarcasm, is the most malicious attack on the patient's character.

In spite of the absurdity of such a comparison between the perpetrator of an act *violating the person and property of other human beings* with the 'perpetrator' of an act *submitting to the violation of one's own person*, the consensus of the guardians of social standards – lawyer, judge, doctor – affirms the criminality ascribed to female 'circumcision,' at least for an 'educated' woman.[4] In fact, however, Sarah, impelled by overpowering psychological, social, and emotional pressure to embrace the cultural practice of 'circumcision,' has indeed become a victim of the ritual. In this way she is comparable to any girl-child who is compelled by family expectations. But, because she is an educated, middle-class adult, Sarah, in addition to being *victimised*, is also *vilified* for her decision. For, even though Sarah's defeat in the child custody case rests on her potential danger to the daughter of eventually having her circumcised, the basis for the judge's view is Sarah's own 'reprehensible' conduct, making her 'an unfit and an untrustworthy person to have access to the children, especially the daughter' (236).

Sarah's story, before and after her 'circumcision,' receives detailed dramatic attention not because the novel makes any real attempt to sympathetically analyse her situation but because she plays a crucial role in the *personal* life of her husband, the anti-FGM activist gynaecologist.

However, throughout the book Sarah's account competes for narrative space and attention with the scores of FGM stories that directly or indirectly make up Dr Blankson's *professional* life, cases he sees in his Accra medical practice of girls and women who suffer from complications of FGM. There are also cases, later in the novel, on which colleague Dr Yvonne Alhassan calls him for consultation when he visits her at her workplace in northern Ghana. Indirectly impacting his professional life are the treatments to which he is exposed through his participation in conferences and seminars, both in Ghana and in Britain. Those experiences bring research data from the 28 countries on the African continent where FGM is practiced. Further, Dr Blankson is exposed to the personal stories of FGM told by African women living in Britain as well as group discussions with African immigrants of both sexes for community education about the particular medical, sociological, and legal issues affecting the practice of FGM as it has been transported to the African Diaspora in Europe.

THE NOVEL'S STRENGTH IS ALSO ITS WEAKNESS

Dr Blankson's education in the various types of FGM is conveyed through copious graphic details of procedures and effects, both in London and later back home in the northern town of Bolgatanga, where Dr Alhassan practices. Dr Blankson is able to take part in examinations and surgeries on girls and women who present him with dimensions of the issue new to him. The seminars, both in Ghana and in Britain, the consultations on cases also in both countries, the testimonies of 'circumcised' women – all are skilfully woven into the text and effectively conveyed by the author. Indeed, this is the strength of the novel. Nimako succeeds in humanising technical medical phenomena, with appropriate anatomical vocabulary, and sociological facts – ranging from the extreme example of FGM performed after death (34), to the common cases of its performance during puberty rites – while maintaining a layperson's level of discourse. Starting with clear definitions of clitoridectomy, excision, and infibulation, the expositions that are set in the various conferences or seminars present all imaginable forms of the practice as well as the harmful physical and mental consequences.

Keloid formation is due to infection and failure of the wound to heal.

The wound therefore produces excess inelastic scar tissue. Keloids form a disfiguring complication. They cause anxiety, shame and fear in women who think that their genitals are re-growing in monstrous shapes. Some fear they have cancer' (55).
'On urine retention, one young woman said she remembered the excruciating pain she had when she was infibulated. She was so afraid to pass urine that her mother had to hold her to do so' (54).

Touching on difficulty with urination, Yvonne explained that it was:

due to inelastic tissue or skin scab covering the urinary meatus...The next slide showed...complete labial fusion in a ten-month old baby with urine escaping from a tiny hole in the midline. Then another depicted a marked scarring of the vaginal opening leading to stenosis or the abnormal narrowing of the opening. 'These developments,' Yvonne said, 'prevent the free flow of urine and can cause retention or chronic kidney infection with stone formation' (56).
'Chronic pelvic infection is another harmful effect. It is the result of infection at the time of circumcision that has gone untreated and undiagnosed. The use of unsterilised surgical tools and infected wound dressings causes infection. Multiple adhesions are then formed around the internal reproductive organs, like the uterus, ovaries and Fallopian tubes, and block the Fallopian tubes' (57).

Other such research presentations reveal secondary damage such as fractured arms and legs caused by limbs bound up for the procedure but which reflexively move in reaction to the pain, a scenario depicted on the cover of the book.
While the previous quotations are taken from the conference lecture setting, the following example occurs in the course of actual medical practice:

'Sister Brew here will confirm that the cases we have to deal with involve children, teenagers, and adults during their first pregnancy.'... They got to the ward and the Nursing Sister in charge joined them. Yvonne spoke with confidence and a satisfied feeling as they stood by the bed of a beautiful teenage girl...[of]...about sixteen. 'She's had surgery for obstetric fistula,' Yvonne told Dr Blankson. 'It's the most disabling of the serious complications of childbirth in this region. The common cause is obstructed labour and that's how she presented. Her condition was due to a contracted pelvis resulting from untreated infection during childhood' (257).

Beyond exposure through conferences and consultations, Blankson gains a wider picture of the phenomenon in its international dimensions through the testimony of articulate women who have been 'circumcised.' He particularly benefits from opportunities to hear educated African women who can speak to the imperative of abolishing the practice from their own perspective. Thus, he comes to recognise that FGM is not socially determined. There is, for example, an open forum, during the course of the London seminar, attended by married women and men as well as teenage girls and boys (but separated for small-group discussion), sponsored by the Foundation for Women's Health Research and Development (FORWARD), 'a non-governmental organisation' whose work 'on female genital mutilation with immigrants from Africa in the United Kingdom had been recognised and was being supported by the United Kingdom Department of Health' (129). The free-for-all brings personal testimonies that are confirmed by others and enlighten many:

'I was tightly infibulated at the age of six. It was an excruciating experience I shall live with throughout my adult life. ... When I got married ten years ago, my first sexual intercourse with my husband was disastrous. I had always dreaded the encounter. I could see the enjoyment on my husband's face while I lay there squirming and struggling. It was for procreation and I had to endure it. It wasn't for my enjoyment.[5] How could I have enjoyed it when my clitoris and other vital organs had been cruelly excised. My mother told me my tight vaginal orifice was for my husband's enjoyment. How stupid! ... I have two [children]. Having the first one was another ordeal. I had prolonged labour. I was sure I would have lost the baby if I hadn't had her here in a London hospital. I had to be deinfibulated. And you know what my husband requested after the baby had been born? Reinfibulation! When I reminded him that it was illegal in Britain, he said we could return to Ethiopia on holidays and have it done there' (130–1).

Another opportunity generated by the forum presents itself to Dr Blankson to hear testimonies from immigrants in London, when:

A group of about fourteen teenagers, mainly from Ethiopia, Somalia and Nigeria, arranged another meeting with [Drs. Alhassan, Blankson, and a locally-based colleague]. Their anxious faces said it all. From their group discussions, they realised with horror the dangers of infibulation and vowed to be deinfibulated before marriage. Some of them talked candidly about other problems (135).

In the course of this deeper immersion into the sociological and cultural contexts of FGM, Blankson evinces sympathy for suffering victims but no understanding for the basis of the practice. He sees it in absolute terms, purely as irrational, barbaric, obnoxious, and criminally dangerous. 'How could people in their right senses not see the stupidity of [it]. Don't they know about the immediate and long-term health hazards of female genital mutilation?... the obstetric complications?' (9) By the end of the novel, however, he shows evidence of recognising at least the force of cultural pressure. After examining a year-old infant on whom 'Yvonne had done a good job to repair with utmost care the mutilated organ of an innocent baby. A baby mutilated because of an obnoxious and harmful traditional practice. His resolve was total. As they left the patient, he looked at the young mother with contempt, but quickly replaced it with sympathy. She might not even have had a hand in the decision to have her baby circumcised' (259).

IRREFUTABLE ARGUMENTS FOR ABOLITION

Whether or not the targeted secondary-school audience is successfully engaged by the very transparent plot of this novel, as a source of insight and an irrefutable argument for abolition, its facts, figures, and attitudes on FGM relevant to Ghanaians and other Africans within and outside the continent make it valuable. Nonetheless, to assess the book as a propaganda piece is not only appropriate but also acknowledges the author's unmitigated condemnation. Narrative diction such as 'concoction,' and 'suspicious herbal medicine' applied to the 'circumcision' wound; 'with deft hands [the traditional surgeon] disgustingly sliced off... [and]... discarded pieces of human flesh' (37); 'Sarah['s] children[s'] questioning about her health after her crude surgery in the North' (140) – unmistakably articulates the intended propaganda. However, in assessing the strength of the novel and its effectiveness at stimulating reaction to a social issue, even a work directed toward a younger audience, its literary quality should not be compromised. In this case, presentation of the argument for abolition compromises some major elements of plot, thus weakening its credibility.

The most significant sacrifice to the author's agenda is the character of Sarah Blankson, the westernised, middle-class, married woman, who allows herself to be pressured into being circumcised. It is not enough that this otherwise self-aware individual, who had boasted to the Alhaji that he could not make a traditional acolyte out of her, simply capitulates to his behind-the-scenes machinations for her surgery, to her family's great joy, of course! In putting the cultural screws to her to submit to 'circumcision' he glibly rebuts her remaining objection, the fear that Ebow should leave her, by promising to marry her himself. Yet, it is simply incongruous that self-possessed Sarah would accept the total subordination of herself implicit in Alhaji's 'contingency plan.' Also clumsily contrived is Sarah's matter-of-fact subsequent conversion from Catholicism to Islam – complete with name change – in order to be able to become the Alhaji's third wife. Sarah's complacent acquiescence cannot even be justified as a marriage of convenience. For the marriage is not to Sarah's ultimate 'convenience,' given Alhaji's expressed ideas about the passive qualities and subordinate role of a wife. On several occasions prior to the wedding, Sarah ponders and voices her disagreement with such a position.

In fact, the awkwardness with which the after-effects of Sarah's 'circumcision' are handled illuminates all the more the sacrifice of characters' subjectivity to the author's agenda. Not only does Sarah's decision cost her an otherwise happy marriage with Ebow, it also forces her or leaves her no other social choice but to change her religion. For the only option she has of being a respected, married woman is to accept the Alhaji's cavalier offer to make her his third wife. Once espoused to the Alhaji, Sarah, now called Salamatu, accepts the obligation to bear her new husband the son that his other wives have not given him – this, in spite of the agony that sexual intercourse has become for her since the cutting. Worried, however – and hassled by her husband – when she does not conceive after an appropriate amount of time, she confides to a friend, who must persuade her (former wife of a gynaecologist!) to see a gynaecologist. No surprise to the reader, Salamatu learns that her Fallopian tubes are blocked from chronic pelvic infection resulting from her 'circumcision.'

So, now having served the novel's agenda by sacrificing her marriage, her religion and her fertility, Sarah as 'pawn' gets deployed for further service to the cause. Divorcing the Alhaji, who has no further interest in her anyway, Sarah renounces the new marriage, the new religion, the new name, and the traditional practice of female 'circumcision' itself, re-locates back to the north, joining the movement championed by her first husband and his new partner in the campaign to eradicate FGM in Ghana. While her conversion to the anti-FGM camp is easily convincing,[6] resulting from her personal trials and tribulations, all of the other elements in Sarah's trajectory are far too obvious. For example, for an all-around happy ending, Sarah gets to marry a nice doctor whom she meets while working for the cause in the North, and together they attend the wedding of Ebow and Yvonne.

But not only Sarah's credibility is sacrificed to the anti-FGM cause in this novel. More damaging than just the contrived trajectory of a character (who should rightfully be the protagonist) is the critique, from the narrative voice, of some aspects of Ghanaian life that are represented as contributors to the scourge of FGM. Inter-ethnic marriage, for instance, is criticised as a cause of marital discord, because it brings out conflicting practices and perspectives. Ebow is admonished by his aunt, who had never approved of his marriage to a woman from the North: 'The rate at which some of these inter-ethnic marriages are breaking up is something to worry about, especially when the traditional people start interfering. ... Sorry, if I seem to be sounding the alarm bells, but these are the realities of life.' Ebow defends his marriage, though, not without an edge of uncertainty: 'It's worth keeping that in view and thank you for the hint. Our love for each other has not waned and I hope she won't do anything foolish' (115). Other thinly veiled criticisms regarding dangers of inter-ethnic marriage occur in the text.

Disapproval also tarnishes rural life depicted as backward and mired in intractable tradition. Thus, the communities where Dr Alhassan's work has been centred are portrayed as the quintessence of rural ignorance and underdevelopment. Even further, Sarah's native village and especially her family are shown to be physically, economically, and culturally under-developed. Indeed, the description of Mongasi, on her visit there with Alhaji, is an exercise in gratuitous denigration of the village scene.

> As the car drew near her house, that old mud house among several others with their thatched roofs, she saw children gathering around with admiration and amazement. It was rare to see a car in the village; a Mercedes-Benz saloon car was certainly beyond their expectations. Then she saw two women walking by. They looked haggard as they carried some wares on their heads towards the market. She recognised them immediately even after all those years of harsh village life and uncontrolled childbearing. They were her childhood friends...(85).
> Amina and Adisa were older than [their sister] Sarah. They were illiterate peasant farmers living in the same village with their husbands who were also farmers. Their huts were further away from their mother's in the dispersed settlement characteristic of the area (87).

In his depiction of Sarah's village the geography teacher-turned-novelist indulges in editorial condemnation with comments such as 'that old mud house among several others with their thatched roofs,' 'uncontrolled childbearing' and 'illiterate peasant farmers.' Of what relevance is this depressed depiction to Sarah's joyous homecoming visit to her widowed mother and sisters except to introduce a smug and unflattering contrast between Sarah's urban and their rural existence? It does not reflect Sarah's perceptions of the village. It is, instead, authorial editorialising that does not serve the action at hand. However, in presenting this depressed image of Sarah's village, the author usefully creates a milieu of backwardness for the setting of the FGM to which Sarah will eventually submit during her sojourn at home.

A TEEN-AGE READERSHIP

A novel such as this one, directed at still-impressionable school-pupils, is certainly justified in weighting the argument toward abolition of FGM. As one or another of the impassioned doctors repeats at several points, 'no ethical defence can be made for perpetuating a traditional or cultural practice that damages women's health and interferes with their sexuality for life' (99). *Mutilated,* as a *scientific* treatise against the perpetuation of the practice, is unassailable by any lay audience.

Unfortunately, however, as a *narrative* treatment critical of the practice this novel's case is considerably less cogent. The story line provides no substantive conflict with, or challenge to, the forces of abolition. It takes up the socio-economic issue of 're-tooling' (!) the traditional practitioners whose livelihood is devastated by the eradication of their vocation, but as NGO's have become aware, despite training, midwives continue to cut as long as demand exists. Crucial is to understand the intractable sources of demand, but a critical reader of this book is not engaged by any substantive socio-psychological and cultural struggle that could illuminate the basis for the practice's strength and magnitude. What is causing such resistance in the face of arguments from medical science? One physician cites increased sexual gratification for men but also emphasises that it is women who perpetuate the practice.[7] Beyond such explanation from the medical community, the book offers only the cultural obligation that confers social respect on a woman. But the issue of social respect is neither interrogated nor problematised in the text. Hence, the hold exerted by the tradition on its adherents can, at best, only appear incomprehensible or irrational, and, hence, indefensible. Or, as it is characterised in this novel, that hold appears simply as a mark of unenlightened, underdeveloped societies, and, hence, indefensible. Consequently, the most unsatisfying aspect of this novel is the absence of consideration accorded to advocates of cutting. Even youthful audiences should not be denied the opportunity to see the picture more comprehensively, in order to intelligently appreciate the conflict as a socio-cultural issue of great historical moment, rather than simply a medical and legal witch-hunt.

Written for youth, *Mutilated* received approval by the Ghana Education Service as an optional literary work for secondary-school use. Because of its potential as a tool for consciousness-raising and social impact, *Mutilated* was subsequently selected by the Ministry of Women's Affairs and by the Ghana National Commission on Children to be distributed to secondary-school students in the sections of the country where FGM is practiced. Those agencies, working together on awareness of the need to abolish excision, have included this novel to engage the next generation of adults who would be in the position to prohibit cutting for their own children. Therefore, the Ministry of Women's Affairs purchased copies to distribute to secondary schools in the Upper West and Upper East regions of Ghana in 2004. Whereas the Accra schools that have bought copies have placed them in libraries for students' extracurricular reading, it is hoped that the schools in the Northern regions will actively encourage the students to read and discuss the work towards the envisioned purpose of changing community perspectives and behavior.

In that regard, this paper rests more on what it cannot do than what it actually does. It should be regarded as the preface for a study that is yet to be executed, to analyse responses to the book by communities in which it is most relevant. Such a field study, conducted preferrably by a social scientist, and after at least a year or two following distribution of the books, would be of great significance to a volume such as this.

However, responses available from the very different population of more urbanised, academically stimulated young women of Accra Girls' School clearly substantiate the novel's representation of limited acquaintance with, and strong criticism of, FGM held by the urbanites of the capital. These students acknowledged that reading this book increased their otherwise limited understanding of the practice, particularly the ways in which it affects women's sexuality. To questions about criminalising the practice, they answered vociferously that, because it endangers lives and sometimes kills, FGM is, without question, a criminal practice.

FGM was, in fact, outlawed in Ghana in 1995. And, indeed, there have been a few convictions. However, because the law has had little deterrence effect, it has been re-visited in recent time and strengthened. In the amended version the name of the offence is changed from 'female circumcision' to 'female genital mutilation,' denoting now its harmful effects rather than its tradition as a cultural ritual. The impetus for the Criminal Code (Amendment) Bill passed by Parliament on June 14, 2007, was to 'widen the scope of the provision to reflect the actual nature of the offence' and 'widen the scope of responsibility... to include all other accomplices to the practice.'[8] Although the penalty of a 4-to-10-year prison sentence remained virtually unchanged, in spite of strong support for increasing it to 10 to 25 years, the necessity of education about the practice was stressed as a more important means of eradication in place of harsher punishment. In view of this prevailing opinion on the part of the Parliamentarians, Mr Nimako's novel should become a primary educational resource.

Tobe Levin

What's Wrong with Mariam?
Gloria Naylor's Infibulated Jew[1]

Perhaps the most seriously under-researched human rights violation in the world, Female Genital Mutilation (FGM) is rarely encountered as a literary theme. Therefore, as a rule, activists welcome it. In *Bailey's Café* (1992), Gloria Naylor courageously presents a young Ethiopian, Mariam, who has undergone an excruciating ordeal, infibulation, and the author clearly disapproves, as do all the fictional characters in her tale. In fact, one of them, Eva, herself a victim of sexual violence, tries to show diners what FGM means. To do so, she eviscerates a plum, and the gesture's brutality is unequivocal. The novel is against FGM.

Why, then, am I troubled by Naylor's infibulated Jew, as though sensing the character's ethnicity is a bad aesthetic choice? Should I not be grateful for exposure of a tabooed subject in a fictional text that also strives, in this increasingly divided world, toward a rapprochement between Muslims and Jews? But if Jews *don't* infibulate, why risk eliciting readers' uncritical assumption that they do? True, Ethiopian immigrants' scarred labia have been examined by gynaecologists in Israel, but none were sewn, and the cutting custom never entered liturgy.[2] It was performed on women *despite* their faith, making Naylor's implication that Jews, too, 'do it' disingenuous. What drives this odd motif?

The question is important, precisely because Naylor is a meticulous stylist, a seductive writer who cocoons you in her fascinating world. Caught up in the author's magic, you miss your U-bahn stop; the microwave pop-corn burns; the yawning dryer waits in vain for the laundered sheets. You keep on reading, captive to the Velcro of Naylor's skilled hand. For that reason, you are wide-eyed when confronted with the following event:

Eva plunged the knife quickly into the middle of the split fruit. With one twist of her wrist, she cut out the large pit. It carried ragged pieces of dark amber flesh with it... (151).

The metaphor precedes reality:

The child's hanging skin is held together with acacia thorns and boiled thread. A clean straw is inserted to ensure there will be a small opening after the body has healed itself shut (151).

Naylor's openness is a mark of courage. As Bernadette K. Kassi notes, an inexcusable silence attaches to a surprisingly large number of African authors whose interest in and as women would suggest inclusion of the 'initiation' theme. Why such indifference, she asks? (178).

One reason for malaise lies in the subject itself. My interest in clitoral ablation and the Beta Israel owes a great deal to the fact that, as a Jew in Frankfurt, I have learned from three decades of opposing genital surgeries how the topic is hostage to an inherent double-bind. On the one hand, it must be exposed and, at the same time, covered up, for the moment FGM is no longer self-evident, taken for granted by a viewpoint from within the culture, it becomes embarrassing. The urge to suppress knowledge about it stems from this: that in the modern world, it has no place[3] and, when confronted by modernity, it instinctively goes underground. As a result, though honouring Gloria Naylor's extraordinary gift, I find it disturbing that infibulation is linked to Judaism. Why this odd aesthetic choice?

MY OWN LIFE WRITING

In April 1998, at the 'First Nashville Conference on Black-Jewish Relations' at Vanderbilt and Fisk Universities, after I had questioned the rationale behind Naylor's having made the genitally mutilated character a Jew, Black activist Tony Martin of Wellesley College peeled his slim, white-clad body from the seat to tell me I had just made matters worse. My use of the terminology, 'female genital mutilation' in place of 'female circumcision' displayed a neocolonial arrogance. I politely referred him to the 1991 UN Seminar on Traditional Practices Affecting the Health of Women and Children, held in Burkina Faso, where African women activists voted to substitute 'female genital mutilation' or FGM for the deceptive 'female circumcision,' their views now codified in the World Health Assembly Resolution WHA46.18 and other international instruments (1994 J2), including the adamant 2005 Bamako Declaration.[4]

Terminology aside, the issue is indeed one of reception. In 1992, an anti-Semitic atmosphere in African American studies, evident on many US campuses,[5] could have neutralised Naylor's attempts to resolve differences between Blacks and Jews in *Bailey's Café* while also disserving abolition campaigns. Activists recognise that, although 3 of 4 Islamic schools of thought claim only male circumcision is required, Muslim women often mistakenly believe they are cutting their daughters with divine support. As Wiebke Walther notes, '... the circumcision of girls is obligatory... in the Sh-fi'ite school; in the M-likite school it is ... customary' (78–79). And the truth is that *infibulation* – among the 4 presently classified types of FGM – is *performed almost exclusively by Muslims.*

If I seem to be admitting that raising the issue at all can elicit a racist reaction that is exactly what I am doing. My discomfort reading Naylor is tied directly to agreement with African activists who, for many years, have insisted that Western allies in the struggle to abolish FGM integrate anti-racist discourse into all discussion, for failure to do so encourages bias. Here is one example. In Germany, since 1994 when during the World Population Conference CNN exposed clitoridectomy's higher-than-90 per cent prevalence in Egypt, an enormous increase in media attention to genital mutilation led some journalists, hitherto quite ignorant of the custom, to employ a racist undertone. For instance, *BRAVO! Girl* (1996), circulation approximately 3 million and aimed at a readership of 10 to 17 year-olds, carried a 'news' item about 'Awa, 17: 'Ich wurde Beschnitten' [Awa, 17: I was circumcised]. Featuring a Sudanese allegedly operated on in Germany,[6] author Petra Göttinger opens with her own incredulity: 'Unbelievable! With knives and razors, tin can tops, blunt scissors or splinters of glass 2 million girls between 7 and 14 are hideously mutilated every year' (10).

Because I had advised the journalist and was listed as an activist, the blatant, exaggerated tone saddened, embarrassed and above all angered me, but worse was to come: bushels of letters from school girls and boys – close to 200 in the week the magazine appeared – flooded in. The children and their teachers expressed empathy with the suffering teens but called for jail, extradition, even lynching of the parents. Typical is this petition from an entire Swiss high school class (Eine Klasse der Oberstufe Suhr 1996): 'Da könnte man doch gleich alle Mädchen erschiessen! Das sind Arschlöcher! Die sind so etwas von behindert, ich bin sprachlos!' ('They might as well just shoot the girls, the ass holes... I'm speechless.').[7]

One Afro-German friend believes that any and all references to FGM in the Western world irritate existing prejudice. The same danger holds, I feel, when the bigotry targets Jews.

AN 'ANTI-ANTI-SEMITE'?

Recipient of the National Book Award for her debut novel, *The Women of Brewster Place* (1982), drafted when she was only 22, Gloria Naylor went on to pen *Linden Hills* (1985), *Mama Day* (1988), *Bailey's Cafe* (1992), *The Men of Brewster Place* (1998), and *1996* (2005)[8] reaping enthusiastic praise which places her in the empyrean of Black women writers, her work on the syllabi in numerous African American studies courses.

Now, for the most part I share in the encomiums, nodding as I read Karen Joy Fowler in *The Chicago Tribune* (October 4, 1992) calling *Bailey's Café* 'memorable and musical, harsh and funny, strange and familiar' (26); or Donna Rifkind in *The Washington Post*, for whom Naylor's is 'a commanding fictional voice: sonorous, graceful, sometimes piercing, often spellbinding' (28). *New York Times* reviewer Dan Wakefield continues the litany, finding in Naylor's fourth novel '[a] virtuoso orchestration of survival, suffering, courage and humor' (30), while Peter Erickson commends Naylor's using 'the medium of fiction to convey the possibility of cooperation' (34) in a contentious realm beyond the book: in the so-called Black-Jewish controversy. Noting that 'the problems of black anti-Semitism and Jewish racism have recently received new attention' (34). Erickson is grateful for Naylor's intervention. Reading the novel for its revaluation of manhood, he goes on to explain:

> The black male proprietor of Bailey's Cafe and Babe [*sic*] the Jewish owner of the pawnshop are brought together specifically to bless the baby boy to whom Miriam [*sic*], an Ethiopian Jew, has given birth. The festive response by the novel's three key male figures to 'the baby's first thin cry' is touching: 'Then Gabe grabbed me, whirled me around, and we started to dance. He could kick pretty high for an old goat. Miss Maple [a male cross-dresser] took his other hand and the three of us

were out in the middle of the floor, hands raised and feet stomping.' The same three men preside over the formal ceremony of [male] circumcision... [so that] through this cross-cultural nurturant concern, the novel provides a final suggestion of a new male identity (34).

Maxine Lavon Montgomery extends this concept of harmonious identity to women. For Montgomery in the *African American Review,* the novel's 'ambiguous climactic scene is [intended] to effect some sort of unity among the widely disparate voices of women.' Mariam promotes this rapport. Described as 'a curiously virginal unwed mother,' the Ethiopian's 'touching account of anti-Semitism and sexism recreates a vital sisterhood among women of colour across the Diaspora who often find themselves at odds with notions of female sexuality prescribed by patriarchy.'

Hinting as well that acerbic relations between certain Blacks and certain Jews result from a confrontational male identity under patriarchy, Erickson places Naylor among the conciliatory female voices for whom machismo (with homophobia and misogyny) has wielded the battering ram against a fragile, 'troubled alliance'. *Bailey's Café* can be read, to borrow the term coined by Henry Louis Gates, Jr., author of the famous *New York Times* op-ed piece 'Black Demagogues and Pseudo-Scholars' (July 20, 1992), as the work of an 'anti-Anti-Semite.' Gates contends that contemporary top-down anti-Semitism has been used 'strategically: as the bid of one black elite to supplant another. It requires me,' he writes; 'to see anti-Semitism as a weapon in the raging battle of who will speak for black America: those who have sought common cause with others, or those who preach a barricaded withdrawal into racial authenticity' (in Berman 221). As the friendship between Bailey the restaurateur and Gabe the pawn-broker clearly aligns Naylor with the former, I have no doubt of her clean hands.

Nonetheless, I argue that *Bailey's Café*, if read by an audience exposed to anti-Semitism, can reinforce hatred of Jews. Why? Because a racist reaction to initial encounters with FGM is not unusual. 'What barbarians,' people think. 'How cruel, uncivilised.' My aim, therefore, is not to disparage Naylor's novel but to warn against believing that Jews desecrate vaginas.

BETA ISRAEL DON'T INFIBULATE

...according to this view, *Firaun* ['name of the Pharaoh during the time of prophet Musa (Moses)'] was told by soothsayers that a male child would be born among the Israelites who will bring his kingdom to an end. He ordered killing all Israelite boys alive and to ensure that every Israelite woman would need a midwife when delivering, he ordered that they should be cut and infibulated, hence the name pharaonic circumcision. This way they would be able to get to know the birth of any boy and kill him. If true, then the practice is not Islamic as it pre-dates it (Maryam Sheikh Abdi 23).

In 'A Religious Oriented Approach to Addressing FGM/C among the Somali Community of Wajir, Kenya,' Maryam Sheikh Abdi aims to show the mistake most Somalis make in thinking that Islam requires FGM. To do this she draws on the above belief and adds 'another historical account.' According to this second view, jealousy drove Sarah to be the first to perform 'circumcision' on Hagar, thus also predating Islam.

Is there any evidence for these tales? According to Harvard's Shaye Cohen, 'When I wrote my book on women and berit [circumcision] I looked long and hard and was unable to find any classical Jewish reference to female circumcision/ infibulation. See chapter two of my book ['Were Jewish Women Ever Circumcised?']. The story referenced [above] (re Pharaoh and Sarah) is Muslim.' In *Why Aren't Jewish Women Circumcised?* Cohen sums up his findings with considerable confidence thus:

Aside from some statements of the geographer Strabo, there is no evidence that any Jewish community—aside from the Beta Israel of Ethiopia – has ever practiced female circumcision. If we reject Strabo's testimony on the grounds that he has incorrectly conflated the Jews with the Egyptians, who did in fact practice female circumcision, and if we set aside the customs of the Beta Israel, on the grounds that their observance of female circumcision is more a function of their Ethiopianness than of their Jewishness, we may restate the sentence more simply: there is no evidence anywhere that any Jewish community has ever practiced female circumcision' (64).[9]

Now, has Naylor simply made an 'innocent' mistake?

An exception even among extremes, Mariam is expelled from her village for pregnancy without disclosure of paternity. A virgin giving birth on both literal and symbolic levels, she becomes a Virgin Mary surrogate, yet her pain is not unusual. She enters a novel whose female clients all share a history of sexual abuse rabid in its intensity (Sadie, Esther, Eve, Mary Take One); and although Eve's mistreatment by her step-father, the minister, certainly stems from Christianity's vilification of the body, the blame for other characters' defilement does not fall on religion itself. Infibulation, however, clearly results from tribal injunction: the Hebrew faith bears responsibility.

But, you object, prior to Operations Moses and Solomon, some Beta Israel engaged in genital cutting. Even so, they are not known to have favoured the total ablation of all external organs.

Now, Naylor did some of her homework. To describe the Beta Israel, she watched Meyer Levin's 1973 film and 'borrowed' several lines (on page 146) from the voice-over. Levin, however, though mentioning male circumcision, does not deal with girls' rituals at all despite the availability of information. For instance, in 1967 D. Harel, in 'Medical Work among the Falasha of Ethiopia,' revealed that infibulation was not performed, while more recent research provides definitive proof.

Grisaru, Lezer and Belmaker (1997) admit that genital surgeries in Tigray (though not in Gondar where Beta Israel also lived) sometimes 'create adhesions that prevent marital intercourse' but by means of natural scar tissue at the site of clitoridectomies or labiotomies. More specifically, the University of Beersheva team examined 113 Ethiopian Jewish women ranging from 16 to 47 years-old and found that:

[only] forty-seven (47 per cent)... had evidence of old scars. In 11 (10 per cent) there was total amputation of the clitoris and prepuce. In 19 (17 per cent) the clitoris was partially amputated. In 8 (7 per cent) other women there was [a] 1 cm square removal of the labia minora beneath the clitoris: in some this was bilateral and in some unilateral. In 4 (3 per cent) [of] women, there were scars of incision only on the clitoral prepuce, about 4 mm long. In the remaining 71 women (63 per cent) there was no evidence of any genital past incision or ablation (211–215).

These facts strongly suggest that, even in the 1940s, Beta Israel were not stitching up vaginas. 'It is strange,' Dr Belmaker wrote (e-mail message 6 March 1998), 'that they would emphasise the Jewish aspect.' Yes, examinations revealed 'a significant incidence of partial clitoridectomy,' but 'we didn't find infibulation' (e-mail message to author).[10]

Nonetheless, critic Rebecca S. Wood, surely not unlike many other readers, simply takes for granted that 'according to Beta Israel custom, George's mother Mariam is prepared for her future marriage by being circumcised, and the village midwives sew her up tighter than usual to raise her value as a wife' (152). Wood takes her lines from the novel (page 152) and appears to believe them true. Likewise, my internet searches have failed to reveal instructors' awareness of an error (Teaching about Violence 3/18/98). The blunder, therefore, is contagious and grave because it makes the victim of the only structured, institutionalised abuse in the novel a Jew. Although Naylor takes great care to have Eve say of Mariam's mother (and by extension of the infibulating community), 'You do understand... how much she loved her daughter?' (152), the rasping knife-edge stripping flesh dominates our knowing. A ritually tortured Mariam, victim of a seeming Hebraic consensus, adds fuel to anti-Jewish fires and weakens Naylor's conciliatory aims.

For Naylor acknowledges anti-Semitism as a problem – witness Gabriel and the pseudonymous Bailey, for instance, discussing Israel. And just as surely, when one of the Gatlins – 'white trash' roughnecks – comments, 'I don't know any Jew who'll take a collect call,' (181) readers won't miss the ironic emblem of a common enemy. Nonetheless, when Nadine begins 'Mary (Take Two)' talking about 'the little Jew gal' (143), her choice of uneducated adjective, like the 'N' word to a Black, makes a Jew uneasy. And as she continues to claim authority to speak in that girl's name, queasiness ensues. Mariam is quoted in the novel - repeating four times 'No man has ever touched me' (143–145) – yet for the most part she is silenced in a script that otherwise makes space for the female voice.

Mariam's muteness, however, supposedly deriving from mental deficiency, produces several ruptures in the story's frame. First, when Gabriel brings Mariam to Eve, he has broken one of the narrative's own rules: you must come to *Bailey's Café*, an allegorical utopia that signals readiness to take your own destiny in hand, by yourself. Arrival signals that you have taken on the responsibility to change. Now, although slow-witted (like Tashi's brain-damaged offspring maimed by the vulva's closure in *Possessing the Secret of Joy* [1992]), Mariam has completed a monumental trek through the highlands to Addis Ababa where the 'white Falasha' – Gabe, a refugee from Hitler – rescues her. This heroic persistence might have plausibly entitled her to find her own way to Bailey's, like the others, but instead Naylor places her in a male mediator's hands. What then do we make of Nadine's assertion, 'This isn't a story any man can tell' (143)? Does Gabriel's complicity - his gallantry or humanity - imply unmanning of the Jew? Sander Gilman points to the Jewish menstruating male, circumcision's flow of blood associating men with menses – 'the altered form of his circumcised genitalia reflecting the form analogous to that of the woman' (76) – as a prominent anti-Semitic stereotype whose trace is here: '... the male Jew is read ... as really nothing but a type of female' (127) in much anti-Semitic literature, Gilman asserts.

Exploring further the effects of twinning Mariam and Gabriel, I see the pair of Jews underscoring the impression that infibulation is indeed a Hebrew custom so debilitating and culturally anchored that its victim cannot possibly heal herself by herself, a conclusion with which I happen to agree, but question in the context of singling out the only Jewish female character to mute, and in light of attributing to Jews a practice many Africans themselves call torture.

Complicating reception even further is anti-Semitism not propagated by Afro-centrists but by feminists. Now, since the early years of the contemporary women's movement, Jewish progressives have critiqued male biases within the religion but have also deplored certain Christian theorists' blaming patriarchy itself on the Jews, responsible for monotheism whose male deity supplanted the polytheistic partly female pantheon. Susannah Heschel, for instance, faults German theologians who claim the ancient Hebrews killed the goddess (144). Thus, infibulation, among the strongest expressions of male will to dominate women, when associated with Israel, may strike Goddess-revivalist readers as supporting their anti-Jewish leanings.

A TEXT FOR ABOLITION?

I wonder, though, whether Naylor herself did not sense the negative effects on audience I have been evoking, evidenced by a contradiction between the gruesome somatic fact of infibulation and timidity in the poetic voice. For one thing, Naylor begs the highly politicised question of who is to speak for whom. Mariam appears as too feeble to represent herself, and, admittedly, the systematic destruction of girls' genitalia is debilitating. Yet, many testimonies have convinced me that its victims do not become uniformly meek. In *Lion-Women: Conversations with Somali Women and Men about Infibulation* (Bern: eFeF, 1997. In German: my translation), Charlotte Beck-Karrer affirms the strength that her refugees – all closed – bring to their new lives in Switzerland.

And even if Mariam 'can't do it for herself [i.e. tell her story], [because] she's a little off in the head' (143) neither can Eve, Nadine, or the intervening narrator (who also departs from the novel's other segments in which, introduced by 'Bailey', each speaks for him/herself). Thus, both wanting to avoid charges of neo-colonialism while at the same time hoping to ally herself with African protest, Naylor hits tones that fall between the keys.

For the rite as a metaphoric plum gutted on Bailey's cafe counter and experienced by the village girl departs from certain standard features in the literature of FGM. Of course, some similarities exist. Other testimony (of which I have read or heard dozens of cases) claims, as Naylor does, 'a white-hot world of pain ... filled with high-pitched screams' (151). But Naylor adds 'the singing of women,' a joyful addenda whose effect I question. Yes, women often ululate, but they do it to cover the nauseating shrieks, the heart- and mind-wrenching howls. And what are we to make of the 'gentle moans of her mother and grandmothers'? 'Gentle' does not fit this scene, for even granted the willing child, this world lacking nuance enacts impotence and force. There is no 'press of soft breasts, soft arms against her heaving body' (51). There is only hardness, for it generally takes four to five adults, one holding firmly to each limb while the fifth sits on the girl's chest, as often a piece of bark is placed between her teeth to prevent – though it does not always work – her biting off her tongue. True, as Naylor notes, the 'world is without end' for the slicing and stitching can proceed, without anesthesia, for a good twenty minutes. But it offers no redeeming douceur or shelter, and although African women, both upholders and critics of tradition, defend their mothers, the 'token torturers' (Mary Daly 163), the maternal serving the patriarchal is, as Alice Walker notes, 'the cruelest aspect of it' (Warrior Marks video).

Yet for Naylor, the surgery is aesthetic: the plum's skin, scraped and severed, 'curls inward like a petal' [151]. The activist in me cringes at this beauty that continues when the omniscient narrator – otherwise absent – intrudes. The sutured vagina will heal, leaving 'a small opening' the girl obviously needs:

> Once she is able to pass her urine. Her mother will be there to comfort her because, at first, the feeling will be strange. The girl may cry when it is time to relieve herself. Drip by drip. But she will know no other way to pass her blocked menstrual blood. Drip by drip (151).

This passage, because succeeded by Biblical encomiums to 'the virtuous woman' (Proverbs 31, verse 10–31), foregrounds once more the Hebraic milieu.Yet its debilitating euphemisms, shrinking meekly away from reality, do not really muffle the horror or rehabilitate the 'surgeons'. Urinating, for example, does not feel 'strange'; in testimony by infibulated women, it will repeat the knifing of live flesh. As former Somali Ambassador to the UN, Edna Adan Ismael told me (November 1997), more than fifty years after her parents had her done she continues to suffer. To write that 'the girl may [*sic*] cry when it is time to relieve herself' erases those moments of keening torment that recur in virtually all memoirs and which, when leading to urine retention to avoid the punishing sensations, can result in additional health damage.

Another problem for readers well-informed about FGM arises in Naylor's treatment of rape and the immaculate conception for semen deposited at the minuscule vaginal opening can in fact lead to pregnancy – and in documented cases has done so. Yet, given the novel's symbolic frame, we are to understand Miriam's only direct claim – 'No man has ever touched me' (143–145) – as physiologically true, with the messianic myth representing Naylor's point:

> So you're telling me, we've got ourselves a miracle?
> Well, Nadine, it won't be the first.
> Yeah, if we're talking the little girl in Galilee...
> She wasn't the first either.
> But you've gotta admit, she's gotten away with it longer.
> And I say, more power to her (153).

This essentially comic passage exemplifies Naylor's indispensable sense of humour yet it is not heretical. It does not pose a serious challenge to the dogma of the virgin birth. On the contrary, the suspension of disbelief required by a surreal reading can easily accommodate Miriam's child born to 'save' the cafe population, since Mary's predicament has already been naturalised for gentile readers. Working against this symbolism of redemption, however, is the fact that conception without intercourse can indeed take place in the absence of defibulation. Thus, Eve's assertion – 'But I've bathed this girl and seen her body; no man has even tried' (152) – escapes interpretation. Eve implies that only rape could have produced an embryo – 'So you see if it had been rape, the whole village would have heard her screams' (152) – but this is simply untrue. No violence was needed. Ejaculation of semen produced by masturbation can cause pregnancy in infibulated virgins.

Normally, of course, force is present, as Eve informs her listeners:

Even on the wedding night...with a willing bride and a cautious husband, the village will hear the screaming. Sometimes it will take months and many trips to the hut of blood, before the wound he slowly makes allows him to penetrate her without pain. And sometimes she's not fully opened until her first child (152).

Obscured by this account of a 'willing' (I prefer docile and terrified) bride and 'cautious' (I would prefer considerate) husband is the injunction to penetrate the wound itself several times a day to assure its stretch. Misleading, too, is the reference to 'many trips to the hut of blood,' the site where infibulation supposedly took place – actually, another *faux pas*, as midwives generally operate not in any hallowed space but in an unhallowed clearing of brush or in the victim's home. In fact, after the seven days' isolation following a wedding which Meyer Levin records, attempts at penetration occur in the marital bed – with ritual dimensions largely absent among those who suture.[11] All this notwithstanding, since the Jews do not infibulate, bringing in the sacral significance in this instance once again reinforces a link between the alleged ancient Hebrew custom and the suffering of girls, a connection that draws meaning from the pre-existence of anti-Semitism in the conceptual framework of the reader.

BUT ISN'T THIS FICTION?

In her review 'Healing the Wounds of Time' (1993), Gay Wilentz contrasts Alice Walker's *Possessing the Secret of Joy* with Naylor's *Bailey's Cafe*, to the detriment of the former. Ironically, Wilentz charges Walker with misrepresenting Africa, pointing to the Georgian's 'incredulity, evidence of a misunderstanding of African culture' and her tendency to 'efface difference [which] will be problematic for readers acquainted with African history' (16). Tashi, Walker's protagonist, belongs to the Olinka, an imaginary, composite community for whom Walker claims no precise geographical referent. Impelled by nationalism, Tashi also differs significantly from Mariam for having chosen to undergo infibulation and Walker's heroine remains the agent of her destiny in equally choosing her revenge, murdering the exciseuse. Now, the Georgian has been accused by African activists of failure to respect those powerful female surgeons, and assassination of the 'Tsunga' certainly counts as disrespect. In agreement with Walker's critics, Wilentz praises Naylor's 'more literary than polemical' presentation. Applauded is the younger author's nuance: for 'unlike Tashi,' Wilentz contends, Naylor's characters 'are not universalised' (16). Yet, it is this very specificity that leads readers to accept as truth the fiction's errors.

This is unfortunate for, as we have seen, genital cutting has been mobilised as a patriotic statement whose implications can be perilous once we consider how, in response to racism encountered in Israel, the younger generation has turned toward Pan African nationalism. As Katya Gibel Azoulay notes: '...colour-based prejudice,' along with a racialised language that speaks – in Hebrew – of white Jews and Black Jews, has led to 'a kind of defiant Ethiopian identity' among the youth. Halevi notes that '[F]or an alienated minority, a Black African identity is becoming a substitute for a failed sense of Israeliness – an ironic reversal of their parents' insistence on being Jews, not Ethiopians' (81–82). More ironic still, genital mutilation has been used in precisely such situations, as an answer to beleaguered nationhood. Ngugi wa Thiong'o's first novel, *The River Between*, presents a heroine, Muthoni, who chooses, like Tashi, to undergo the rite in order to 'be made beautiful in the tribe' (Levin 213). Jomo Kenyatta's first act of state, to give another instance, once independence had been won from the British, was to reinstate permission to perform clitoridectomy, a gesture that may have inspired the following.

In the Gambia, 'Jammeh Says His Government Will Not Ban FGM' (January 22, 1999):

> Banjul – President Jammeh on Tuesday told a group of Muslim elders that his government will not ban Female Genital Mutilation (FGM)...
> 'FGM is part of our culture and we should not allow anyone to dictate to us how we should conduct ourselves,' he said.

That the Beta Israel abandoned genital scarring on arrival in the Holy Land confirms the older generations' desire to be Jewish – as Jews do not 'circumcise' females. And to underscore Ethiopians relinquishing the custom, their abandoning cutting contrasts sharply with its exportation by refugees and immigrants residing elsewhere. It continues in Europe, the USA, Australia, New Zealand – wherever practitioners have settled in the world. Judaism therefore sanctions abolition, not maintenance as Naylor implies.

'It's the law of the Blue Nile,' Eve says of FGM. 'And along these shores ... no woman in her right mind – Jew or Muslim – ... would want her daughter to grow up a whore' (150). As a result, the story of the Beta Israel's shearing and stitching leads Nadine in a rare line to insist, 'I was so angry I wanted to break something. Blame somebody' (152). As a man, 'Bailey' feels accused, but I am uncomfortably close to, even while resisting of another implication: blame the Jews.

Marianne Sarkis

Somali Womanhood: A Re-visioning

Recent attention to life writing has not yet embraced the Somali woman, leaving what little is known about her largely to the inventiveness of androcentric anthropologists and historians. To them, she is a pawn exchanged between clans to further the economic interests of her parents. Her sexuality excised, and access to her body closed, she lives by codes of honour and shame inculcated via customs, poetry, song, and proverbs. Because infibulation ensures 'chastity' and marital acceptability, the surgery inaugurates a process of indoctrination into the responsibilities of women to their husbands, children, and kin; and because women's bodies have been thus literally inscribed with social values, rejection of FGM becomes akin to dismissal of the culture's core ideals of 'womanhood.' This chapter introduces three Somali-born authors who challenge their society and scholars' conservative interpretations. Witnesses to women's agency, they suffer estrangement from kin and threats to their lives, but show that, despite a rigid social structure, dynamic women hold the keys to change.

In the last three years, at least two women have seen their lives threatened for speaking out on FGM and the status of women in Islam. Both argued that outdated customs needed urgent reform. The response was brutal. In April 2007, Kadra, a Norwegian-Somali anti-FGM activist, was beaten unconscious by a gang of young men in downtown Oslo. A week later, two Somali men were arrested on assault charges while six other suspects remained (as of this writing) still at large.

Two years earlier, another Somali, Ayaan Hirsi Ali, a high-profile politician in the Netherlands, was forced underground after repeated threats on her life. She had just released a documentary with her friend, Theo van Gogh. The film, *Submission,* blamed Islam for women's abuse and provoked a Moroccan man to murder Van Gogh.

These two events are unquestionably vicious. They also reveal an underlying tension between gender normativity and identity. Because Islam prescribes the woman's place, Kadra and Hirsi Ali's criticisms were inevitably (mis)construed as an assault on the religion itself. In *Infidel,* Hirsi Ali anchors this dissonance in an abyss between religious dictates and people's ability to live accordingly; a rift between the real and the ideal. But, as Hirsi Ali, Waris Dirie, and Fadumo Korn show, despite Islam's dominance in Somalia, when they were growing up its influence was more relaxed, allowing women flexibility in managing their lives. Islamism's relentless encroachment in Africa and the Middle East in the last thirty years has changed that. Gender normativity became increasingly dogmatic, and thus more perilous for individual women to challenge.

This chapter contextualises these tensions, arguing that FGM, usually considered a one-time event, in fact initiates a life-long process of gender construction sanctioned by kin relations, social mores, and cultural products such as proverbs, poems, and interpretation of religious texts. If then, in Somalia, an 'open' girl is labeled unchaste and, therefore, unmarriageable, and infibulation creates a 'woman,' to reject FGM is to refuse gender identity per se – clearly impossible, yet resourceful women work around it.

What does historiography say about this? Early analyses profile women as helpless victims in a highly oppressive social structure, an image the personal narratives revise. Such traditional misunderstandings stem from three main faults. First, scholars failed to consider the contributions of gender and age to social inequality, the division of labour and means of production (Kapteijns 1995). Second, they neglected to factor into women's status the multiplicity of options implied by lineage, class, education, and social standing. Third, despite political upheavals and migration, analyses ignored the Diaspora, where women maintain Somali identity despite the rejection of FGM and, in some cases, Islam.

Somali women's memoirs therefore complement the existing body of historical literature on three levels. First, they show how girls, while growing up, learn to become women, starting with infibulation at or before the age of reason. Second, they reveal obstacles to detachment from a subservient gendered position as they move toward self-determination and integration into Western host cultures. Last, they document agency in that new identities arise.

BACKGROUND: EARLY HISTORIOGRAHIES AND CULTURAL PROFILES

From 1840 to 1960, colonialists employed cultural anthropologists to profile weak points in African and Arab countries so that European powers could exploit them. Until recently, intelligence about Northern Somalia came from Ioan Lewis. For Lewis, Somalis are 'intelligent, sophisticated, subtle, proud, and extremely individualistic' (1955: 130) who value lineages, tribes, and clans that influence every facet of society. Published in 1955, *Peoples of the Horn of Africa: Somali, Afar, and Saho* (Lewis 1955) stressed that all three societies organised themselves along a decentralised segmentary lineage system with a chief at the top.

According to Lewis, the two largest clans are the Darod (with Marehan and Kablalla sub clans) and the Hawiya. At the time of Lewis' fieldwork, the Darods lived roughly along the Shebelle and south of the Juba, southwestern Somalia, northern Kenya, and parts of Ethiopia (principally the Ogaden) (Lewis 1955: 20). They were mainly nomadic, herding camels, goats, and cattle. The Darod and the largest and most important Southern tribe, the Hawiya, claim descent from an original Arab *sharif* founder.

During colonialism, the Darod were the main force behind the Somali Youth League (SYL), a nationalistic anti-colonialist movement. Of importance here is that Siad Barre who ruled from 1969 to 1991 under 'scientific socialism' was a Darod and installed many of his kin into important government positions. As a result, other major clans felt increasingly alienated, and with Ethiopian aid, overthrew Barre in January 1991. The period that led to the coup, known as the First Genocide, saw violence worse than Somalia had ever experienced, as dissenters, fueled by their hatred for Barre, raped and tortured thousands. In retaliation, Barre ordered the slaughter of hundreds of Muslims from all clans as he tried to crush opposition to his increasingly brutal regime. Since that time, many transitional and interim governments have come and gone, and Somalia remains in a state of anarchy ruled by warlords. Northern Somalia, or what has become known as Somaliland, has been relatively stable since the coup, having established a system of self-government independent from the rest of the country.

These events took place at about the time when Hirsi Ali, Dirie and Korn left Somalia. Each describes in detail how seeing the death of kin from the Darod and Hawiye clans affected them and influenced their relationships in Somalia and Europe.

POSITION OF WOMEN IN SOMALI SOCIETY – THE 'IDEAL'
Colonial anthropologists, historians, and political scientists explained Somali social dynamics in terms of lineages and clans rather than relationships among individuals, and tended to be either silent or ambiguous regarding women's social position. These representations privileged men's views of women who appeared stifled by oppressive institutions like marriage, kinship, religion, and pastoralism. Largely unchallenged, such stereotypes dominated discourse on Somali gender identity and seemingly compelled women to choose between equality and inherited cultural mores. 'It is ... pastoral tradition that, like millstones around the neck, weighs down any contemporary Somali woman who wants to challenge the limiting gender ideology' (Kapteijns and Ali 1999).

Contributing to this complexity, Ioan Lewis documented extensively the lineage system and life cycle from the 1950s to the present and included cursory descriptions of infibulation and women's position in the overall structure. Ahmed (1995) charges Lewis for defining the national character of Somalia, his works largely responsible for misunderstanding of gender normativity.

Ioan Lewis' treatment of Somali women is confusing and contradictory. For example, the 1955 *Peoples of the Horn of Africa: Somali, Afar, and Saho* suggests that women can be nearly as influential as men (2004 [1955]: 128): '...the Somali woman [may have] low rank but... considerable standing. She appears in segmentary relations as a dependant with rights only through the agnatic group to which she is attached by marriage or birth' (Lewis 2004 [1955]: 128). That is, she *has* rights, even if these are undermined: she is excluded from political positions or participation in the assembly of elders; cannot obtain redress in case of insult or injury; has her testimony, inheritance, and blood-compensation weighted as being worth half the man's, nor can she own substantial property or marry without her father's consent. She is physically abused by her husband upon consummation of the marriage.

And last, Lewis notes, 'in a sense, women are outside the agnatic lineage structure... [For] when they appear in social relations involving segmentary groups they do so as clients attached to agnatic units, never directly or *sui juris*' (Lewis 2004 [1955]: 129). Furthermore, a woman owes her husband obedience, submission, and subservience.

Lewis writes:

Throughout her married life a wife is expected to sustain this ideal of male domination, at least publicly, whatever the affective character of the relationship between the couple. ... Thus publicly a woman must defer to her spouse – whatever happens in private – cook for him but eat apart from him, and when... together in public walk behind [him]. The women of a hamlet may, however, publicly ridicule those of their menfolk who return ignominiously from an unsuccessful... raid [suggesting] strong sentiments of female solidarity. (Lewis 1994:57)

In other words, although Lewis wants to portray women as voiceless and dutiful, he also appeals to the old canard of 'power behind the throne.' Women benefit, then, from a certain negative bonding, and, although clearly marginalised by a rigid kinship structure, they retain sufficient agency to express their needs.

Both Waris Dirie and Hirsi Ali substantiate Lewis. They maintain that women's fate hangs largely on submission to the will of their families' males. Dirie likens this subordination to a child's helplessness (45). Hirsi Ali explains it in terms of *baari*, an ideal for which women must always strive or jeopardise their 'honour':

A woman who is *baari* is like a pious slave. She honours her husband's family and feeds them without question or complaint. She never whines or makes demands of any kind. She is strong in service, but her head is bowed. If her husband is cruel, if he rapes her and then taunts her about it, if he decides to take another wife, or beats her, she lowers her gaze and hides her tears. And she works hard, faultlessly. She is a devoted, welcoming, well-trained work animal. That is *baari* (Hirsi Ali 2007:12).

A strict division of labour along gender lines follows from this:

Men travel, and women guard livestock and children. In Somalia, the relationship between the sexes is clearly defined. A man never does women's work. He takes care of camels, kills lions, and attacks enemy clans. His wife does everything else. Men take themselves seriously, and women treat them as if they are right to do so. Even as small children, girls learn to serve and respect their brothers, fathers, and uncles. A girl rises when a man enters because he might like that precise spot where she has been squatting. Men are always served the best meat, and women the leftovers. ... In Somalia, the world belongs to men (Korn and Eichhorst 19).

As the three quotes confirm, women's status, work, and nutrition depend on their semblance of deference to men. Further, girls are taught young through poems and songs about their 'proper' inferior role. They must lower their voices, behave modestly and shy away from males (Kapteijns and Ali 1999:23). Indeed, practically from birth, mothers' lullabies praise domesticity and docility, as the following song suggests:

> Daughter, the wealth that comes by night
> Belongs to the girl who is quiet
> Daughter, where there is no girl
> Daughter, no wealth is received
> Daughter, and no camels are milked...
> A marriageable young woman is in the house
> And men pass by its side
> Quiet down for us
> Lest we become an empty space
> [by not receiving bride wealth for you].
> Quiet down for us (Kapteijns 1995: 248).

This lullaby links a girl's behaviour to her family's (hopefully improving) socio-economic status. The five camels paid for Waris Dirie, for example, comprised a respectable sum. But such amounts are given only for infibulated girls who are thought immune to predators and sexual temptation. Here FGM becomes a form of 'patriarchal bargaining' (Kandiyoti 1988), whereby a bridge of skin is presumed to seal virginity and, consequently, the female's future. In return for her conformity in not

131

shaming the family, she can access an extensive, often international, kin network whose benevolence, if withdrawn, can spell disaster. Note Hirsi Ali's grandmother's proverb: 'A woman alone is like a piece of sheep fat in the sun. ... Everything will come and feed on that fat. Before you known it, the ants and insects are crawling all over it, until there is nothing left but a smear of grease' (Hirsi Ali 2007: 9).

POSITION OF WOMEN IN SOMALI SOCIETY – THE 'REAL'

Yet paradoxically, scholars also argue that, from precolonial times to the present, Somali kinship has undergone radical change (Besteman 1995; Helander 2003; Kapteijns 1995; Samatar 1992). Some describe a dynamic system that alters with contexts and needs. Although women lacked explicit political power, they bore significant social capital since they linked various lineages and at times shaped their relationships. Most important, however, women widened their social networks, enjoying protection from paternal, maternal, and husband's clans (Kapteijns 1995: 247). Therefore, although responsibilities and roles differed by sex, communities valued both women's and men's contributions. Children, too, learned to participate early as little girls tended sheep and goats, men and small boys herded camels, and women maintained the home (Kapteijns 1995: 244). In this view, integration into the world economy shifted gender roles, and the emphasis on access to trade resources has enhanced visibility and significance of clans. These new economic dynamics necessitated women's moving (often alone) from the interior to the city in the hope of accessing better opportunities and networks.

Yet with the shift from pastoral to urban life women began to lose their social capital, and 'apart from their reproductive labour, which continued to be crucial..., women's most important contribution lay in...their creation and maintenance of a...middle-class lifestyle' (Kapteijns 1995: 285). Newly urbanised formerly nomadic women, however, came to constitute the new underclass. Unprotected by kin, they had to rely on mat production, day labour, or prostitution. The state also saw them as a threat and often returned them to their families or arrested them for selling sex. Yet many women redefined their roles by pursuing education, postponing marriage, and earning their own income.

Women's changing status is revealed in the three memoirs, demonstrating that the homogeneity of women's inherent social inferiority was largely a myth. None of the authors' mothers, for instance, was submissive. Each eloped. All accessed maternal and paternal lineages, even as fugitives running away from bad marriages or family situations. All three had rich and educated relatives who insisted that they attend school, and be exposed to a value system different from the pastoralists' and nomads'. Their urban female kin dressed differently, achieved high status jobs in the government, and earned their own income. Korn's uncle had even married a Christian woman who did not circumcise her daughters and openly condemned FGM. Yet the distance between the city and the desert proved inadequate protection for Waris and Ayaan, both forced to flee arranged unions. All three left Somalia.

Despite the historical and socio-economic changes and significant out-migration as a result of war and conflicts in the last thirty years, academic analyses of women's social position have remained static. Once in the West, they tend to be written off as uninteresting refugees, largely helpless, without consideration of their agency in negotiating newly-minted selves. Or, they are interesting only because of their infibulated state, which brands them as medical monsters to an offended biomedical establishment.

Yet, as we shall see, women are actively engaged in restructuring their lives, their gendered identities, and their integration into a society that reduces them to mutilated bodies. They are much more than that. Hirsi Ali, Dirie, and Korn provide three different experiences of the Diaspora that scholars can draw from in revising the model of Somali womanhood. Here's how.

AYAAN HIRSI ALI'S *INFIDEL*

Certainly neither abject nor submissive, Ayaan Hirsi Ali is among the most controversial Somali and Islamic figures of the present day. Not since Salman Rushdie has anyone raised the ire of so many Imams, sheikhs, and other Muslims. *Infidel* opens with van Gogh's harrowing assassination and then flashes back to Somalia. It chronicles the author's life in several nations before she moves to Washington, DC.

Darod, Harti, Macherten and Osman Mahmud: Part I, chapter 1 ('Bloodlines') shows Ayaan, coached by Grandma, reciting this important genealogy. Born in 1970, the second child of parents from two different lineages, Ayaan leaves behind a tumultuous life. An irate Quranic teacher had fractured her skull and her mother regularly beat her. Yet she so badly wanted her mother's love that she became, for a time, the practicing Muslim child her mother valued. Wearing a chador, the dutiful daughter prayed five times a day. Her faith, however, soon faltered.

Why? Throughout, Ayaan reveals the sources of malaise. One drawback was indeed women's status. As a teen, having learned from romance novels that gender equality was possible, once Ayaan felt attracted to her cousin, she wed him. Desire trumped fear (140). Yet the bridge of skin was unforgiving. Ayaan recalls: 'It wasn't rape. I wanted ... sex with Mahmoud – just not this way. He gasped and shoved and sweated [trying to force] ... my scar. It was horribly painful and took so long. I gritted my teeth and endured ... until ... numb. [Then] I went and washed ...' (2006: 143).

After Mahmoud's one night stand (he left to study in Russia), Ayaan kept her marriage secret. Her father, however, arranged another union to a relative in Canada, the prospective groom wanting a 'pure' Somali woman. Resisting this betrothal, Ayaan failed to attend her own wedding (though her absence did not matter, the *nikah* signing being official without her). Her brother, discovering her ruse by accident, declared invalid her prior secret bond. He tore up her marriage certificate thereby freeing Ayaan from an awkward position, yet at the same time, negating her act of defiance. Meanwhile, with formalities complete for the newly sanctioned wedding, her husband left for Canada. Ayaan never joined him. During a layover in Bonn, she fled, eventually making her way to Holland where, despite residing in a camp for refugees, she began to enjoy her freedom. With Somalia engulfed in civil war and Ayaan's asylum plea approved, she slowly altered her identity, wanting to 'become a person, an individual, with a life of [her] own' (Hirsi Ali, 2006: 187). Exchanging the veil for Western clothing, she also decided to stay in the Netherlands and earned a degree in political science. While a student, she worked as a government interpreter serving asylum seekers, immigrants, and Somalis overrepresented in the city jails.

Audacious and principled, Hirsi Ali rose through the political ranks to become a member of parliament who publicly renounced Islam, since she perceived it as hypocritical and oppressive to women. Speaking out, however, did not bode well with other MPs in her own party. And *Submission*, the short film she authored on women's religious and social subjugation for director Theo van Gogh, brought her repeated death threats at home, at work, and abroad. Van Gogh's murder sent her into hiding where she remained until constant surveillance strained the state budget. Her Dutch citizenship revoked (and then reinstated), she left the country to work for the American Enterprise Institute in the United States.

Hirsi Ali has written two books, *The Caged Virgin* (2006) and *Infidel* (2007); both condemn traditional practices, Islam, and domestic violence. Yet their tone is apologetic, their mission to show how her dissident views took shape. To discredit her, some of her recollections have been challenged. A Dutch documentary, *The Holy Ayaan,* conducted interviews with her parents, brother, and kin in an effort to expose alleged deceit in depictions of, for instance, her forced marriage.

Ayaan's public presentations are also at times problematic, due not only to their dogmatic tone (Ghorashi 2007), but also her self-perception. When asked why she is fighting Islam, she claimed to be the first 'Muslim woman of [her] generation' to speak in public about 'excision' and 'forced marriage' (*New Perspective*, 2006: 20). Not true, of course, but none-theless, Ayaan has not been called the 'little Voltaire' for nothing: far more radical than Dirie or Korn, she has developed a coherent emancipatory philosophy that sees Islam in need of its Enlightenment, and women needing to resist.

Among Ayaan's ideological sources is surely her excision, justified because, she was taught, should her 'hideous *kintir*,' the clitoris, not be removed, it 'would one day grow so long that it would swing.' To avoid that embarrassing eventuality, and to ensure 'purity,' at Grandma's instigation, the cut comes. In Ayaan's words:

> [Grandma]...gripped my upper body...Two other women held my legs apart. .... Then the scissors went down between my legs and...my inner labia and clitoris [were shorn]. I heard it, like a butcher snipping the fat off a piece of meat. A piercing pain shot up my legs, indescribable, and I howled. Then came the sewing, the long blunt needle clumsily pushed into my bleeding outer labia, my loud and anguished protests, Grandma's words of comfort and encouragement. 'It's just this once in your life, Ayaan. Be brave, he's almost finished.'...the man cut the thread off with this teeth.

That is all I can recall of it (30–31).

Ayaan took two weeks to recover, and while she was able to bounce back, her sister was never the same. The trauma had been too much for her, and she struggled with psychological aftereffects for the rest of a short life she ended herself. Ayaan, unlike Dirie and Korn, does not discuss this matter further. Yet she critiques FGM as an assault on women's bodies and human rights, and considers it endemic to a faith unjust to women.

WARIS DIRIE'S *DESERT FLOWER*

More consistently outspoken about FGM, Waris Dirie has written four books, *Desert Flower* (1998), *Desert Dawn* (2004), *Desert Children* (2007) and *Brief an meiner Mutter* (2007). Here I focus only on *Desert Flower*, which describes her escape from Somalia, her modelling career, and her eventual involvement with the United Nations.

The book opens with Waris on the run, waking to find a lion in her face, fortunately after he has had his dinner. Only thirteen, she had recently discovered that the family planned to marry her to a sixty-year-old man. Dirie's father was to receive a handsome bride-price, five camels, introducing the economics of infibulation into the tale. 'Virginity is a hot commodity in the African marriage market,' Dirie writes, 'one of the largest unspoken reasons for... female circumcision' (50). So, early one morning, the intrepid child walks off into the desert, alone, en route to Mogadishu. While hitchhiking, Waris barely escapes being raped by a forty-year-old; and her paternal uncle tries to send her back. A sister in Mogadishu, who had also escaped a forced marriage, finally provides refuge. But tending her sister Aman's children becomes tedious, so Waris leaves in search of better prospects. She then resides with an aunt, works as a day labourer on a construction site, and finally enjoys a turn of fortune: the Somali Ambassador to London, married to one of Dirie's aunts, had come to Mogadishu looking for a maid. Waris goes with him, and the rest, as they say, is history. Working at McDonalds's, Waris is discovered by a fashion photographer and becomes a successful model – but one with a painful difference compared to her Western colleagues.

Dirie's infibulation is as vividly described as Hirsi Ali's. She is cut by the 'Killer Woman' responsible for the deaths of innumerable girls. At first, of course, like many children, Dirie wanted to 'get fixed,' to become like the others. Although witnessing in secret her sister's operation, which sickened her, she did not change her mind.

Thus, on the appointed day, Dirie's mother wakes her early; the two walk to the brush to await the cold and 'strictly business' gypsy woman (42). Blindfolded, Waris becomes even more intensely focused on her body. She describes the dull blade 'sawing back and forth through [her] skin' (42). She recalls in a passage repeated in each of her books:

> When I think back, I honestly can't believe that this happened to me. There's no way in the world I can explain what it feels like. It's like somebody is slicing through the meat of your thigh, or cutting off your arm, except this is the most sensitive part of your body. However, I didn't move an inch, because I remembered Aman and knew there was no escape. I just sat there as if I were made of stone, telling myself the more I moved around, the longer the torture would take. Unfortunately, my legs began to quiver of their own accord, and shake uncontrollably, and I prayed: Please, God, let it be over quickly. Soon it was, because I passed out (42).

She comes to, however, only to suffer more excruciating pain as thorns and thread invade her flesh. She wants to die and, indeed, – very much like Fadumo Korn, as we shall see, – nears death:

> I felt myself floating up, away from the ground, leaving my pain behind, and I hovered some feet above the scene looking down, watching this woman sew my body back together... At this moment, I felt... peace;... no longer worried or afraid (43).

Worry will return, however. The procedure over, Waris says: 'I looked ...for my mother, but she was gone...so I lay there alone, wondering what would happen next. I turned my head toward the rock; it was drenched with blood as if an animal had been slaughtered there. Pieces of my meat, my sex, lay on top, drying undisturbed in the sun' (43). Later, Waris is drawn back to this rock. Are her genitals still there? No, 'they were gone – no doubt eaten by a vulture or hyena...scavengers [who] clear... carrion, the morbid evidence of our harsh desert [lives]' (45).

Subsequently, her legs tied together for a month, she 'heals':

When the ties...were removed...I discovered a patch of skin completely smooth except for a scar down the middle like a zipper. And that zipper was definitely closed. My genitals were sealed up like a brick wall until my wedding night, when my husband would either cut me open with a knife or force his way in (45).

In London, suffering intense menstrual pain, Dirie seeks defibulation and, from her platform as a world-class model, starts to speak out. Attracting the UN's attention, she is appointed special Ambassador against FGM and, having become an Austrian citizen, founds The Waris Dirie Foundation in Vienna.

Desert Flower's final chapter, 'The Ambassador,' reveals the author's feelings about her ordeal. Clearly enraged, she calls the practice a 'ritual of ignorance' (213) promoted and demanded by men '—ignorant, selfish men – who want to assure ownership of 'their' women's sexual favours. They demand circumcised – that is, genitally mutilated – wives' (220). Dirie insists that enough is enough.

Like Hirsi Ali, Waris sees herself as advocating for the mute, placing her suffering from FGM within the larger purview of female subjugation. Increasing education taught her she was not alone, and that her health problems also plagued millions. She wonders, 'Who is going to help the woman in the desert – like my mother – with no money and no power? Somebody must speak out for the [voiceless] little girl...And since I began as a nomad...like them, it [remains] my destiny to help' (213).

FADUMO KORN'S *BORN IN THE BIG RAINS*: *A MEMOIR OF SOMALIA AND SURVIVAL*

Author (with Sabine Eichhorst) of *Born in the Big Rains. A Memoir of Somalia and Survival,* Fadumo Korn, like Hirsi Ali and Dirie, recalls her nomadic upbringing in Somalia, her painful circumcision, lifetime suffering from complications, treatment in Europe, and eventual action as Vice-President of an anti-FGM organisation, FORWARD - Germany. Korn's story, while quite moving, increases in interest once we learn that Siad Barre, the former Somali President, is her uncle. The memoirs offer an insider's view of the politician's family.

As a result of debilitating rheumatic symptoms unresponsive to treatment in the desert – and clearly resulting from inflammation following FGM—, Fadumo's parents send her to live with her rich uncle Abdulkadir in Mogadishu where the former goatherd enjoys an upper-class lifestyle with maids, chauffeurs, and cooks. Yet, she suffers: unable to eat or bend her fingers, she is ridiculed for being 'disabled' and 'disfigured.' Like Dirie, she also confesses to excruciating menses lasting for a week and her eventual de-infibulation after marrying a German, Walter.

Fadumo's life-shattering event, much like Waris' and Ayaan's, conveys the trauma of her cutting. Like Waris, she is taken to a bare clearing at daybreak. The exciser, stooped and heavy-lidded, appears as an ancient figure that, with neither ceremony nor civility, poses her tools and begins 'reciting a secret spell to ward off evil spirits and the devil. A witch. ...certainly a witch' (37). Again like Waris, Korn is tortured. Suppressed by 'a horde of hands, pressing, tearing, pulling,' she feels the 'ice cold' cut, 'a lightening bolt to the head' (37). And Fadumo bucks, a shriek 'stuck in [her] throat,' as, again, a girl nears death. 'The world stopped spinning. Everything went numb' (39) as body and spirit divide. Has she really come to?

> ...floating [I was] looking on from overhead, seeing myself on the ground...stiff as a board,...a block of wood in my mouth, and an old woman squatting between my legs, carrying out her barbaric craft.
> At some point I could breathe again. I screamed: 'Mommy, help me!'
> But it didn't stop. It didn't stop for a very long time (39).

Fadumo realises the extent of her ordeal only when exposed to a television documentary, years later in Munich, showing another little girl being cut. The child's shrieks elicit flashbacks and rage that lead to action. '...then I got angry and took the floor myself' (162). At the opening of an exhibition, Nigerian artists depicting FGM, this is what Fadumo said:

> Hello...My name is Fadumo Korn...[and] I want to tell you why I am happy to be an African woman. You'll probably wonder about that, since this is a meeting about human rights and genital mutilation, so the fact that I'm happy might come as a surprise.

Yes, she had been cut, and sewn, and 'what happened that morning in the clearing [she will] l will never forget.' Nor the aftermath: the wound infected, the fever high, the coma, the fear. 'But girls are always dying [of] circumcision.' Nothing unusual in that. 'People would say, 'Allah has taken the child to himself' (161).

Fadumo survived but at a price. The 'curious, undisciplined, sometimes willful girl' had been erased, replaced by a silent, morose figure 'never hungry,' 'infinitely sad' and chronically ill:

> My joints swelled; my fingers and toes became deformed...Years went
> by before I was diagnosed with rheumatism. Then my family sent me
> to Germany for therapy.
> Now I was fortunate to find a country with good doctors and clinics. I
> was treated and operated on. My pain was eased although I can't be
> cured. I'll have rheumatism for the rest of my days, but I've accepted it
> because, despite my handicap, I can live a happy life. I got to know my
> husband. I met a sensitive physician who opened me up. Both supported
> me in becoming a woman who likes her body and is able to enjoy sex.
> I'm eternally grateful for that and want to share my happiness. For
> women who went through a similar trauma, I want to be an example
> and source of support. And I want to prevent what is happening daily:
> little girls being subjected to this horrible custom. If I can save even one
> little girl, the effort will have been worthwhile (161).

CONCLUSION

Ayaan Hirsi Ali, Waris Dirie, and Fadumo Korn, three Somali women settled in Europe or the USA, have gained international attention as a controversial politician, a top model, and a popular activist. They reject female genital mutilation, a custom that affects approximately 98 per cent of Somali girls, and publicly challenge the institutions that demand such practices, questioning marriage, religion, and the clan-based kinship system.

Despite the problematic nature of personal narratives, they provide an insight into processes of identity formation around gender normativity through an intentional molding by social institutions in the homeland and change through personal choice in the Diaspora. Individually, autobiographies are a testimony to women's resiliency in the light of the hardships of pastoralist, cultural traditions and religion. When we read these three together, we find that life-writing provides a multivalent narrative that articulates values common in culture. As a group, the tales also complement each other, providing insights into situations that might appear briefly in one but not the other. Lastly, they elaborate on or challenge the accuracy of historical and anthropological interpretations.

This chapter has shown that current historiography in which Somali women are subservient, submissive victims of society is flawed. The distance that migration affords allowed the protagonists to experience newly found freedoms and discover alternate means of self-expression through international human rights work or participation in the electoral process. Though the roles that Hirsi Ali, Dirie and Korn play are, according to Lewis and other scholars, antithetical to 'ideally subordinate' Somali womanhood, these women have pioneered a new identity, for, as Korn writes, 'Even after *Gudniin*... a fulfilling life [is possible].' It's not easy, of course, and 'a pity to struggle to achieve what we should [naturally] enjoy – love for our bodies and sexual pleasure. But African women are strong' (167), and Alice Walker is probably right: 'Resistance is the secret of joy.'

ENGAGED

Pierrette Herzberger-Fofana

Excision and African Literature: An Activist Annotated Bibliographical Excursion[1]

Translated from the French and edited by Tobe Levin

'If God felt that certain body parts were superfluous,
why did He create them?'

Waris Dirie

To demand that an anachronistic custom be abolished is not malevolent, nor does it exhibit 'a weakness for 'white' habits' ('L'excision' 32). It simply means acknowledging that although physical and mental violence is taking place in full view of humanity, euphemism buries it under the shibboleth of 'culture'. The truth is that the health of millions of girls is at risk, sacrificed to backward beliefs and so-called 'venerable' traditions. As Jean Pliya, author from Benin, puts it:

> Construction of a modern nation demands the destruction of certain relics from the past. As long as the women of Benin continue to be victims of a useless and dangerous practice, we will lose out on their contribution to the process of national development.[2] Everyone concerned with the tragedy of excision must link arms and intensify the crusade. Ceaselessly, we must alert the public to the fact that, as we enter the 21st century, a custom that has existed for 2500 years, and has preceded both Islam and Christianity, continues today. ...We must dare to shout 'STOP' ('L'excision' 3: Translation mine).

142

Sadly, we find any number of novelists who deal with the subject and yet fail to cry 'stop' while others, in their fictions, simply remain uncritical. Let us take just one example, *Efuru* by Flora Nwapa. The author describes preparation for excision without in any way questioning the custom. Once Efuru's husband comes home he is informed that his wife will soon be excised, since 'it must be done now... this is the time. Let's not leave it until she gets pregnant' (12).

Because excision is deeply embedded in Igbo culture, Nwapa 'naturally' uses the euphemism to 'take a bath' (15), meaning clitoridectomy, the 'ceremony' recommended to precede marriage though it may be postponed until just before the first baby is born. Why must it be done by then? According to local belief, the clitoris endangers the infant's life should the head touch it, so the offending organ must be removed. Nwapa invites this conviction into her plot at the point where Nwakaego's mother is criticised. She had hoped to spare her daughter, but a baby boy has died and the mother is blamed, his death confirming the threat of organs left intact. The novelist thus presents a feudal society whose codes she accepts. Her sympathies, in other words, are with those whose behaviour in fact justifies it. Far from being the sorceress of story and legend, the elderly midwife's motives are good as she provides after-care, showing concern for the well-being of the patient, and even refusing to cut should the woman be pregnant. Ironically, however, clitoridectomy's danger and *schmerz* also appear clear to its victims, hence the promises to minimise them: 'I will be gentle with you. Don't be afraid. It is painful no doubt, but the pain disappears like hunger' (13–14). Furthermore, surrounded by her neighbours, the newly excised woman, now 'fully feminine,' is the object of vivid community attention. 'Gbonu, my daughter. It is what every woman undergoes. So don't worry' (15), the initiate hears, as the author approves.

Nwapa was not the first woman writer to expose the custom on her pages. Already in 1939, in *Femmes d'Afrique noire* Sister Marie-André mentions the operation to which girls in Burkina Faso were (and are) subjected, alluding to the risks involved. But her publication generated no greater discussion during the colonial period than the few nods to it from the medical milieux after Annie de Villeneuve, in 1937, published her description of an infibulation in both a professional journal on tropical diseases and another directed at Africanists (30).

The tone changed in the 1970s when Fran Hosken with biting and often unacceptable denunciation and, in particular for French-speaking countries, Awa Thiam[3] launched their personal 'crusades' against what they considered an unmitigated evil. Polemics propelled and polarised an incipient movement, until, in 1979, Nawal el Saadawi, gynaecologist and novelist from Egypt, shifted the focus from outsider to insider when she testified to her own clitoridectomy in an autobiographical account, *The Hidden Face of Eve*. Excised at age six, el Sadaawi has been fighting all her life against the practice. As a medical doctor, she has often outlined clitoridectomy's health risks for women. Her political engagement earned her a prison term and later, exile. The Arab Women's Solidarity Association that she founded in Cairo saw itself forcefully disbanded and its goods confiscated by the government. Nonetheless, following the Population Conference in Cairo in 1994, and the passage of favourable laws in 1997, the aim to lower the incidence of excision in Egypt has been confirmed, if modestly (Femme-Afrique-Info. Service d'information électronique 16 February 1999).[4]

Whether reduction in the numbers of the wounded is desired in the first *novel* to deal with excision is difficult to say. In any case, in *The River Between* (1966), Kenyan Ngugi wa Thiong'o elevates excision to the apex of the plot and makes it the touchstone of political strife. Indeed, the Church of Scotland had decreed a policy in Kenya, to expel any child, girl or boy, from its schools if he or she had undergone the rite of 'circumcision.' Fictionalising Jomo Kenyatta's reaction to this, Ngugi shows how the Church's draconian measure was interpreted as an attempt to destabilise the militants in the struggle for Kenyan independence. In retaliation, circumcision and excision became rallying cries within a tense political arena.

Politicised as well but in another sense, FGM in Alice Walker's *Possessing the Secret of Joy* (1992) appears without euphemism as a faulty choice. Because Walker borrows certain elements of plot from Ngugi, it is a good idea to include the later artist here. Whereas in Ngugi the action comes to a head when the daughter of the Christian leader changes sides – from Church to tribe – by opting to be excised, Walker's protagonist Tashi does the same, deciding to undergo infibulation as a young adult in a misguided gesture of solidarity with those who think as Kenyatta would have them do. The parallel ends, however, rather quickly in Ngugi as the excised girl dies. In Walker she lives on to be the living proof of psychological disturbance, showing how the pain which, in Nwapa, is supposed to disappear like hunger, does not but haunts the victim throughout her life as the aftermath, both mental and physical, of trauma. Ultimately, Walker shows how deception is part of the pressure for tradition, and to what extent a woman finds herself diminished after having gone through FGM.

Following an associative path, I think of Awa Thiam as appropriate to mention next, a feminist who both precedes and collaborates with Walker. Thiam's book *La parole aux Négresses*, 1978, was one of the first in the Francophone world to express outrage with the widespread fatalist approach to women's daily lives. It placed excision and, to a lesser extent, infibulation on the public agenda. As a researcher, Thiam solicited statements from Islamic scholars, the elderly, excised women and others, her results stimulating considerable controversy, for no one touches such a taboo subject, let alone displays it openly in Africa – at that time—, with impunity. Nonetheless, Thiam's accomplishment lay in privileging the voices of women – one of whom, PK, wound up as the speaking heart of Walker's *Warrior Marks* – and in showing that, not expressly approved in any Surat, Islam does not recommend excision.

Western feminist movements took up Thiam's text with great enthusiasm, making it the 'little red book' behind their cry to 'stop the barbarism!' Inspired to raise public awareness, they brought to Europe the struggle begun in Africa but, with a certain awkwardness, they relied perhaps too heavily on shock publicity.

What happened? Photographs of excised private parts were shown,[5] an exhibition that outraged African participants in Copenhagen (at the UN Mid-Decade for Women Conference in 1980) who considered it a breach of courtesy and sign of disrespect, because no prior consultation with them, who were also activists, had taken place. The general feeling was that the movement, whose centre and leadership should naturally have been in Africa, had been coopted. Women from the South, confounded by an attitude they found haughty at worst or maternal at best, walked out. Thus, on both sides dialogue was blocked. Or, even worse: the most articulate among African participants drew together to express as one their discontent. If they did not go so far as to defend excision, their lively assault on activists of European and North American origins had perhaps the unintended consequence of making incipient international cooperation considerably more difficult. As the Association des Femmes Africaines pour la Recherche et le Développement (AFARD/ AAWORD) explained, what was amiss in representations of the issue on the part of 'Westerners' was failure to recognise that African society cannot be understood solely in terms of oppression. Instead, AAWORD was looking for 'solidarity' possible only if based on 'mutual respect' ('A Statement' 217). Furthermore, suspicion greeted occidental attention to FGM if unaccompanied by concern for violence against Black women in the West and if detached from any clear awareness that racism, too, made all campaigns against excision particularly perilous. How would black women be served and their lot improved if African culture, already thought 'barbaric' by too many living outside it, should be uniformly represented as sadistic and cruel?

Even authors like Nawal el Saadawi in her novels *God Dies by the Nile* or *Woman at Point Zero* whose opposition to FGM cannot be more virulent questioned a kind of feminism seemingly inappropriate to represent aspirations of women in the South. In other words, the problem having been posed in impractical ways led many African women avid to avoid charges of playing to white sympathies or, worse, being pawns of Euro-American influence, to distance themselves from the issue. Hence, no sooner had it emerged from the shadow of taboo than it slipped back under cover. And in all the years since, frank discussion within mixed African and European movements has been made more arduous by a hard-to-dispel wariness on the part of African women, many of whom know all too well what excision is: they wish to avoid being objects of others' curiosity or passive subjects of others' research.

Thiam's direct heir, attorney Linda Weil-Curiel, continued with the French section of CAMS, Commission pour l'Abolition des Mutilations sexuelles, launched by Thiam in 1982. For three decades, Weil-Curiel has guided the world in her court battles against excision, and under her leadership, France, via its PMI (Protection Maternelle et Infantile, government-run clinics for mother-child health), has become the only country that can show significant decline in incidence of mutilation over the years. Weil-Curiel has also made good use of artistic means of publicising this 'evil'. Among the first to commission a CD – Bafing Kul sings four songs against excision – she has also produced a work of fiction, available on video and DVD, *Bintou in Paris,* set within a West African community in the Diaspora, as well as in comic form for young people, 'La Suite du Pari de Bintou,' or 'Bintou in Paris,' – http://www.cams-fgm.org/bd/intro.php.

Levin describes the drama:

Dawn leaks into the room, taking the census of ordinary objects, couch, crib and mother who suddenly bolts upright. The baby is miss-ing! In a shattered voice Bintou pleads into the phone, 'Aminata. Are they with you?... Adama and Issatou...' No, they aren't. 'Where then?' she rasps. Desperate, Bintou sprints to encounter her sister in a north-ern arrondissement of Paris. They assault a door. It opens, cautiously. 'No,' the exciseuse replies, sucking her teeth, 'no one has been here this morning.' Cut to Bintou's key entering its lock and her husband Adama invading the frame. 'Where is she?' shrieks Bintou, rushing to hold her tranquil daughter. 'I've changed my mind,' the father states. 'She'll never be cut.' (Levin 111–112)

These lines close *Bintou in Paris* [which] features a young Malian from Bamako who decides, without consulting her husband, to spare her daughter from excision. Learning of this, Adama spurns his wife and, together with his mother, pressures her to have the surgery performed. Self-assured, the mother-in-law lifts the receiver, promising to solve this 'one-time little problem...' Bintou, however, has the support of her sister Aminata who educates against FGM whenever she can, for instance at the check-out counter and the beauty parlour where the subtext is, of course, 'il faut souffrir pour être belle.' Nonetheless, salon progressives sit in judgement. Viewed as bad for health or as a dispens-able ethnic marker – 'Cut or not, we're still African,' one woman proclaims – in the last analysis, FGM is denounced by these immi-grants in human rights terms, for why should violence be done to them? Why repress their sexuality? Why mistreat them because they are women? ('Creative' 111–112).

Inspiration drawn from art appears again in Dakar to publicise the passage of a law against excision, using 'Bintou' as a principal motif. In 2000, the NGO Enda-Tiers Monde with the Belgian Free Clinic asbl (family planning) published a comic called *Le choix de Bintou* [Bintou's Choice]. Written in simple language everyone can understand, it explains excision's health risks and the strain it puts on marital relations. The publication concludes with a quiz reminding readers that legislation now exists and that the practice will be prosecuted. Posed in an African context, the questions compel youth to think about their sexuality. The last frame clarifies that you can remain a good Muslim without excision and the back cover reinforces this message: 'Ignorance of the law is no excuse.' The legal text in its entirety is clearly reproduced and warns: 'You will be sentenced to three years in prison if you excise your daughter.' The brochure, available free of charge, appears wherever youth frequent, including clubs, sports associations, discotheques, etc.

Additional appeals include television and radio shows, theatre in local languages, concerts all over Africa featuring well-known stars such as Pierrette Adams, art exhibitions and pupils' drawings, as well as the allure of the big screen. In particular, the stunning *Moolaadé*, filmed in Burkina Faso by renowned author and *cinéaste* Ousmane Sembène, denounces the practice as violence against women and an attack on their physical integrity. In Africa, his profound influence has undoubtedly increased vocal opposition. Dedicated to 'women who fight to abolish this custom from a by-gone era,' the script features Collé Ardo Sy, an excised mother, who had refused to have her only living daughter cut, one child already lost and Collé herself the victim of crude caesarian sections. As the tale takes place, two 'initiates' disappear while four girls flee the ceremony, seeking sanctuary – known as Moolaadé – in Collé Sy's home. Collé agrees, but her generous act sets her against her husband, his family and the village. Here two value systems collide: belief in Moolaadé as asylum and belief in clitoridectomy as 'purification'. Collé's claim – 'You won't do it to my daughter!' – transmits a troublesome message, and her resolve, immune to threats of divorce, exile, and a brutal public whipping meant to force utterance of the word to end aslyum, seriously challenge the Salindé, the excisers. Although FGM is normally considered a woman's issue, the men's council feels compelled to mediate. Clearly understanding Collé's opposition as a step toward women's insubordination, they confiscate all women's radios, symbols of modernity, and burn them in front of the mosque. Thus, the traditional and the progressive air their conflicting views, but Collé's courageous example moves the undecided to her side. The final image, in which women shout Wassa Wassa! ('We have won!'), places the seal of approval on abolition.

IMAGES OR WORDS?

This clearly feminist approach, shown convincingly in Sembène and Bintou to belong to African women and men themselves, has nonetheless been badly received when presented in neither elegant nor diplomatic ways. As a result, at the UN Mid-Decade for Women Conference in Copenhagen (1980), as noted above, awkward encounters escalated into open hostility and signified a years' long setback for the international movement.

Despite such difficulties, however, great strides have been made on both sides to continue the struggle to end FGM. For instance, encouraged by FORWARD International in the early 1980s, two African women published both scientific and autobiobiographical works: Sudanese physician Asma El Dareer, *Woman, Why Do You Weep?* (1982) and Somali citizen Dualeh Raqiya Haji Abdalah, *Sisters in Affliction: Circumcision and Infibulation* (1983).

Also in 1983, after having been in touch with El Dareer and Abdalah, Efua Dorkenoo, President of FORWARD in London ventured into another genre, producing an allegory for children (and adults): *Tradition! Tradition.* Dorkenoo portrays a society crippled by genital assaults on half its population, her heroines systematically deprived of one leg as symbolic counterpart to the severed clitoris and, although certainly amazingly adroit on crutches, they are clearly less agile than on both legs. Including comic moments as well as irony, Dorkenoo hopes to reach African immigrants in the UK, most of whom remain attached to their ancestral 'rite'.

Working with other African women wishing to oppose it, Dorkenoo tells Alice Walker in *Warrior Marks* about a stage play these participants at FORWARD meetings wrote but, when about to put on, did not dare. The script concerns an imported bride who arrives in Great Britain sewn. 'She can't possibly go to a general practitioner,' Dorkenoo says, 'back then, in 1985. He would just freak out. So they do it by themselves, here, in the UK, turning up the radio, television, anything to muffle the noise and cover the hideous shrieks as the razor does its chore – again. Why couldn't the play be performed? Its authors feared threats of death' (*Warrior Marks*).

In the 1980s, joining Dorkenoo, El Saadawi, and Thiam in protest were other African writers whose books, regrettably, often remained in the shadows. In 1985, for instance, in her novella *La Voie du salut* followed by *Le miroir de la vie*, Senegalese novelist Aminata Maïga Kâ, inspired by a French newspaper clipping, told the story of a three-month-old who bled to death following excision in Paris. 'How dare you excise an infant at that age?' Baba shouted. The young mother burst into tears. 'Doctor, it's tradition!' (19: my translation). A cultural insider, Kâ inserts the plot line into Halpular life.

One year later, Nuruddin Farah would do the same for Somalia. In *From a Crooked Rib*, he describes infibulation. For his heroine Ebla, the experience was among the worst of her life: 'My god, it hurt so much, she recalled. On two occasions I regretted being born and that was one' (110: back translation). Here Farah gestures toward the entire Horn of Africa, where fusion of the labia majora is de rigeuer, so that in Somalia, Sudan, parts of Ethiopia, Kenya, Djibouti, and Eritrea, defloration becomes an excruciating act achieved at the cost of additional cuts. After childbirth widens the vagina again, subsequent stitching often obtains. Ebla becomes acutely aware of the injustice implied by these procedures, revealing Nuruddin Farah to be one of the rare male voices in the region who condemns mutilation in his work. Not surprisingly, his novels were judged blasphemous, put on an index of forbidden literature, and their author constrained to go into exile.

The trauma of excision also plays a role in Kesso Barry's 1988 memoir, *Kesso, Princesse Peule*. A former top model from Guinea, she presented an autobiography which, like many others, was received in relative silence both in Paris where the text was published and in Dakar where it was a book fair feature the same year.

Alice Walker, celebrated American author, joins Barry in describing the traumatic after-effects of infibulation in *Possessing the Secret of Joy* whose heroine, as we have seen, chooses mutilation in a misguided patriotic gesture of militant solidarity. But instead of growing strong, she is weakened by her ordeal, and comes to realise the extent to which she has been duped. As Tashi, also called by her Western name Evelyn, suffers recurrent psychological distress as a result of the debilitating intervention, Walker is suggesting a broad interpretation that may be extended to all the female population whose genitals are customarily sewn.

Whereas *Possessing the Secret of Joy* has been fairly well received – published in 1992 it is only now in 2007 reported as no longer in print – the film *Warrior Marks* enjoyed a timid if positive reception in some places, but quite a negative one in others, eliciting criticism that implied the subject might only be approached with a certain restraint.[6]

The same is true of Fauziya Kassindja's *Do They Hear You When You Cry?* When it appeared in 1996, the book elicited hardly an echo in either France or Germany though translated into both French and German. Fauziya, a native of Togo, fled the country on the eve of her arranged marriage in order to avoid excision. Thus, she resisted the will of an aunt who had agreed to give her in marriage to a much older man. When alive, Fauziya's father, who disapproved of cutting, had protected his daughters from it. Yet Fauziya's future husband demanded his wife have her clitoris removed. As a result, aided by her mother and sister, the teen succeeds in reaching Germany where she stays illegally for three months before travelling on to the USA. Erroneously informed that she need only utter the word 'asylum' to gain acceptance into the country, she winds up imprisoned for close to two years, all the while attempting to make valid her claims to refugee status if US law could be interpreted to recognise the legitimate fear of FGM as grounds for asylum.

INCREASING ARTISTIC MILITANCY?

Nearly twenty years separate publication of the works by Flora Nwapa and Aminata Maiga Kâ as well as a number of other texts already mentioned: Calixthe Beyala's *Tu t'appelleras Tanga*, Aicha Fofana's *Mariage, on copie*, and Fatou Keïta's *Rebelle*. In her novel, Beyala denounces not only the dissolution of values she sees occurring as a result of excision but also the psychic trauma her heroines suffer (24). After all, the cut is no longer embedded in any kind of traditional education such as that described by Salimata's mother in Kourouma's *Les Soleils des Indépendances* or Nwapa's *Efuru*. Salimata still receives instruction as a future homemaker and bride in the company of age-mates, thereby inscribing her clitoridectomy in a communal project characterised by transmission of rites and precepts that perpetuate tradition:

> You'll see, my child: for a month you'll live with others and while we sing songs you'll learn about the tribe's taboos. Excision is a watershed

in your life, a rupture that marks the end of equivocal years, the time of impurity as a young girl and entrance into the life of a woman (Kourouma 32: my translation).

For Nga Taba, mother of Tanga in Beyala's novel, not necessarily 'purity' for its own sake but rather the mercantile aspect dominates all other considerations. Deviating from its original significance, excision has become for the parents a means of appropriating their daughters' bodies like merchandise responding to economic laws of supply and demand. Nga Taba's reaction, dancing and emitting cries of joy in anticipation of the benefit she will draw from her daughter's prospects, highlights excision in terms of mercenary motives. Tanga has been obedient to her mother's will only to satisfy the older woman's lust for lucre, placing herself for the sake of a suspect 'honour' in the hands of the 'clitoris snatcher' ('arracheuse de clitoris,' 24).

If a certain militant clarity had now entered into representation of the subject, publication of Waris Dirie's best-selling *Desert Flower* and the publicity campaign accompanying it brought specific problems of their own. After Alice Walker, the first famous person to condemn FGM in the English-speaking world, Dirie would find herself facing a certain doubt among African readers, skeptical of the motives for such spectacular success in Western book markets. As a result, and paradoxically, excision's ravages to health, body and spirit would once again be obscured, partly because the autobiography includes FGM but is not limited to that single theme which, however, would be the most often cited and commented on. Although she has certainly done so since, in *Desert Flower* Dirie never states outright that the operation caused her irreparable psychological harm – this comes out in subsequent books that describe in clinical detail what can only be understood as post traumatic stress disorder (*Desert Children, Brief an meiner Mutter* and the Waris Dirie Foundation website). Nonetheless, in her first opus, which can be construed to represent the suffering millions of little girls, who pass through the excisers' hands, what follows for Dirie remains idiosyncratic and personal. Paradoxically, as a result of the book, extensive documentation focusing on FGM, for instance in *Le Monde* ('Dossier') based on the *Marie-Claire* campaign, run ten years earlier ('Excision, le combat des Africaines' 1985), results not in consensus but balkanisation, not in dialogue but a hardening of fronts. Such frontal attacks on 'circumcision' also lead retrograde voices in the African press to react, showing just how much territory is left for activists to cover. In a virulent article, a journalist from Benin writes, for instance:

> Besides, Waris Dirie should be grateful to her grandparents and her parents, thanks to whose foresight she was excised and therefore spared the trap of prostitution into which so many European models fall. Excision prevented her from becoming a woman out of control. In fact, we can easily see how, with the reduction in excision, girls are becoming increasingly disloyal and promiscuous (Sovide 1).

NEGOTIATING CHANGE?

What the President of Gambia has said about the issue also suggests that solutions to the problem do not result from unilateral intervention generated in the North and imposed from above but rather result from negotiation and dialogue with all parties involved:

> If Europeans are so concerned with the well-being of African women why haven't they air-lifted them out of combat zones? Why, to this day, have there been no mobilisation campaigns against depigmentation when it is well known that attempts to whiten skin cause cancer? ('Jammeh')

Voices raised against abolition campaigns have based their opposition on the motives of Western funders and feminist movements. The publicity generated by Dirie's first tome, regardless of the book's origins and aims, has become a double-edged sword. In some hands, it allows the grand gesture toward major injustices of our times demanding response on a magnificent scale. For these advocates, nothing justifies compromise when it comes to eradicating harmful practices that gnaw away at any hope of future equality or even complementarity between women and men. For others, it underlines the hegemony of a world that turns away from Africa's 'real' problems and highlights the failure of ideas and models of social relationship imposed on the continent against its will. From this it is easy to conclude that men and women of good will are bound to shy away from confronting such an urgent issue at the dawn of the 21st century whose only prospect of resolution lies, in my view, in accepting the call of true solidarity.

During interviews that I have undertaken with a number of African novelists (see P. Herzberger-Fofana. *Littérature féminine francophone d'Afrique noire*. Paris: Harmattan, 2000), most women of letters have shared their dismay regarding the curse of excision and have accentuated the work of persuasion, sensitisation and information that remains to be undertaken. Kesso Barry, in *Princesse Peule*, seconds their collective concern, proposing that 'Like all suffering, this, too, passes. But really, we've been tormented for nothing. We can't blame religion for imposing an oriental custom on us, and then defend it as inherent to our culture, our Africanness.'

An elderly mid-wife, Adja Ndèye Boury Ndiaye, author of *Collier de chevilles*, remembers the purely medical aspect of excision and regrets that victims are doomed to give birth while suffering more useless pain: 'Belonging to an ethnic group that practices exicison, the Lébou, I have known the discomfort attendant on the practice of my trade. Women suffer episiotomies, i.e. involuntary tearing that leads to urinary retention, or to fistula.' Terrible as all this sounds, Annette Mbaye d'Erneville reminds us that, it's 'no use blaming parents, calling them criminals and savages, but by the force of persuasion, we can better put an end to such practices, just like tatooing of lips has disappeared' (Herzberger-Fofana: *Littérature* 389–90).

But are tattoos and sex the same thing? Whereas tribal marks of all kinds have been decreasing, and as a custom, can be addressed without too much ado, *jouissance* seems to be a different matter. Mame Seck Mbacké, author of *Le froid et le piment*, deplores the fact that feminist movements have placed sexual pleasure high on the agenda, because here we enter a domain both sensitive and difficult to measure. For quite some time now, Africans have been posing questions and searching for appropriate solutions. Do we really need to accentuate desire? She asks. In nations where women's sexuality is rarely openly discussed, it is a risk that pioneering critiques must consider. Mme Mariama Lamizana, President of the National Committee against Excision in Burkina Faso, thinks it is premature to frame the question in terms of sexual pleasure because such a political standpoint will only incite detractors to view the movement as a call to debauchery and excess ('Mariama' 32).

Ousmane Sembène would appear to disagree. A key scene in *Moolaadé* superimposes circumcision on the marital act, blending the excruciating pain into one monstrous assault in which the victim bites her finger bloody, having inserted it in her mouth like the bit of wood between an excisee's teeth, placed there to stifle screams and save the tongue.

Nor would Fatou Keïta bracket out the discourse of sex. In *Rebelle*, she prizes a radical courage as the only means to alter points of view, as does Khady Koita in her defiant *Mutilée*, translated as of this writing (October 2007) into fourteen languages, but not English.

Let us give Khady the last word. President of the European Network against FGM, she writes:

> Mutilated as a small child, married before adolescence, pregnant before I had become an adult, I had known nothing but submission. It's what men want, for their pleasure, and what women perpetuate, to their own regret (222. Translation: Levin).

Like Fatou Keïta, Khady suspects that beneath a conformist exterior there is in fact more opposition than many suspect, much of it in thrall to fear. Yet, even if the majority says, 'I was cut and lived through it, so why shouldn't my daughter experience the same?' (222) Khady has met 'grandmothers in African villages, ninety-years-old sometimes, who use another idiom. 'Daughter, do you know why men invented that?' One granny said. 'To shut our mouths! To control our women's lives!' (222).

And with regard to sex:

> The word 'orgasm' doesn't exist in [Soninké]. A woman's sexual pleasure is not only taboo, it's simply unknown. The first time a woman talked about it in front of me, I had to rush over to a dictionary. And then I saw the immensity of what had been done to me (223).

Immense as well remains the task ahead.

Muthoni Mathai
Who's Afraid of Female Sexuality?

Editors' note: In this creative non-fiction memoir, physician, activist and researcher Dr Muthoni Mathai (University of Nairobi, School of Health Sciences, Department of Psychiatry), remembers an invitation to 'take Kenyatta's tea,' a euphemism for oathing ceremonies that threatened to coerce 'female circumcision.' Though to her knowledge no one was actually cut, a climate of opinion was then established that carried over into more recent eras of crisis. A perceived loss of Kikuyu male leaders' power has repeatedly renewed calls for FGM, women's departure from mutilation blamed as a cause of the group's political weakness. In this blend of personal narrative, research results, and interviews concerning FGM, AIDS, and male superiority, Mathai illuminates reasons why the practice continues and reveals alarming resistance to change.

A TEA PARTY

Many years have passed since primary school and some things are long forgotten, but others will always remain. I still remember the day the Head Master announced that on Friday the children would go to take 'Chai wa Kenyatta' – Kenyatta's tea. A truck would come at about 3:00 o'clock to bring us to Naromoru, about 20 kilometres away.

In those days, school outings were rare and usually exciting. Normally we wished for such occasions and hoped that our parents would come up with ticket money plus a few coins for something extra on the way. But this was not to be any ordinary excursion, nor did the announcement elicit the usual cheers. Rather, not quite sure how to respond, the children were mute and confused. This trip would not end up at a bottling plant where we could drink as much soda as we liked, or at a coffee factory, or with dancing and singing for the President at his home in Gatundu. This was something quite different and mysterious.

At school, some of the older children who were always in the know had, for weeks, been murmuring about strange and frightening things. To catch some of the tales, we 'little ones', as the bigger girls called us, had been creeping around trying to be invisible but the stories stopped whenever we were noticed. To glean just such secret intelligence, we practiced being inconspicuous though it was never really hard to find out when something big was in the air. Alone or in pairs we would watch out for groups in serious conversation, creep up on them without a word and scribble in the dust with a finger or stick, but with both ears open wide. This way we heard things about a tea ceremony where nothing about tea was ever mentioned. What we picked up instead were stories of people made to eat raw, fatty meat dripping with blood. Whispers told of strange and scary figures armed with cutlasses, who threatened anyone trying to spit out the flesh. Those present also took an oath of silence.

It was during such a tale that one of the older girls turned round as if she'd known we had been there all along, as she probably had, and sneered, 'You're in big trouble!' Why? Because participants would be asked to remove all their clothes, and we would have to, too. Then, when they found out that we had not been circumcised[1] they would chop off our hair and, with their cutlasses, excise us on the spot. 'Because it's the likes of you who abandon tradition that have weakened the Kikuyu people.'

I still see this girl's face before me, smirking, as if she really enjoyed seeing us squirm, even though her family had lived in our neighbourhood and we had walked to school together for years. Twelve months before she had become a *Muiritu*, a grown up girl who had undergone FGM. She had then stopped playing with us and started calling us *Turigu*, a term that taunts girls not yet cut. A wave of anxiety swept through me, and without a word, eyes to the ground, my friends and I crept away to contemplate this latest piece of news.

That night we told my mother we needed money for transport to go and drink Kenyatta's tea. For the first time I remember seeing fear in her eyes but she quickly glanced away, saying she would talk to my father. His arrival produced more whispering and muted phone calls to another family. We could hear the ringing back and forth but no disappearing act enabled us to dissolve through the door and re-assemble in the sitting room where consultations were taking place.

In the morning my father delivered the verdict. 'When the other children are picked up, you're to come home.' Later, my parents said, they would take us to the tea party themselves.

On Friday, with mixed feelings, I watched the truck. On the one hand, it looked like any other school trip, with children singing, pushing and shoving. On the other, however, I could not forget the story of the cutlass. Whether it was true or not, I remembered the look in my mother's eyes.

When the children returned, nothing in their behaviour suggested that anything traumatic had happened. Yet they were quiet and, for some time, avoided those of us who hadn't gone to drink the tea. One of our friends told us she couldn't afford to be seen with us any more; it might be rumoured that she had revealed the ceremony's secrets to us. Gradually I found out more about that afternoon, but most of what I knew I had read in the paper.

It was 1969, a time of political instability. The ruling KANU (Kenya African National Union) government headed by Jomo Kenyatta had banned the opposition party KPU (Kenya Political Union), sending all its leaders into detention, and Tom Mboya, a popular politician, had been assassinated. Any challenge to the ruling President and the Kikuyu-dominated Kanu political party was seen as a threat to the leadership of the Kikuyu People at a time when the Kikuyu were convinced they had won the right to Kenyan leadership.

Drinking Kenyatta's tea turned out to be the pseudonym for an oathing ceremony. According to R. Ajulu, 'Kenyatta's reaction to the...Mboya crisis was to invoke narrow national [identity] and seek cover under Kikuyu ethnicity' (137). The oathing ritual, a move to organise the Kikuyu people behind the Kenyatta regime, consisted of participants being made to swear they would fight to keep the flag in the house of Mumbi.[2]

Stories of forced female circumcision continued to circulate at school but I never heard of any girls actually excised against their will during these rites. Later some revealed they had been asked to undress but were allowed to retain their underwear. Whether the call to return to our roots may have influenced some parents to have their daughters cut, I cannot tell.

What I learned from the papers is that some people were beaten up and badly injured because they had refused to take part in oathing ceremonies. The main oathing locality was Gatundu in Kiambu, the home area of President Kenyatta. Later, all over Kikuyu land, other, smaller oathing stations opened.

My younger sisters, brother and I, in primary school at the time, never went to drink Kenyatta's tea, and, after several months, the hullabaloo died down. It became history.

Yet, not entirely. The oathing ceremony of 1969 had much in common with an earlier oathing ritual during colonial times as the Kikuyu and their neighbours were engaged in a liberation struggle. Both events were committed to strengthening group identity and directing the Kikuyu toward a common goal, the former being to fight for independence and recapture the land stolen from them by the colonial masters. Surprising, or maybe not so, is that discourse on female genital mutilation, which was already on a downward trend, was revived during this second oathing.

During the earlier ceremony referred to as the Mau Mau oath, most adult Kikuyu women had already undergone clitoridectomy. During that era, the cutting of female genitals had generated considerable controversy and been a bone of contention between the Kikuyu on the one side and colonial rulers and colonial church on the other. European rulers' attempt to forbid FGM had been met with massive resistance, eventually forcing the British, in 1958, to rescind all efforts to restrict it. In 1930 the issue of female circumcision had actually been raised in the House of Commons and a committee appointed to investigate the matter. Assigned to the group to represent the Kikuyu people was anthropologist Jomo Kenyatta, the man who was later to become the first President of Kenya. During this meeting Kenyatta made his (in)famous pronouncement, that to abolish female circumcision would be to destroy the very structure of Kikuyu society (*Facing Mount Kenya* 135).

By the time of this second oathing, however, a number of parents like mine had turned away from FGM; increasingly, it failed to earn for its present-day initiates as much recognition as had been enjoyed in earlier times. Yet traditionalists, who saw the rite's demise as one factor weakening the Kikuyu People, continued to revert to this line of argument with each new crisis.

BACK TO OUR ROOTS

Several years later the discourse on FGM reared its head again. Kenyatta had long been dead, and the aim of the tea drinking had failed. The Flag had left the house of Mumbi. The next president hailed from the Kalenjin people. President Moi had stripped the Kikuyu of their powerful positions in the government; they had also lost property and were being driven out of their homes in the Rift Valley. In fact, never in postcolonial times had the Kikuyu experienced so much oppression. In addition, hard hit by inflation, Kenya witnessed a dramatic increase in unemployment. Why had all this occurred? In 1999, I remember talking to a woman who told me what the older men were saying (I paraphrase): the Kikuyu's weakness stemmed from women's increasing reluctance to part with their clitoris.

It is in this context that pseudo religio-political traditionalist groups appeared among the Kikuyu. At first there was *Hama ya Ngai uri mwoyo* (Tent of the Living God), led by a man named Ngonya wa Gakonya. You would often find his faction in Nairobi at the Jevanjee Gardens facing Mount Kenya preaching and offering traditional prayers to *Ngai*, the God of the Kikuyu. Members dressed in a kind of neo-traditional costume, calling out for the Kikuyu to return to their roots, which meant to embrace polygamous marriages, traditional wedding ceremonies and female circumcision. Later Ngonya wa Gakonya tried to register his religion as a political party, but his bid was rejected.

Shortly thereafter the *Mungiki* arose, a religio-political group difficult to define which seemed to attract a lot of young Kikuyu men and women. Like the 'Tent of the Living God,' *Mungiki* called out to the Kikuyu People to return to their roots, worship facing Mount Kenya and revert to female circumcision (among other things). The members don't wear traditional clothes but reject some western symbols and have dreadlocks like the Mau Mau freedom fighters of earlier days. This crowd would gain notoriety for its ruthlessness in conducting oathing ceremonies, fighting other ethnic gangs, and implicating innocent bystanders who were often mowed down. The struggle for territorial control of the thriving *matatu* industry (public transport system) became one of *Mungiki*'s identifying features. Like other ethnic groups the *Mungiki* were also hired by politicians to fight political rivals in ethnic conflicts as the multiparty elections approached. 'The sect has always left a trail of arson, coerced oathing and forced circumcision in its wake. Its operations have focused on Central Province, especially in

160

Nyeri, Nakuru and Laikipia districts. Its exact membership remains unknown' (*The Nation*/Africa News Online: 2000).

Mungiki, like other ethnic thugs, was spreading terror in the land, but in addition started threatening Kikuyu women. Members beat up females wearing short skirts or trousers that they judged inappropriate. It was the same old story: by turning away from traditions and abandoning female circumcision, women had weakened the Kikuyu People. But *Mungiki* went a step further than the 'Tent of the Living God.' Not merely calling for women to undergo clitoridectomy, they were rumoured to be capturing women and girls and excising them by force. In Kiambu in 2002, I talked to a class and learned the girls were afraid to walk home after school because *Mungiki* had dropped leaflets at the shopping centres threatening them with FGM.

The pupils' words were confirmed by the *East African Standard* reporting that the sects' handouts had given females up to 7 July – also known in Kenya as *Sabasaba* (seven-seven) – to be cut; otherwise, they would be excised by force. Usually celebrated by opposition groups, *Sabasaba* marks the introduction on 7 July 1992 of Kenyan multiparty politics (Kenya Rights activists).

Thus, over and over again, Kikuyu women have been accused of treason when resisting amputation of their genitals.

A TICKET TO PARLIAMENT

In the early nineties, an anecdote circulated among the Meru, another FGM practicing Bantu group who are neighbours of the Kikuyu. It was about a rich young man who wanted to go into politics as a member of parliament. He approached the elders with his intention. They replied, 'We can't allow you to represent us, because you are a boy, not a man. When we come to your house, who will serve us food and drink since you don't have a wife?' In fact, the man was married but to a foreign woman whom his people did not acknowledge. As a result, he received too few votes and his parliamentary aspirations failed. Undeterred, however, he prepared himself for the next elections, separating from his foreign wife and marrying a new one from among his own people. Returning to the elders, this time he was sure of a positive answer, but again they said, 'No,' reasoning that he remained 'a boy.' 'How can you expect to represent us, a whole people, when you are not even in charge of your own house? A man who doesn't have control over his wife has no control over his house and can not represent us.' The man's second bride had not been circumcised. Eventually, the third time around, he did get into Parliament, having done the needful: he subjected his wife to FGM.

True or not, I don't know. The point is that FGM is seen not only as the measure of a man's control over his wife but also as a yardstick of his individual might and the vigour of the group as a whole. Uncircumcised women, lacking docility and thereby challenging male dominance, are thus thought to weaken the collective, for men derive their strength from dominating women. Yet how much stronger the whole would become if women's potential were added to men's!

No one asks whether or not excised women still enjoy sex. Of primary interest is the Kikuyu claim that women, unless cut, cannot suppress their sexual urges, hence the need for FGM, and this fear of uncontrolled female sexuality is shared by both women and men, often argued especially by women who see clitoridectomy as liberating them from troubling sexual longings. It is thought to spare them the frustration of unfulfilled desire.

This call to restrain female sexuality has also found resonance in another discourse. Parallel to the political and economic threats of the 90s and early 2000, the Kikuyu and all Kenyans have had to face an added challenge, AIDS. And yes, you guessed it. Once again, FGM or, rather, the failure to have it performed is often cited as the source of the epidemic among the Kikuyu.

AT A MEAT-EATING LUNCH

In the heart of Kikuyu land, it's the year 2001 at a small shopping centre in Kenya's central province, hilly and green where coffee grows alongside maize, beans and potatoes. In this densely populated region, most people live on small plots that shrink with every generation leaving little room for cultivation between houses. These, too, have changed over time. The square, mud-walled, grass thatched huts of our grandparents' and great grandparents' day first lost their thatch to corrugated iron roofing and then ceded their form to three room rectangles with walls of wooden cut-off planks and, if budgets permit, concrete floors. Whenever it rains, the new houses are so loud you have to shout to be heard; and the temperature, too, makes trouble. In the cold season you shiver, and in the heat you might as well live in an oven. But the structures are durable, and you can collect rainwater from the roof. In any case, there is no more thatch to be had. Here and there, scattered between these modest dwellings are stone homes of all sizes, from tiny to palatial, with either corrugated iron or red tiled roofs. The roads that lead here used to be tarmac but are now so worn out that, during the rainy season, cars literally wade from one pothole to the next.

But this is not the rainy season; it is hot, dry and dusty, and we are at the local shopping centre where it is hottest and driest. One street runs through to the next shopping district as several paths crisscross here and there. The road, lower than the shops along both sides, is splayed out between deep gullies that become raging rivers when it rains. Now, however, they are filled with garbage. When you want to get to the merchandise you jump over the gullies or walk until you reach that spot where a desperate shopkeeper has bridged the gap with a wooden plank. Wherever you look, you see a modern form of vegetation – plastic sacks, in every form and shape. A slight breeze shakes the dust off a few, wafting them several paces where they settle again to wait for a new coating. When the wind really blows, like today, even long-anchored synthetic frees itself and swirls around in circles. The chickens, goats, sheep and several cows push the intruders aside or tug at them, trying to get to any bit of green that might lie beneath.

The shopping centre itself is vibrant, with people everywhere. Voices call out in greeting; laughter echoes; tales are told and, from time to time, a young man or woman breaks off from one group, jumps across the dry ditch and joins a new clique on the other side. New bursts of hilarity and loud clapping of hands fill the air. At the bus stop, KISS 100, one of the new independent radio stations, is pouring music from the waiting *matatus* (mini buses), and, when not shouting for passengers, the young men who work as loaders and conductors, here called 'matatu touts', sing along. What an incredible feeling of energy and life!

Built of stone or wood and corrugated iron, the small shops and kiosks, all selling the same things, lean one on the next and are half empty. On the main street you see young muscular men dripping with sweat, pushing heavy wheelbarrows loaded with Jerry cans containing water. Water selling is a trade; the taps have been dry for years. There is no garbage disposal or drainage system anymore. This place has been hit hard by inflation and yet the people have not lost the ability to laugh and sing. It is difficult to believe how challenging it is to live here from day to day, to accept that so many of the young people hanging around have little chance of finding a job or earning enough money to support themselves.

It is here that I have come to meet a young man with whom I have been working on a project. Today we are having lunch together and he has taken me to one of those local restaurants that are really butcheries known as *Nyama choma* places, Kiswahili for roasting meat. Like many Kenyans I relish roasted goat and have been looking forward to this meal with great pleasure.

We jump over one of the ever-present ditches to get to the place. It is a small stone structure with a glass display window. On the window a huge red and black bull with long horns is painted behind a man with a curved knife. Above the drawing is written 'Haraka butchery and Nyama choma.' It means the service here is quick. Through the image you can see, hanging from hooks, huge chunks of meat.

We walk in through a narrow entrance to a counter on the right. My friend, well known here, offers the usual greeting, asks for *choma* or *chamcha* (roasted or boiled) and orders. An expert at this, he knows what parts of the goat are good and watches carefully to see that he gets what he wants. With one slash of a huge cleaver the butcher severs our cut, one and a half kilos to the gram. The man rushes off and hands over our meat to the cook who salts it rapidly and throws it on an open grill. We walk on to the smoky interior, passing by a small tank with heated water where we wash our hands. Taking one of the two tables, we sit on a long bench, sip coca-colas and continue talking. Soon another young man joins us, a friend of my friend, who had ordered his meat earlier and so, as we wait for ours, we share his portion. The huge chunk on a wooden board is rapidly chopped and enjoyed with a side serving of *ugali*, a solid porridge made from white maize flour[3] as well as *Kachumbari*, a salad of tomatoes, onions, hot green and red chillies and coriander.

Somehow we begin to talk about what I have been doing for the last few years so I tell them about the campaign against FGM. My friend's friend, about twenty-five-years old and a primary school teacher, looks at me with a serious expression and asks whether, 'considering the way the situation is with AIDS now,' I don't agree that 'it is probably better to encourage female circumcision so that women would be faithful and not move around?' After a moment of silence, I answer, 'Yes, but only if we cut off men's penises as well.' Silence. Heavy silence. No further comments. I can see the message has sunk in. Our meat is served, we share it and move on to other topics.

As in other parts of Kenya, the AIDS threat is being felt acutely here. And again the Kikuyu, unpacking old stories, are suggesting reviving FGM. Illogical and senseless as the argument may be, it now touches directly on control of female sexuality.

Although the strongest voices are men's, women too are part of this call. Whether you are talking about Ngonya wa Gakonya's 'Tent of the Living God' or the *Mungiki*, or those who think the community can fight AIDS through FGM, women, even if they are not usually movement leaders, are certainly among the followers.

PASSING WHERE WE PASSED

Six months after the incident with the young man, on a very hot Sunday, I am on my way to see Mama Kabui whom I met two weeks earlier during a women's self help group discussion in her village. The agenda over, we agreed I should go to her house and conduct an interview. That is the research I have been doing for several months, asking women to relate their experiences with HIV/AIDS. I don't usually visit on Sundays but Mama K works as subordinate staff with a parastatal. She cleans and makes tea at the office. On Saturdays she does her own housework, so Sunday afternoon after church is her only option.

I have been to this village several times but never before on a Sunday. The streets are full of people, so many everywhere you would think everyone was partying. Mama K lives on what used to be a coffee farm, part of which was converted and allocated to landless squatters. Mama K was not herself a squatter, but, after her husband died of malaria, she bought her plot from the allocation's beneficiaries. Now a huge village in the middle of agricultural land, the enclave is inhabited by a large number of single mothers who earn a living as casual labourers on the coffee farms and wherever else opportunities arise. Sometimes people refer to it as the village with three generations of single mothers. The oldest are in their 70s and came here in the fifties and early sixties; the second generation, in their thirties and forties, was born here; and the third generation, in their twenties and below, have dropped out of school after getting pregnant. Three generations of unskilled workers with no benefits and they live from job to job and on the good will or, more accurately, at the mercy of male overseers who take advantage of their position by sexually exploiting them. It has been going on for nearly fifty years. The village has been very hard hit by AIDS.

After asking for directions several times, a woman sends a small boy to accompany me. He might be about five-years-old and is still dressed in his Sunday clothes, a pair of dark blue trousers with a yellow stripe running down the side, a red t-shirt two sizes too big and sports shoes. He does not say a word but runs on ahead pushing an old tire and, as we come to a green gate made of corrugated iron sheets, he points with a finger and scoots down the hill.

Mama K is at home with two of her daughters; the other two and her younger sister who live with her have gone off to see the grandmother. After the usual exchange of greetings and hand-shakes, I give her the food basket containing gift items visitors usually bring from town for their village hosts: two packets of flour, rice, sugar and bread. I am shown into the sitting room.

Mama K lives in a standard three-room house with corrugated iron sheet walls and roof with a concrete floor. She has, however, covered the inside walls with soft-board, making it a little bit cooler. Still, there's no real respite from the over 40-degree heat and I am grateful for the big jug of orange juice she puts on the table. The house is pleasant, clean and tidy. The main door opens directly into the sitting room; another, to the left, leads to the kitchen that, I suspect, also serves as bedroom to some of the children. A third door to the right, shows where the mother and the younger girls sleep.

It is a standard arrangement. Mama K has several sofa seats and small tables all decorated with embroidered cloth. One wall displays a black and white photo of a man; on another is the snapshot of two children. Unusual here is the absence of 'Jesus is the head of this house...', a wall hanging to be found in nearly every home I have visited here as well as at my mother's. Instead, an old calendar deploys a similar Christian saying.

Two pretty girls in pale blue, frilly Sunday dresses huddle on one corner of a sofa. Almost clinging to each other, they look ill at ease in my presence but try to remain still. Soon, however, they start fidgeting, and I ask the mother if I can photograph them. My request breaks the ice for they love having their picture taken. It also provides the opportunity to bring out the family album. While we are thumbing through it, Mama K slips into the kitchen and returns with food, excusing herself because the rice has not turned out too well. Although I have already eaten, she insists I take at least a little meat that she had bought just for me. I find it delicious. After we have finished, Mama K sends the girls out to amuse themselves although they don't really want to go, obviously preferring to sit around, play invisible and hear what we are about to discuss. It is also hot outside and they would prefer to watch the small black and white television that has been running soundlessly all the while in a corner of the room.

The interview begins, with Mama K very open and ready to talk. Indeed, she talks and talks: about her sisters who have died of AIDS and her mother who has never cared much for them, among other things. I have also been asking about women's sexual lives, their sex education and initiation rites. In other words, I ask them to tell me about FGM. Perhaps a quarter of the group has suffered clitoridectomy, but, as is common among Kikuyu women, they don't talk much about it. What I hear is something like, 'I was circumcised because it was like that then.' 'Then it was the tradition, but now it is different.' 'People don't do it any more, or maybe there are some who still do it but in secret.' The women are reluctant to go beyond this, to relate how it affects their lives or what it means to them now. Any attempt to find out more is blocked. It was and it happened, because it was so at the time and that's it. As for the children, the daughters, it's irrelevant. Why discuss it if it isn't happening now? 'Those things are finished,' as one woman said.

But Mama K is different: she is willing to reveal her views on FGM.

Now about 40-years-old, Mama K underwent clitoridectomy at the age of 10 and dropped out of school to become a household servant. Her education had lasted six years. Who arranged for her to be cut? Not her mother but the paternal grandmother, after whom she is named, sent her for circumcision. Her younger sister was spared but, motivated by 'a kind of [family] curse,' her grandmother insisted she, Mama K, be 'done.' How? Women of a certain age organise it, 'even borrowing money' if needed to ensure that they have 'taken you.'

I: Were you asked whether you would like to go, or how did she put it?

K: It had to be; my grandmother used to say there is a curse ... in her family. You couldn't live like that. That's what she used to tell us.

I: Did you go to someone's house or where?

K: It was someone's house. A woman named Waringa. In fact, I think she is still alive. Now I hear that those things are forbidden; but in my family it was a must. When a girl matures at the age of 10 she is taken.

I: It was your grandmother who used to say it must be done.

K: Yes...and she still says it, that in her family you can't stay like that. That the grandfather died after saying no one should stay like that.

I: Your grandfather?

K: The grandfather we never knew.[4]

There was no ceremony or counselling attached to the event, Mama K goes on, for immediately afterward, Waringa took her money and the girls were dismissed. Only while they were hobbling home did the assistant try to advise them.

K: She would tell you, now if you start, if you have contact with a man, you will get pregnant, such things.

Mama K doesn't talk about the pain, nor does she remember having any problems. She healed well.

I go on to ask about plans for her children. Although she feels they 'have become very spoilt and now know many things even before they pass through there,' she takes pride in 'bring[ing] them up the modern way, and [wants] especially to avoid [AIDS],' a danger 'because [of what] she uses, you know, [no] disinfectant to clean them.' But Mama K is torn, recalling when there was no AIDS.

I: Yes, back then no disease was transmitted through blood by cutting.

K: But now I say they stay like that [uncut], and, in fact, I would not want anybody telling me to do it. I even told my grandmother, 'You keep saying there is a curse. But you will have to finish with those things. Then was then and now is now.'

I: You explained how it is now.

K: Yes, I told her my children, seeing the way it is, will stay like that. I could say there is a curse, grandmother says there is a curse, but in the process I bring them more problems. I say I am avoiding the curse, but then the curse is preferable to [AIDS which] is worse than a curse. So I say they stay [intact]. I won't even try to take them... even if they tell me to. Maybe some people haven't stopped [cutting, and one of the girls] may have had contact with a man. [Then] those [tools] are used [on her] and on the one who hasn't [yet caught] anything. You see, it has been spread like that. So I won't even try. I don't agree. I say let them stay [as they are, intact].

Yes, Mama K has given FGM a lot of thought, even talking to her grandmother about it. But let's be clear: not because there is anything wrong or unpleasant about FGM does she reject it. No. It is rather the fear of contracting AIDS through contaminated instruments that holds her back. Ironically, she feels that particularly now, when sex itself has become lethal, it is actually advantageous to have undergone excision in her youth. And if there were no disease?

K: I would say let them pass the same way we passed. Because like now, for example, like that woman I have been talking about. A lot of people who were not done [when we were] are very bad. That woman would even sit here crying like a child and when I would ask her, 'what is it?' she would say she needs something and can only be happy when she gets it. So those people who have not been done, a lot of them (laughs)... are making things worse because their bodies control them.

I: What woman are you talking about?

K: That one who I told you started with the man who was my friend.

I: Yes?

K: She had not been done, and a lot of them who did not pass there are suffering now. Because the body gets used to that thing, and now she can't do without it. If it had not been for the disease, [I'd recommend excision because] a person who passed that way... isn't concerned with [sex]. You can go for ten years without thinking about it. You can decide to stay without... Like I tell people, [abstinence] will not make you sick [but]... I see [the unexcised] are really bothered by bodily needs.

Thus, Mama K judges as 'bad women' those who have not undergone FGM. Their sexuality endangers the community. It is an interesting argument when you know the background story. A year after her husband's death, Mama K made friends with a married man who set her up and promised to help raise her three children. She even conceived a fourth. During the pregnancy, however, her lover started sleeping with her best friend, the woman she refers to, so after the baby's birth she broke up with him. Although her rival's unexcised state is blamed for the attraction, how ironic that Mama K's own excision didn't stop her from getting involved! In fact, both women failed to control their sexuality, at least with this particular (already married) man. Naturally Mama K is sour at her friend, and still thinks she could protect her daughters by having them cut, thereby translating the problem of AIDS into one of uncontrolled female sexuality. Men's role, as usual, goes under.

Mama K introduces another dimension of control when she talks about her sister-in-law. In her husband's family, the 'older ones' had been excised, but her mother-in-law successfully opposed circumcision for a younger sister, the one for whom Mama K named her daughter Lucy. However, sister-in-law Lucy 'was taken recently when she was already in her husband's house.'

I: Already with husband?

K: (Laughs). With four children because of her getting sick. The grandmother, the one I have been telling you about, said it was a curse...both she and the other grandmother who died, the grandmother of my husband...She used to tell us stories [about] how that woman got sick. And [Grandmother would warn] her, 'You ... must be done. Even if you have ten children, you have to pass there.' I tell you they pushed her, so when she went to deliver her last child it was done.

I: When she went to deliver a baby?

K: Yes. They said it was that thing [the clitoris] that used to affect her and make her run mad. So, the way I see it, some beliefs are not good. Because the way the grandmother kept on about it being a curse made that woman anxious.

Did clitoridectomy help? Mama K admits that even afterward, Lucy 'kept on getting mad, getting funny illnesses, and frequently fighting with her husband.'

Mama K's ambivalence is clear. On the one hand, she wants to be up-to-date and bring up her children the modern way, but on the other, she is afraid if she doesn't have them cut they will run wild, be sexually out of control, and contract AIDS. At the same time, if she takes them to a cutter like Waringa so that they can 'pass where she passed' as she puts it, she also exposes them to AIDS. Add to that the grandmothers' stories about curses that she obviously fears for leading a woman into madness and uncontrolled behaviour like fighting with her husband and the difficulty becomes clear. Nonetheless, she, too, quarrels with the grandmothers, whose stories she sees as a possible cause of the trouble.

Time and again I have thought about Mama K and her daughters. Will she or will she not have them circumcised? Practical considerations aside – that the girls are growing older every year and are more likely to put up a fight—, I believe she wouldn't want to make them 'pass,' trying as she is to be modern.

AN ILLUSORY STRENGTH
It is a discourse that covers a period of almost 60 years.

You could argue that every time the Kikuyu community is under threat, advocacy for FGM revives.

What I have presented here seems like two lines of argument that excision's supporters would advance. The first sees FGM's abandonment at the root of the Kikuyu's depleted political power. The call to renew clitoridectomy, programmatic for the oathers of Kenyatta's tea, the 'Tent of the Living God' and *Mungiki,* hinges on this point. The issue here doesn't seem to be that women, mature in their strength, can contribute to society and better it. Rather, the opposite. By tightening control over women, weakening them, men propose to increase their strength. The norm must remain acquiescence, women prepared to acknowledge the superiority of men and not fight them (like Mama K's sister-in-law did). This is clearly illustrated by *Njuri Njeke,*[5] our politician's story. A man who marries an uncircumcised woman is not in control of his home and cannot represent the People. He is impotent.

I don't think that FGM necessarily makes women weak. It does, however, affect their sexuality in such a way that men feel in control, and this control bequeaths them an illusion of strength.

The second line of argument is an old one as well but has been renewed in relation to the threat of AIDS. Women cannot master their sexual needs; these needs must be controlled by FGM; otherwise women will spread

AIDS, go mad, or sit and cry because of unfulfilled desires. Reviving the old stories of woman, the weak creature driven by anatomy, this reasoning refuses to acknowledge the role of men in the spread of AIDS.

On second thought, these seem to be not two different lines of argument at all but different faces of the same thing.

AIDS is not merely threatening the community. It has already considerably weakened it and been the source of great anxiety. It touches on a sensitive area for men and women alike, sexuality. And AIDS seems to be challenging men in both their sexuality and masculinity. Men are therefore turning more and more to desperate measures to prove their manhood; this may partly explain the increasing incidence of rape.

The call to revive FGM is another frantic measure, a reversion to worn out patterns of re-establishing control over women to boost male strength. It is the same tired premise; if women are circumcised men can more easily control and command them and, therefore, their power returns.[6] The point that I am trying to make here is that masculine identity and prowess are defined and experienced relative to feminine weakness. This perspective is not new and can be found in various guises in different cultures in all parts of the world. Among the Kikuyu, as in other FGM practicing communities, however, it takes the extreme form of inflicting physiological and psychological damage on women. Is there an end in sight?

Nura Abdi and Leo G. Linder

Tränen im Sand/Desert Tears (Excerpts)

Translated from the German by Tobe Levin[1]

Dedication ...
***To all the world's women, victims and non-victims of FGM
(Female Genital Mutilation). Let's reach out to one another
to protect coming generations from the torture that continues
to threaten girls today.***

... One or another of the neighbours might actually let you look from a distance at what was going on, but not all by any means. Most permitted no observers and shooed you impatiently out of the house. So, if we really wanted to know, we could find out a little. But in the end, the only thing you knew for sure was that they were going to do something with a piece of you, down there between your legs.

Excerpts from Chapter 7

'Who'll be most courageous?'

We also knew why. Because it had always been done to girls and because that's how you became a woman and because otherwise you could just forget about ever getting married – no man would want you as long as you were dirty and stank. And that's why I jumped all over our courtyard with exuberance, clapping my hands and shouting how happy I was, just having learned that in one week's time, right after the holidays began, my older sisters Fatma and Yurop and I would be circumcised. Even though I wasn't yet five and therefore really much too young...

Before the *halaleiso* had even touched her, Yurop cried out. At once, one of the women slapped her in the face. The general consensus held that this was no time to exercise forbearance. And maybe this advice was not so far off the mark, but in Yurop's case it didn't quieten her down. She went right on screaming so they stuffed the gag in her mouth, ready for that purpose. I remember, I thought that was funny. I still hadn't understood a thing. And anyway, there were still enough girls in line ahead of me. I was not next, so I could just keep on sniggering. But as the line grew smaller, laughter stuck in my throat.

From Yurop came nothing but groans by now, and a couple of minutes later a woman came out holding a narrow band of cloth. This she wrapped around Yurop from her hips to her big toe, so tightly that she couldn't move her legs. Then two women carried her carefully into the room with mats on the floor.

I had not been able to take in very much of it. Once they had gagged her, I sort of took off. Because there were so many women pulling on her and standing around, I could not have seen much anyway. Now it was Ifra's turn, and like all the others, she turned and fled, screaming her throat out. So first the women had to catch her and, with fanatical violence, threw her onto the box. Then, repeat performance: Ifra screamed and tried to free herself, and again the women fought and gagged her. And so it went with Fatma, Muna, Suleiha and Nasra. All shrieked, all were gagged, the halaleiso never slowed down. Between girls she wiped blood off the box and with her foot kicked sand over the puddle on the floor. And now there was only one left, and that was me.

When my turn came, I burst into tears. I was scared but froze instead of running away. Still, I screamed as they approached me, I shrieked, 'I don't want to!' But that didn't help at all. They grabbed me, dragged me to the box that had once held oranges, and sat me down on it. I hollered and kicked, but was overpowered from all sides. Not one of the women made the slightest move to help me. One of them reminded me that yesterday, I had promised to be the bravest of them all. I sat there as if on a stage, a circle of women around me. They imprisoned me, tossed my skirt aside, pulled my legs apart, and that was the moment when one of the neighbour women burst into song.

She saw my stomach and thighs – body parts that, even on a four-year-old girl, remain hidden – and was enchanted. I was the lightest of us all anyway, but down there my skin was almost white. And this woman began to sing, 'Nura, how beautiful you are, how white you are, your skin is whiter than white camel's milk.' And although they kept me in their violent grasp, the women answered her, one after another, repeating the verse: 'Nura, how white you are, whiter than white camel's milk.' And I really did calm down. Are you really so white? I thought. But at that very moment the *halaleiso* grabbed me and cut.

The sound was sharp, like knifing a burlap sack or heavy-mesh. Now the women competed with each other in shouting. They screamed across each other, all the while pulling on my arms and legs and nearly crushing the breath out of me. 'Yes, yes, that side is good!' 'But there, there you've forgotten something!' 'So, that's it!' 'Done already! Done!'

A witches' cauldron. But louder than their screeching was this scratching when the razor sliced through flesh. I was in such shock that no scream came out. No matter what they cut jack-hammered in my ear, louder than all screams in the world.

But the worst was yet to come.

The worst is when they sew you up.

Sweat poured out of me. I had invested all my strength in surviving the first pain. Now I had no power left. In the meantime it had grown warm. The sun had wandered in over the courtyard and blinded me. I was nauseous. I had the feeling I was going to throw up. And between my legs someone was busy with a needle in an open wound. It was as if with all my senses, wholly conscious, I was being slaughtered. I tried to defend myself, but what can a four year old do against six grown-up women? Maybe I moaned, maybe I gasped for breath. But I didn't scream, for I was spared the gag. And then I fainted.

Before they began to bind me up, I came to. It was a new pain this time, the *halaleiso* rubbing herbs on the fresh wound. These herbs are supposed to speed up healing. It felt like I was being held over an open fire.

Again I fainted.

While conscious, I had not looked. I could not look while they were cutting me up. But I remember: when they wanted to carry me away, I opened my eyes. I saw blood on the floor and those parts that had been hacked off swimming in a bowl. What had been sawed off all of us, including the other girls. The *halaleiso* had tossed them in a pile in a bowl. Later I learned that someone had dug a hole and buried them somewhere in the courtyard. Exactly where we were never to learn. 'What do you need to know for?' was all they would say. 'It's long gone to where it belongs. Under the earth.'

Excerpt from chapter 8

'I was bravest'

To this very day I can recall my father's face in front of me. On the second day the door opened and he stepped inside. That is, he stood on the threshold and gazed at us girls on the floor. I can still see the look in his eyes. He was close to tears. Spying us lying there, words stuck in his throat. Saying nothing, he quickly turned around and shut the door...

Notes & References

Notes to Preface

1   Good news from Eritrea (a new law in 2007); Egypt (another ban in 2007); and sanctions proclaimed elsewhere promise long-term benefits but short term failure in the absence of other incentives to alter conduct. Weighing against such headlines is the news about infibulation tourism from Europe. *Afrol News*, 26 June 2007: 'Hargeisa, the peaceful capital of the self-proclaimed state of Somaliland, has become a new centre for the Somali Diaspora to perform female genital mutilation (FGM) on their daughters.' 27 June 2007 <http://www.afrol.com/articles/25884>. See also Nicola Woolcock. 'Parents Fly in African Village Elders to Circumcise Their Young Daughters.' *The Times*. 23 Oct. 2006. 11 Oct. 2006. <http://www.timesonline.co.uk/article/0,,8122-2416783,00.html>

2   See Levin, Tobe. 'Cutting out Circumcision.' Rev. of Olayinka Koso-Thomas. *The Circumcision of Women: A Strategy for Eradication*. London: Zed, 1988. *The Women's Review of Books*. 5/8, May 1988. 5-6.

References

Ottah, Comfort. 'Enough is Enough'. In *Through the Eyes of Nigerian Artists: Confronting Female Genital Mutilation*. Exhibition Catalogue. Eds. Shulamit Reinharz, Tobe Levin, Joy Walker. Waltham: The Brandeis University Women's Studies Research Centre, 2006. 20.

Notes to Levin: 'Assaults on Female Genitalia: Activists, Authors, and the Arts'

1   The World Health Organisation recognises 4 types: 1) so-called sunna, or legitimate circumcision removing only the clitoral prepuce; 2) clitoridectomy or excision, which amputates either a) the visible part of the clitoris alone and/or b) the labia minora, in whole or in part; 3) infibulation, which may or may not remove the visible part of the clitoris and the labia majora and then stitches the vulva shut, leaving a pencil point opening for the passage of urine and menstrual blood; 4) a pot pourri of additional techniques including cauterisation, scarring, introduction of irritating substances into the vagina, etc. Of the estimated 140 million victims worldwide, 15% undergo infibulation (the vast majority of women in Somalia, Sudan, Djibouti, Eritrea, and among Somali ethnics in Ogaden, Ethiopia; southern Egypt; Kenya; Saudi Arabia; Yemen; and everywhere in the Diaspora).

2   Of the innumerable publications critical of Walker's interventions against FGM, I will single out Obioma Nnaemeka's 'If Female Circumcision Did Not Exist, Western Feminism Would Invent It' for its brilliance and unexpected deficits. Though Nnaemeka's disagreement with many individual aspects of Walker's and Parmar's film and book make sense, overall she under-estimates the extent of African activist input into and advice on the production of *Warrior Marks* and appreciation, after the fact, of the preceding novel. In light of the Bamako Declaration as well, the argument regarding language may appear in a different light. See both my essay 'Alice Walker: Matron of FORWARD' and further discussion of Walker criticism below.

3 Among innumerable possible examples, I'll showcase Egypt's Marie Assaad (age 84), 'who has been campaigning against FGM since the 1950s' (Salonen 2).

4 Dorkenoo confirmed this exchange, noting that in fact one of the Tashis – whose name will remain confidential – had been sharing her flat (Telephone interview with the author, 3 October 2007).

5 In Asaah's words, 'So it is that the very woman, Walker, whose views on womanism provided an African-oriented conceptual framework to reconfigure gender politics and who, on account of her selfless devotion to African spiritual renewal, is praised by no less a person than the committed Pan Africanist writer Ayi Kwei Armah' (436), ironically finds herself now vilified for using 'language, discourse and epistemic modes of Western culture' (Nako 5).

6 Thanks to Augustine H. Asaah for the arguments in this and the following paragraph.

7 It is worth invoking here Mamadou Kante's considered opinion that the practice of cutting/excising/circumcising is Africa's contribution to world culture (Patterson 178–79). Reference thanks to Augustine H. Asaah.

8 The Well Woman Clinics, initially directed by Dr Harry Gordon, were pioneered in the mid-90s in the UK under the auspices of FORWARD.

9 Or, an impressive alternative formulation from Clark Fountain reviewing Soraya Mire's *Fire Eyes*: 'The intent is to make procreation a necessary but unpleasant duty which wives and concubines, viewed as possessions, will reluctantly perform, and then only for those in authority over them' (Mire in email to Tobe Levin, 29 September 2007).

10 Miré, prize-winning director of *Fire Eyes: Female Circumcision* (1994) is also writing a memoir about her mutilation.

11 'Academia's fixation on cultural sensitivity is changing the debate around female genital mutilation, with a growing number of professors and women's rights activists becoming hesitant to condemn the practice.' Thus writes Zosia Bielski for the *National Post* as though in direct response to the point I have been trying to make. She is reviewing Janice Boddy's *Civilizing Women: British Crusades in Colonial Sudan* on 26 August 2007.

12 'An issue of concern at the 6th General Assembly…have been attempts to dilute the terminology Female Genital Mutilation (FGM) and replace it with the following: 'Female Circumcision,' 'Female Genital Alteration,' 'Female Genital Excision,' 'Female Genital Surgery,' and more recently 'Female Genital Cutting' (FGC). …Female Genital Cutting (FGC) does not reflect the accurate extent of harm and mutilation caused by all types of FGM' (Bamako Declaration).

13 Speaking polemically in *Warrior Marks*, Comfort Ottah declares, 'This is not culture. It's torture, and these girls suffer for life.' Sadly, the one does not exclude the other.

14 Visibly shaken and in many cases moved to tears is the audience of midwives in Mali filmed by Erica Pomerance in *Dabla! Excision* as they watch the gruesome scene in Nigeria IAC's video *Beliefs and Misbeliefs* in which a baby is being butchered on a Lagos sidewalk. The clip was included in a training session for exciseuses en route to abandoning their profession to become active in the movement against the practice.

15 See also Julie Okoh. *Edewede* (2000) and Yao Lassana Justin. *Pourquoi donc l'excision? Why excision?* (1995) performed by the Tériya Theatre Troupe in Banfora, Burkina Faso, in the Dioula language (52 minutes; visual synopsis 10 minutes). Information thanks to Chantal Zabus.

16 The conference was called 'Weibliche Genitalverstümmelung beenden: Erfahrungen aus Afrika und Europa – Perspektiven für Deutschland' [Ending FGM: Experience in Africa

and Europe – Lessons for Germany] (Bundesministerium). A second multi-media performance, *Respekt,* conceived by the girls and directed by Preba Pather Magdefrau and Isabelle Ihring, was performed in March, May, and July 2008 by a new group of teens whose parents emigrated from Eritrea.

17   Imagine my surprise as FORWARD-Germany's Present Girls' Theatre Group, composed mainly of Eritreans, spent the afternoon of September 30, 2007, writing the next play: the script at first took the shape of Williams-Garcia's novel without any of the participants, all German speakers, having read the untranslated book!

18   Africa is not the only venue to have incorporated protest into song. Among other manifestations in popular culture is 'Bravebird' sung by Amel Larrieux (FGC); 'Infibulation' written by Tony Parker for the Buccaneers ('Musicsquare'); and 'Cornflake Girl,' by Tori Amos, whose 'inspiration… came from Alice Walker's novel *Possessing the Secret of Joy*' ('Cornflake'). Popular culture has also included the theme in tv shows, for instance in the series *Law & Order*, an episode called 'Ritual' aired on 12/17/97 ('Law and Order'). Documentaries, as well, such as *La Duperie* (Burkina Faso) or *Ma fille ne sera pas excisée* (Bourema Niwema) produced by local activists are screened in villages. Pioneering artistic work by Malian film-maker Cheikh Omar Sissoko (*Finzan*, 1989) has also raised awareness as have productions directed by Zara Mahamat Yacoub, *Dilemme au Féminin* (Tchad 1994) and Anne-Laure Folly, *Femmes aux yeux ouverts* (Togo), both major figures in African cinema. In their documentaries, the wounded speak.

19   In the Stop Excision collection. Bomboté's lyrics, roughly translated, read:
I was an exciseuse. I excised little girls.
It's not good to excise girls. I won't do it anymore.
The bad things I've seen about excision are enough for me.
Excision is bad. [Chorus] There are too many terrible consequences.
Excision is bad. [Chorus] Women suffer a lot from it.
Excision is bad. [Chorus] Lots of diseases come from it.
Excision of little girls is bad, my family. [Chorus] It causes lots of serious diseases.
Lots of diseases come from excision [Chorus] like tetanus.
Incurable diseases come from excision [Chorus] like AIDS.
Married couples have lots of problems [Chorus] because of excision.
In childbirth there are lots of problems [Chorus] because of excision.
Excision is bad, my family, [Chorus] women's problems never end. ·
(2nd part repeated three times.)

20   At last a famous *Lancet* article, 'Female Genital Mutilation and Obstetric outcomes: WHO Collaborative prospective study in six African countries,' had adequate funding for a major inquiry showing FGM's negative effects on maternity.

References

Abdi, Maryam Sheikh. 'The Cut.' Population Council. 2 February 2007 <http://www.popcouncil.org/rh/thecut.html>.

Abdi, Nura and Leo G. Linder. *Tränen im Sand*. Bergisch Gladbach: Verlagsgruppe Lübbe, 2003.

Afele, Enyonam. 'Grausames Ritual. Die Verstümmelung weiblicher Geschlechtsorgane verstößt gegen die Menschenrechte.' *Der Überblick* 2/93. 29–34.

AHOI Artists & Event-Management. Email to Tobe Levin. 5 Oct. 2007.

Armah, Ayi Kwei. *The Eloquence of the Scribes: A Memoir on the Sources and Resources of*

African Literature. Popenguine: Per Ankh, 2006.

Asaah, Augustine H. 'Challenges of Our Times: Responses of African/Diasporan Intellectuals to FGM.' *Afroeuropa* 2 .1 (2008). Forthcoming.

Barry, Mariama. *La Petite Peule.* Paris: Mazarine, 2000.

BENKADI homepage. 15 October 2007 <http://www.benkadi.org/Bilder/Flyer3.pdf>.

Bielski, Zosia. 'Canada/Sudan: Cautious Criticism.' *National Post.* 26/08/2007. 28 August 2007. <http://www.fgmnetwork.org/gonews.php?subaction=showfull&id=1188134557&archiv>.

Bomboté, Ténin. 'I Abandon.' Music DVD. Bamako, Mali: Sini Sanuman, 2006.

Bowers, Emily. 'FGM Practitioners Sway Elections in Sierra Leone.' *Women's Enews.* 10 June 2007. <http://www.womensenews.org:80/article.cfm?aid=3305>.

Bundesministerium für wirtschaftliche Zusammenarbeit und Entwicklung. Themen und Schwerpunkte. Konferenz. 11 December 2006. <file://C:\DOKUME~1\Temp\1ZHRD0EV.htm>

Conteh, Osman. *Unanswered Cries.* Oxford: Macmillan, 2002.

Diallo, Khadidiatou. *Mon destin est entre les mains de mon père.* Bruxelles: Les Editions du Collectif Alpha, 2007.

Dirie, Waris with Corinna Milborn. *Desert Children.* Trans. Sheelagh Alabaster. London: Virago, 2005.

—. *Desert Flower: The Extraordinary Life of a Desert Nomad.* London, Virago, 1998.

Dorkenoo, Efua. Telephone Interview with Tobe Levin. 3 October 2007.

'Drama Changes attitudes towards genital mutilation.' 15 March 2006. 26 June 2007. <http://www.stopfgmc.org/client/sheet.aspx?root=268&sheet=1383&lang=en-US>.

'Female Genital Mutilation Can Be Overcome.' 1 October 2007. <http://www.fulda-mosocho-project.com/Unterseiten/News.htm#Scarred>.

'Experten: Genitalverstümmelung ist Menschenrechtsverletzung. Öffentliches Anhörung des Ausschusses für Familie, Senioren, Frauen und Jugend.' 26 September 2007. <http://www.bundestag.de/cgibin/druck.pl>.

Foundation for Women's Health, Research and Development Annual Report 2005-2006. London: FORWARD, nd.

Ganusah, Rebecca Y. 'Community versus Individual Rights in Africa: A Viewpoint.' *Legon Journal of the Humanities* 15 (2004) : 1-21.

'Die Geschichte (Chronik) des Vereins [Terre des Femmes].' 15 October 2007 <http://www.frauenrechte.de/tdf/index.php?option=com_content&task=view&id=37&Itemid=80>.

Groult, Benoite. *Ainsi soit-elle.* Paris: Grasset, 1975.

'Help Stop Female Genital Mutilation. Support Women and Girls in Mali!' Flyer. Susan McLucas. November 2006.

Henry, Natacha, Linda Weil-Curiel, Hawa Gréou. *Exciseuse.* Paris: City Editions, 2007.

Horton, Stephanie. 'Somervillian gets Malian rock star enlisted in cause.' <www.somervillejournal.com>. 2006. From Susan McLucas' files.

Inter-African Committee. *DECLARATION: on the Terminology FGM; 6th IAC General Assembly, 4 - 7 April, 2005, Bamako/Mali.* 15 November 2006. <http://www.iac-ciaf.org/index.php?option=com_content&task=view&id=28&Itemid=44&PHPSESSID=ccab7400b78c4c9a3d1c37b99817fa52>

Khady. *Mutilée.* Paris: Oh! Editions, 2005.

Koulibaly, Isaïe Biton. 'Madame Ba Maïna Sow.' [Interview]. *Amina* 354 (Oct. 1999): 68.

Kourouma, Ahmadou. *Les Soleils des indépendances.* Paris: Seuil, 1970 (1968).

—. *Allah n'est pas obligé.* Paris: Seuil, 2000.

Kul, Bafing. 'C'est pas bon.' *Africa Paris.* CD. Paris: Editions musicales Dava Musique, Linda Weil-Curiel and la CAMS, n.d.

Levin, Tobe. 'Alice Walker in the Bundestag.' CAAR 2005 in Tours. Unpublished conference paper. 1–10.

—. 'Alice Walker: Matron of FORWARD.' *Black Imagination and the Middle Passage.* Eds. Maria Diedrich, Henry Louis Gates, Jr., and Carl Pedersen. NY: Oxford UP, 1999. 240–254.

—. 'Cutting out Circumcision.' Rev. of Olayinka Koso-Thomas. *The Circumcision of Women: A Strategy for Eradication.* London: Zed, 1988. *The Women's Review of Books.* 5/8, May 1988. 5–6.

Melching, Molly. 'Abandoning Female Genital Cutting in Africa.' In Susan Perry and Celeste Schenck. *Eye to Eye. Women Practising Development Across Cultures.* London: Zed Books, 2001. 156–170.

Mire, Soraya. Email to Tobe Levin. 29 September 2007.

Nnaemeka, Obioma. 'If Female Circumcision Did Not Exist, Western Feminism Would Invent It.' In Susan Perry and Celeste Schenck. *Eye to Eye. Women Practising Development Across Cultures.* London: Zed Books, 2001. 171–189.

Nako, Nontsasa. 'Possessing the Voice of the Other: African Women and the 'Crisis of Representation' in Alice Walker's *Possessing the Secret of Joy.' Jenda: A Journal of Culture and African Women Studies* 1.2 (2001) : 1–8.

—. 'Genital Landscaping, Labia Remodelling, and Vestal Vagina: Female Genital Mutilation or Female Genital Cosmetic Surgery?' *Jenda: A Journal of Culture and African Women Studies.* 1.1 (2000): 1–24.

Ngugi wa Thiong'o. 'Responses' in Clifford Geertz ''Local Knowledge' and its Limits.' *Yale Journal of Criticism* 5 (Spring 1992): 129–57.

Nimako, Annor. *Mutilated.* Tema, Ghana: Ronna Publishers, 2001.

Nukunya, G.K. *Tradition and Change in Ghana: An Introduction to Sociology.* Accra, Ghana: Universities Press, 2003 (1992). 2nd Edition.

Ottah, Comfort. 'Enough is Enough.' *Through the Eyes of Nigerian Artists: Confronting Female Genital Mutilation.* Exhibition Catalogue. Eds. Shulamit Reinharz, Tobe Levin, and Joy Keshi Walker. Brandeis University, 2007. 20.

Oyewúmi, Oyèrónké. 'Alice in Motherland: Reading Alice Walker on Africa and Screening the Colour Black.' *Jenda: A Journal of Culture and African Women Studies* 1.2. (2001): 1–23.

Parmar, Pratibha, dir. *Warrior Marks.* Prod. Alice Walker. NY: Our Daughters Have Mothers, 1993.

Patterson, Chantal. 'Les Mutilations sexuelles féminines: L'excision en question.' *Présence Africaine* 141 (1987): 161–80.

Pliya, Jean qtd. in 'L'excision dans les sociétés africaines.' *Le Matinal.* 4 November 1998. 3.

Pomerance, Erica, dir. *Dabla! Excision.* DVD. Québec, CA: Les Productions Virage, Inc., 2003.

Robinson, Jenefer. *Deeper Than Reason. Emotion and its Role in Literature, Music, and Art.* NY: Oxford UP, 2005.

Salonen, Rebecca. 'Egypt Bans FGM (Again).' *Godparents News.* 9.10. (Oct. 2007): 1–2.

Sembène, Ousmane, dir. *Moolaadé.* Dakar & Paris: Filmi Doomirew & Ciné Sud Promotion, 2004.

Stellar, Tom. 'Death to the Unchaste. Europe's Muslim women – and the men who murder them. Two Islam-themed plays at St. Ann's Warehouse.' 5 October 2007.

<http://www.villagevoice.com/generic/show_print.php?id=77929&page=sellar&issue=07
40&printcde=MzU3NDYwMTQ5Mw==&refpage=L3RoZWF0ZXIvMDc0MCxzZWxssY
XIsNzc5MjksMTEuaHRtbA==>

Theunen, Patrick and El Hadji Sidy Ndiaye. *Diariatou and the Tradition*. Trans. Marleen Fannes, Ba Oumar, Samba Mamadou. Brussels: GAMS Belgique, nd.

Thiam, Awa. *La Parole aux négresses*. Paris: Denoël, 1978.

Ukhun, Christopher E. 'On the Moral Basis of Clitoridectomy in Africa.' Ed. Christopher E. Ukhun. *Critical Gender Discourse in Africa* I. Ibadan: Hope Publications, 2002.

Vrouwen, een Leven vol Pijn. Genitale verminking: Eeen kunstzinnige confrontatie. Tentoonstellingscatalogus [Exhibition Catalogue]. Ghent: Forum van Vlaamse Vrouwen, 2008.

Walker, Alice. *Possessing the Secret of Joy.* New York: Harcourt Brace Jovanovich, 1992.

Washington, Harriet. 'The Rite of Female Circumcision.' *Emerge.* (Sept. 1996): 30.

Weil-Curiel, Linda. Personal Communication. 9 October 2007.

Williams-Garcia, Rita. *No Laughter Here.* NY: Penguin, 2005.

WHO study group on female genital mutilation and obstetric outcome. 'Female genital mutilation and obstetric outcome: WHO collaborative prospective study in six African countries.' *Lancet.* 377. (2006): 1835–41.

Zabus, Chantal. *Between Rites and Rights. Excision in Women's Experiential Texts and Human Contexts.* Palo Alto: Stanford UP, 2007.

Notes to Bekers: 'From Women's Rite to Human Rights Issue: Literary Explorations of Female Genital Excision since *Facing Mount Kenya* (1938)'

1   Until the mid 1980s the most commonly used term for female genital modifications was 'female circumcision.' Since the United Nations International Decade for Women (1975–1985) this misleading concept –genital operations on women are generally far more drastic than circumcising the clitoral hood – has been criticised by opponents of the practice, most of whom insist on 'female genital mutilation.' The extremely pejorative wording, however, has upset many African men and women, whether they support or denounce female genital excision, as they feel it reinforces the Western racist portrayal of Africans. Motivated by desire not to foreclose discussion through use of the term 'mutilation,' a number of scholars shy away from the derogatory label and opt for 'female genital surgeries' (Gunning 1992; Obermeyer 1999), 'excision' and 'clitoridectomy' (Nnaemeka 1994), '(female) excision' (Lionnet 1994 & 1995), 'female genital cutting' (Carr 1997; James and Robertson 2002), or even 'female 'circumcision' (Shell-Duncan and Hernlund 2000). I use 'female genital excision' as a transparent and non-partisan cover term, all the more appropriate because it facilitates discussion of literary texts on female genital excision, as not all present the practice as a mutilation. Wherever appropriate in a particular context, I distinguish between excision and the more extreme variant of infibulation. Although WHO and others have proposed more detailed categorisations, the literary texts do not always provide enough information to determine which (sub) type of operation has taken place.

2   Although the distinction between autobiography and fiction is not always easy to make, I focus on those texts generally regarded as literary works and do not examine autobiographical texts dealing with female genital excision, such as *Two Lives: My Spirit and I* (1986) by the Kenyan Jane Tapsubei Creider, *Kesso Princesse Peule* (1988) by the Guinean Kesso Barry, the anonymous memoir *Aman: The Story of a Somali Girl* (1994),

Desert Flower (1998) *Desert Dawn* (2002) and *Brief an meiner Mutter* (2007) by the Somali Waris Dirie, *Do They Hear You When You Cry* (1998) by the Togolese Faussiya Kassindja, *Tränen im Sand* (2003) and *Geboren im Großen Regen: Mein Leben zwischen Afrika und Deutschland* (2004) respectively by Nura Abdi and Fadumo Korn, both from Somalia, and most recently *Mutilée* (2005) by the Senegalese Khady Koita. While all authors give the (Western) reader insight into the experiences of excised women, not all condemn female genital excision as an instrument of gender repression. Creider, for instance, does not oppose the practice itself, only the way in which her suitor uses it to marry her against her will, while Aman (a pseudonym) urges medicalisation of the operation rather than its discontinuation.

3   The novel remained on the *New York Times* best-seller list for twelve weeks and was a hot topic on various television shows, including Oprah Winfrey's.

4   Female genital excision is briefly mentioned in Ikonné 1984, Ngandu Nkashama 1985 and O'Barr 1987. It appears more centrally in Tobe Levin's 1986 article entitled 'Women as Scapegoats of Culture and Cult: An Activist's View of Female Circumcision in Ngugi's *The River Between*.' Levin's review, which is interspersed with a commentary on the Western feminist debate on the practice, appears to be guided not so much by a literary interest in *The River Between* and the other texts mentioned as by a more pragmatic preoccupation with the practical 'value of Ngugi's work for feminists' involved in campaigns against female genital excision (Levin 1986: 218). Even when African literary criticism on gender issues begins to flourish in the 1990s (with full-length studies such as Wilentz 1992; Boyce Davies 1994; Stratton 1994; D'Almeida 1994; Lionnet 1995; Ogunyemi 1995; Cazenave 1996; Nnaemeka 1997; Nfah-Abbenyi 1997; Brahimi and Trevarthen 1998), the practice is rarely the focal point of analysis and is usually mentioned only in passing. Those articles that do focus on the literary representation of female genital excision (e.g. Lionnet 1994; Zabus 1999; Levin 2000) do not compare different literary explorations of the practice. Although two unpublished theses (Strong-Leek 1994 and Bekers 1994) went some way in remedying this neglect by dealing with a handful of Anglophone texts on female genital excision, an extensive diachronic comparison of literary works in various languages was conducted only recently (see Bekers 2002, forthcoming The University Press of Wisconsin, 2009). This comparative study is the main source for this chapter, which is an elaboration and an update of an earlier overview of my research findings (see Bekers 2003).

5   Although various ethnographic studies, published both before and after Kenyatta's, have dealt with female genital excision (e.g. Vergiat 1937; Bettelheim 1954; Tucker 1987; Muller 1993), *Facing Mount Kenya* can be regarded as a landmark in that it was the first ethnographic account of the operation written by a member of a female genital excision-practicing ethnic group. It also seriously stimulated debate on the issue, which may help explain why literary texts published before 1938, such as Réné Maran's novel *Batouala* (1921), make little more than a passing reference to the practice.

6   I have found a majority of works in English, in addition to a number of texts in Arabic, French and other European languages and have run across hardly any references to, let alone analyses of, texts in African languages dealing with the practice. The only exceptions are a condensed allusion to a few contemporary Somali poems denouncing infibulation (Talle 1993: 105, fn. 5), a two-line reference to a 1972 Arabophone novel entitled *Aswât* (*Voices*) by the male Egyptian author Sulaymân Fayyâd about a recently immigrated excised Western woman (Malti-Douglas 1995: 152), and Fedwa Malti-Douglas's discussion of the not yet translated play *Izîs* (1986) by El Saadawi (Malti-Douglas 1995:

141–158). In this feminist rewriting of an eponymous Egyptian play (1955) by the male dramatist Tawfîq al-Hakîm, El Saadawi links female genital excision to male castration and relates how it was introduced to control women's desire. Although the tradition of Arabophone African creative writing is much older than its Europhone counterpart, this does not seem to have resulted in a longer tradition of literary explorations of female genital excision. I am well aware that the apparent scarcity of creative writing on the subject in African languages may be explained by the fact that the Europhone African literary criticism that I have consulted is hindered by the same linguistic restrictions as I am. Nevertheless, it is surely no coincidence that literary discussions of female genital excision are primarily conducted in Europhone languages, because the debate has pre-eminently appeared as a multi-cultural affair, both historically and recently.

7   Although female genital excision is a global phenomenon, most excised women are of African descent. In Africa, the operations are routinely performed on girls in the vast Sub-Saharan region stretching from the Atlantic to the Indian Ocean as well as in the Arabic Northeast of the continent, regardless of their social position or religious affiliation, be they Christian (Catholic, Protestant, or Copt), Muslim, Jewish, animist, or atheist. Although female genital excision has no solid basis in any of the large monotheist religions, it is often associated with Islam because many mistakenly believe it is demanded by their faith. The practice, however, is not mentioned in the Koran, and *hadîth* (the tradition of sayings and actions attributed to Mohammed) have been interpreted both to support and renounce the practice (Dorkenoo 1995: 37; El Dareer 1982: 72; 79; El Saadawi 1980: 39). In fact, while its origins remain uncertain, female genital excision predates Islam and Christianity by several millennia. Archaeological evidence shows the practice even dates as far back as the 16th century BC, as traces of genital operations have been found in female Egyptian mummies (Hosken 1982: 54). These ancient roots may well explain why in North East Africa one type of operation is commonly referred to as 'pharaonic circumcision.' Also, Nawal El Saadawi in her earlier-mentioned play *Izîs*, a feminist rewriting of the Osiris-myth, situates the practice in ancient Egypt and by doing so, as Fedwa Malti-Douglas points out, 'sidestep[s] the question of its relation to Islam' (Malti-Douglas 1995: 153).

8   Kenyatta 1956: 127–128. In a more recent plea for African self-disposition with regard to the practice Joséphine Guidy Wandja, a mathematician from Ivory Coast trained in Paris, explained that ethnic groups practicing female genital excision believe 'les femmes non excisées soient moins femmes que les autres [a non-excised woman is less of a woman than an excised one]' (Guidy Wandja 1987: 57, my translation).

9   The crisis over female genital excision erupts when in the late 1920s the Church of Scotland Mission requires all its converts, as well as those whose children attend their schools, to renounce the ritual. Their campaign only increases the popularity of the Kikuyu Central Association, which strongly advocates Gikuyu traditions including female genital excision, and leads to the institution of independent Gikuyu schools.

10 For a detailed comparison of Ngugi's novel and the Elizabethan play, see Bekers 1998.

11 Elspeth Huxley bases this episode on the tragic murder of the African Inland missionary Hilda Stumpf by members of the Gikuyu resistance in January 1930. Although Carol Sicherman writes that Stumpf's excision is often dismissed as an 'unfounded European myth, based on hints in [the] inquest report' (Sicherman 1990: 64), it is not disputed that the missionary was murdered because she tried to prevent her pupils from being excised.

12 *The Scar*, together with another of Njau's plays entitled *The Round Chain*, was first

published in March 1963 in the third volume (n° 8–13) of the Uganda-based journal *Transition: A Journal of the Arts, Culture and Society*. It was first performed in 1960, and by the time it was republished in Tanzania in 1965, it had not only won first prize at the 1960 Uganda Drama Festival and the 1964 Kenya Drama Festival but had also been staged in Ghana and the United States (Njau 1965: [3]).

13 In *Efuru* all characters refer to it as a 'bath,' while an excised woman is said to have 'washed' (Nwapa 1966: 15), the euphemisms being close translations of the Igbo *iwu ahu*, meaning 'to wash the body.' I would like to thank Chika Unigwe for providing me with the information; Nwapa herself uses only English.

14 Already in the late seventies four groundbreaking feminist publications presented the practice as an example of phallocratic violence against women. The first feminist to discuss the issue at length was the Egyptian writer and physician Nawal El Saadawi in her best-known work *The Hidden Face of Eve: Women in the Arab World* (written in Arabic in 1977, translated into English in 1980). In the first part of this book, entitled 'The Mutilated Half,' the author uses her own genital operation as the point of departure for her investigation into the role of female genital excision in the repression of Arab women. She supports her arguments with information she obtained from the many girls and women whom she interviewed for her medical research and also exposes the (inter)national economic and political forces that perpetuate women's inferior status in her own society. Barely a year later, the Senegalese feminist Awa Thiam strikes a similar tone in *La parole aux négresses* (1978; *Speak Out, Black Sisters: Feminism and Oppression in Black Africa*, 1986). Thiam discusses 'clitoridectomy and infibulation' in Africa alongside other practices such as 'institutionalized polygamy,' sexual initiation, and skin whitening. Like El Saadawi, she sees African women's struggle against patriarchy linked to economic and political liberation, and, following El Saadawi's example in her preface to the UK edition, she too strongly exhorts African women to speak out for themselves.

Both these African denunciations differ from two contemporary publications on the practice by American feminists. In *Gyn/ecology: The Metaethics of Radical Feminism*, Mary Daly compares female genital excision to other 'sado-rituals,' misogynist cultural practices across the world and throughout time, such as Chinese footbinding, Indian suttee or widow immolation, European witch-burning and American gynaecology, which she sees as only 'variations on the theme of [patriarchal] oppression, [for] the phenomenon is planetary' (Daly 1979: 111). Also the American journalist Fran Hosken, who had collected an impressive amount of data for Women's International Network News in *The Hosken Report: Genital and Sexual Mutilation of Females* (1979), denounces the practice as an example of global patriarchal victimisation of women. Driven by their ideological premises, Daly and Hosken put more emphasis on (gathering medical evidence in support of) their condemnation of female genital excision on the grounds of women's universal oppression than on the concrete circumstances of the African women who are affected by the practice. Unlike El Saadawi and especially Thiam, they give little or no voice to excised women's opinions or experiences.

15 In *Sweet and Sour Milk* (1979) and in *Maps* (1986) Farah adds to this list the pains of menstruation (*dysmenorrhoea*). In particular the repeated and detailed descriptions Askar gives of his adopted mother's discomfort in the latter novel are reminiscent of non-fictional testimonies by infibulated women, whose monthly agonies are aggravated and extended because the extreme narrowing of their vaginal orifices obstructs the free flow of menstrual blood. See for example Lightfoot-Klein (1989) for women's accounts and

185

Dorkenoo (1995) for medical reports.

16 Though I have found no evidence of the usage of such a device as an accompaniment to the ritual of female genital excision, the practice (especially infibulation) is frequently likened to the medieaval chastity belt, as El Saadawi herself does in *The Hidden Face of Eve* (1980).

17 For a more detailed comparison of *Tu t'appelleras Tanga* and *Woman at Point Zero* and in particular the act of narration in both novels, see Bekers 2005.

18 This link is not so surprising for already in *Le devoir de violence* (*Bound To Violence*) (1968), a satire on African dictatorship, the Malian writer Yambo Ouologuem exposes the correlation between political and gender oppression through the practice of female genital excision. In a minor episode at the beginning of the novel in which Ouologuem is savagely critical of patriarchy, the author describes with ample scorn how the 'dreaded and magnificent' Saif ben Isaac al-Heit, descendant of the dynasty of Saifs that ruled the ancient African Empire of Nakem, adds to his popularity with his male subjects by regularising the infibulation of women (Ouologuem 1971: 48).

19 Female genital excision is 'really just a part of the global mutilation of women' the author states in an interview in *Warrior Marks*, endorsing her own universalising approach in *Possessing the Secret of Joy* (Walker and Parmar 1993a: 308).

20 I respect the author's preference for non-capitalisation.

21 A World Health Organisation study published in *Lancet* in June 2006 confirms, based on information provided by nearly thirty thousand respondents at 28 obstetric centres in 6 African nations, that excised and infibulated women have a higher complication rate in childbearing. Much earlier, however, Asma El Dareer had already explained how the progress of labour for many infibulated women is severely delayed because 'the fibrous vulvar tissue fails to dilate to allow normal passage. The woman will continue bearing down until she is exhausted, and the baby's head will continue to push into this fibrous tissue, and cannot emerge unless incisions are made to widen the opening. If this is not done the head, in pushing hard against the scar tissue, may cause perineal tears and laceration' (El Dareer 1982: 38). Complications may also arise post partum, such as vesico-vaginal fistula, which are openings between vagina and urethra or vagina and anus due to the death of tissues during prolonged labour.

22 In her review of the novel Maxine Lavon Montgomery does not explain how she can read Eve's gutting of the plum as a '*reversal* of the genital mutilation that Mariam has endured' (Montgomery 1995: 31, my emphasis).

23 Isegawa 1999: 587–588, my translation. I am citing from the Dutch translation, which appeared in 1998, as this passage is omitted from the English language editions that appeared in 2000. This deletion only confirms the poor narrative embeddedness of the infibulator episode. For a more elaborate discussion of Isegawa's treatment of female genital excision in *Abessijnse Kronieken*, see Bekers, 'Culture in Transit: The Migration of Female Genital Excision to Europe in African Writing' (2008).

24 'It is [African women's] voices,' Margaret Bass, for instance, suggests in her discussion of *Possessing the Secret of Joy*, 'we should hear and offer our invited support – for they tell the whole story' (Bass 1994: 9).

25 See also Bekers 1999, which contrasts Herzi's and Walker's recent (third-generation) explorations of female genital excision with Alifa Rifaat's in the earlier (second-generation) short-story 'Who Will Be the Man' (1981).

26 Although Clarke and Dickerson's Aminata reminds the audience of her namesake, the

Malian Aminata Diop who escaped female genital excision by fleeing to France in 1989, the playwrights nowhere acknowledge that the fragment on Aminata is based on real events, not even in their 1993 article on the genesis of *Re/membering Aunt Jemima*.

27 In March 1999 I saw one of the group's three performances at the Wereldculturencentrum Zuiderpershuis in Antwerp, a whirling mix of dialogue, song, dance and music.

28 Later that same year I had the opportunity to see part of this exhibition at the 2nd Women in Africa and the African Diaspora conference. In her promotional leaflet, Joy Keshi (Ashibuogwu) Walker, co-ordinator of the NGO, expresses the hope that this 'visual presentation of the theme would conscientize people and ... trigger [increased] commitment from [...] decision makers [who would in turn] change attitudes in their constituencies.' By visualising excised women's pain – the artists' imagery cannot be misapprehended – these painters are clearly subscribing themselves to the same discourses of violence and oppression employed in recent African creative writing on female genital excision. The exhibition including 20 artifacts has been travelling since 2000. In 2006, it left Germany for the United States and has been shown at Brandeis, Harvard, and Cornell Universities, among other venues.

29 I here borrow the words of Dr Omofolabo Ajayi-Soyinka (University of Kansas), who used the saying to confirm the valuable contribution of literature to the debate on female genital excision during a session on the subject at the second Women From Africa and the African Diaspora (WAAD) conference on *Health and Human Rights* at Indiana University/Purdue University in October 1998. Rather than use this proverb to endorse the role of creative writing in the *abolition* of excision, I here apply it somewhat more broadly.

References

Abdi, Nura, and Leo G. Linder. *Tränen im Sand*. Bergisch Gladbach: Ehrenwirt/Lübbe, 2003.

Accad, Evelyne. *L'excisée*. Paris: L'Harmattan, 1982.

Achebe, Chinua. *A Man of the People*. London: Heinemann, 1966.

Allas, Yasmine. *Idil: Een Meisje*. Breda: De Geus, 1998.

Aman: The Story of a Somali Girl [As Told to Virginia Lee Barnes and Janice Boddy]. New York: Pantheon Books, 1994.

Anthias, Floya, and Nira Yuval-Davis, eds. *Woman-Nation-State*. London: Macmillan, 1989.

Armah, Ayi Kwei. *The Beautyful Ones Are Not Yet Born*. Oxford: Heinemann, 1968.

Barry, Kesso. *Kesso Princesse Peule*. Paris: Seghers, 1988.

Barry, Mariama. *La Petite Peule*. Paris: Arthème Fayard/Mazarine, 2000.

Bass, Margaret. 'Alice's Secret.' *College Language Association Journal* 38.1 (1994): 1–10.

Bekers, Elisabeth. 'Ngugi wa Thiong'o's *The River Between*: Romeo and Juliet in a Postcolonial African Context.' *BELL* (*Belgian Essays on Language and Literature*), (1998): 29–37.

—. 'Daughters of Africa W/Riting Change: Female Genital Excision in Two African Short Stories and in Alice Walker's *Possessing the Secret of Joy*.' *Thamyris* (1999) 6.2 (*Special Issue, 'Africa on the Cusp of the 21st Century*'): 255–271.

—. *Dissecting Anthills of W/Human Insurrection. A Comparative Study of African Creative Writing on Female Genital Excision*. PhD diss., University of Antwerp, 2002 (commercial edition forthcoming 2009).

—. 'Painful Entanglements: African and African American Literary Engagements in the International Debate on Female Genital Excision.' *Thamyris* 11:3 (2003) (*Special Issue in Honour of Mineke Schipper, 'Africa and Its Significant Others: Forty Years of Intercultural*

Entanglement'): 45–59.

—. 'Captive/ating Women Warriors: Nawal El Saadawi's Firdaus and Calixthe Beyala's Tanga.' Eds. Edris Makward, Mark Lilleleth and Ahmed Saber. *North-South Linkages and Connections in Continental and Diaspora African Literature*. Trenton, NJ/Asmara, Eritrea: Africa World Press, 2005. 66–77.

—. 'Culture in Transit: The Migration of Female Genital Excision in African Women's Lifewriting.' *Transcultural Modernities: Narrating Africa in Europe*. Eds. Elisabeth Bekers, Sissy Helff and Daniela Merolla. (Forthcoming).

Bettelheim, Bruno. *Symbolic Wounds. Puberty Rites and the Envious Male*. Glencoe, IL: Free Press, 1954.

Beyala, Calixthe. *Your Name Shall be Tanga* (1988), trans. Marjolijn de Jager. Oxford: Heinemann, 1996 (b).

Boyce Davies, Carole. *Black Women, Writing and Identity: Migrations of the Subject*. London/New York: Routledge, 1994.

Brahimi, Denise, and Anne Trevarthen. *Les femmes dans la littérature africaine: Portraits*. Paris/Abidjan: Karthala/ CEDA, 1998.

Brown, Lloyd W. *Women Writers in Black Africa*. London: Greenwood Press, 1981.

Cazenave, Odile. *Femmes rebelles: Naissance d'un nouveau roman africain au féminin*. Paris: L'Harmattan, 1996.

Carr, D. *Female Genital Cutting: Findings from the Demographic and Health Surveys Program*. Calverton, MD: Macro International, 1997.

Clarke, Breena, and Glenda Dickerson. 'Re/membering Aunt Jemima: Rescuing the Secret Voice.' *Women and Performance* 6.1 (1993): 77–92.

—. 'Re/membering Aunt Jemima: A Menstrual Show.' *Contemporary Plays by Women of Color: An Anthology* [sic]. Eds. Kathy A. Perkins and Roberta Uno. London/New York: Routledge, 1996. 35–45.

Creider, Jane Tapsubei. *Two Lives: My Spirit and I*. London: The Women's Press, 1986.

d'Almeida, Irène Assiba. *Francophone African Women Writers: Destroying the Emptiness of Silence*. Gainesville: U of Florida P, 1994.

Daly, Mary. *Gyn/ecology: The Metaethics of Radical Feminism*. London: The Women's Press, 1979.

DeLuca, Laura, and Shadrack Kamenya. 'Representation of Female Circumcision in *Finzan, a Dance for the Heroes*.' *Research in African Literatures* 26.3 (1995): 83–87.

Dirie, Waris. *Brief an meiner Mutter*. Berlin: Ulstein, 2007.

—. and Cathleen Miller. *Desert Flower: The Extraordinary Journey of a Desert Nomad*. William Morrow: New York, 1998.

Dirie, Waris, and Jeanne D'Haem. *Desert Dawn*. London: Virago, 2002.

Dorkenoo, Efua. *Cutting the Rose: Female Genital Mutilation: The Practice and its Prevention*. London: Minority Rights Publications, 1995.

Dorsinville, Roger. *Renaître à Dendé*. Paris: L'Harmattan, 1980.

El Dareer, Asma. *Woman, Why Do You Weep? Circumcision and Its Consequences*. London: Zed Press, 1982.

El Saadawi, Nawal. *The Hidden Face of Eve: Women in the Arab World*. Trans. Sherif Hetata. London: Zed Books, 1980 [1977].

—. *Woman at Point Zero*. Trans. Sherif Hetata. London/New Jersey: Zed Books, 1983 [1973].

—. *The Circling Song*. Trans. Marilyn Booth. London /New Jersey: Zed Books, 1989 [1976].

—. *Two Women in One*. Trans. Osman Nusairi and Jana Gough. Seattle: Women in Translation, 1991 [1971].

Farah, Nuruddin. *From a Crooked Rib*. Oxford: Heinemann, 1970.
—. *Sweet and Sour Milk*. Oxford: Heinemann, 1980.
—. *Sardines*. Oxford: Heinemann, 1982.
Maps. New York: Penguin, 2000.
gossett, hattie. 'is it true what they say about coloured pussy?' Ed. Carole S. Vance. *Pleasure and Danger: Exploring Female Sexuality*. London: Routledge/ Paul Kegan, 1984. 411–412.
Guidy Wandja, Joséphine. 'Excision? Mutilation sexuelle? Mythe ou réalité?' *Présence africaine* 141 (1987): 54–58.
Gunning, Isabelle. 'Arrogant Perception, World-Travelling and Multicultural Feminism: The Case of Female Genital Surgeries.' *Columbia Human Rights Law Review* 23.2 (1992): 189–248.
Herzi, Saida Hagi-Dirie. 'Against the Pleasure Principle.' Ed. Margaret Busby. *Daughters of Africa: An International Anthology of Words and Writings by Women of African Descent from the Ancient Egyptian to the Present*. NY: Vintage, 1993.
Hosken, Fran P. *The Hosken Report: Genital and Sexual Mutilation of Females*. Lexington, MA: Women's International Network News, 1982.
Huxley, Elspeth. *Red Strangers: A Novel*. London, Chatto and Windus, 1952 [1939].
Ikonné, Chidi. 'The Society and Woman's Quest for Selfhood in Flora Nwapa's Early Novels.' *Kunapipi* 4 (1984): 68–78.
Isegawa, Moses. *Abessijnse Kronieken*. Amsterdam: De Bezige Bij, 1999.
James, Stanlie, and Claire C. Robertson. *Genital Cutting and Transnational Sisterhood. Disputing US Polemics*. Urbana/ Chicago: U of Illinois P, 2002.
Ka, Aminata Maïga. *La voie du salut* (suivi de *Le mirroir de la vie*). Paris/Dakar: Présence Africaine, 1985.
Kassindja, Faussiya, and Layli Miller Bashir. *Do They Hear You When You Cry?* New York: Delacorte Press, 1998.
Keïta, Fatou. *Rebelle*. Abidjan/ Paris : Nouvelles Éditions Ivoiriennes/ Présence Africaine, 1998.
Kenyatta, Jomo. *Facing Mount Kenya: The Tribal Life of the Gikuyu*. New York: Vintage, 1965 [1938].
[Koita], Khady and Marie-Thérèse Cuny. *Mutilée*. Paris: Oh! Editions, 2005.
Korn, Fadumo and Sabine Eichhorst. *Geboren im Großen Regen: Mein Leben zwischen Afrika und Deutschland*. Reinbek: Rowohlt, 2004.
Kourouma, Ahmadou. *Les soleils des indépendances*. Paris: Seuil, 1970.
—. *The Suns of Independence*. London: Heinemann, 1981.
Levin, Tobe. 'Women as Scapegoats of Culture and Cult: An Activist's View of Female Circumcision in Ngugi's *The River Between*.' Eds. Carole Boyce Davies and Anne Adams Graves. *Ngambika: Studies of Women in African Literature*. Trenton, NJ: Africa World Press, 1986. 205–221.
Lightfoot-Klein, Hanny. *Prisoners of Ritual: An Odyssey into Female Genital Circumcision in Africa*. New York/ London: Harrington Park Press, 1989.
Likimani, Muthoni. *They Shall Be Chastised*. Nairobi: East African Literature Bureau, 1974.
Lionnet, Françoise. 'Dissymmetry Embodied: Feminism, Universalism, and the Practice of Excision.' Ed. Margaret Higonnet. *Borderwork: Feminist Engagements with Comparative Literature*. Ithaca/London: Cornell UP, 1974. 19–41. (repr. with minor modifications in Lionnet (1995). 129-153).
—. *Postcolonial Representations: Women, Literature and Identity*. Ithaca/London: Cornell UP, 1995.

Malti-Douglas, Fedwa. *Woman's Body, Woman's Words: Gender and Discourse in Arabo-Islamic Writing.* Princeton: UP, 1991.

—. *Men, Women, and Gods: Nawal El Saadawi and Arab Feminist Poetics.* Berkeley: U of California P, 1995.

Maran, René. *Batouala.* Paris: Albin Michel, 1921.

Mire Soraya, dir. *Fire Eyes.* 60 min., Somalia, 1993. Documentary.

Montgomery, Maxine Lavon. 'Authority, Multivocality, and the New World Order in Gloria Naylor's *Bailey's Café.*' *African American Review* 29.1 (1995): 27–33.

Muller, Jean-Claude. 'Les deux fois circoncis et les presque excisées. Le cas des Dìi de l'Adamaoua (Nord Cameroun).' *Cahiers d'études africaines* 33.4 (1993): 531–544.

Naylor, Gloria. *Bailey's Café.* New York: Harcourt, 1992.

Nama, Charles A. 'Daughters of Moombi: Ngugi's Heroines and Traditional Gikuyu Aesthetics.' Eds. Carole Boyce Davies and Anne Adams Graves. *Ngambika: Studies of Women in African Literature.* Trenton, NJ: Africa World Press, 1982. 139–149.

Nfah-Abbenyi, Juliana Makuchi. *Gender in African Women's Writing: Identity, Sexuality and Difference.* Bloomington/Indianapolis: Indiana UP, 1979.

Ngandu Nkashama, Pius. *Kourouma et le mythe: Une lecture de Les Soleils des Indépendances.* Paris: Silex, 1985.

Ngugi wa Thiong'o [James Ngugi]. *The River Between.* Oxford: Heinemann, 1965.

—. *Writers in Politics: A Re-engagement with Issues of Literature and Society.* London: James Currey, 1997.

Njau, Rebecca [Rebeka]. 'The Scar: A Tragedy.' *Transition: A Journal of the Arts, Culture and Society* 3.8-13 (1963): 23–28.

—. *The Scar: A Tragedy in One Act.* Kilimanjaro/Moshi (Tanzania): Kibo Art Gallery, 1965.

Nnaemeka, Obioma. 'Bringing African Women into the Classroom. Rethinking Pedagogy and Epistemology.' *Borderwork. Feminist Engagements with Comparative Literature.* Ed. Margaret Higonnet. Ithaca/London: Cornell UP, 1994. 300–318.

—. ed. *The Politics of (M)Othering: Womanhood, Identity, and Resistance in African Literature.* London/New York: Routledge, 1997.

Nwapa, Flora. *Efuru.* Oxford/Ibadan: Heinemann, 1966.

O'Barr, Jean F. 'Feminist Issues in the Fiction of Kenya's Women Writers.' *African Literature Today: Women in African Literature Today* 15 (1987): 55–70.

Obermeyer, Carla Makhlouf. 'Female Genital Surgeries: The Known, the Unknown, and the Unknowable.' *Medical Anthropology Quarterly* 13.1 (1999): 79–105.

Ogunyemi, Chikwenye Okonjo. *Africa Wo/man Palava: The Nigerian Novel by Women.* Chicago/London: U of Chicago P, 1995.

Ouologuem, Yambo. *Le devoir de violence,* Paris: Seuil, 1968.

Parmar, Pratibha, dir. *Warrior Marks.* Colour, 54 min. Documentary. London: Hauer Rawlence Productions, 1993b.

Rifaat, Alifa. 'Bahiyya's Eyes.' *Distant View of a Minaret and Other Stories.* Trans. Denys Johnson-Davies. London/Ibadan/Nairobi: Heinemann, 1985 [1983]. 5–11.

—. 'Who Will be The Man?' Trans. Elise Goldwasser and Miriam Cooke. *Opening the Gates: A Century of Arab Feminist Writing.* Eds. Margot Badran and Miriam Cooke. Bloomington/Indianapolis: Indiana UP, 1990 [1981]. 74–83.

Scarry, Elaine. *The Body in Pain: The Making and the Unmaking of the World.* Oxford: Oxford UP, 1987 [1985].

Sembène, Ousmane, dir. *Moolaadé,* 2004. Colour, 124 minutes, Senegal. Film.

Sicherman, Carol M. *Ngugi wa Thiong'o: The Making of a Rebel: A Source Book in Kenyan Literature and Resistance.* London: Hans Zell, 1990.

Shakespeare, William. *Romeo and Juliet.* Ed. Brian Gibbons. London/New York: Routledge (The Arden Shakespeare), 1997.

Shell-Duncan, Bettina, and Ylva Hernlund, eds. *Female 'Circumcision' in Africa: Culture, Controversy, and Change.* Boulder/London: Lynne Rienner, 2001 [2000].

Sissoko, Cheick Oumar, dir. *Finzan, a Dance for the Heroes,* 1989. Colour, 107 minutes Mali. Film.

Stratton, Florence. *Contemporary African Literature and the Politics of Gender.* London/New York: Routledge, 1994.

Strong-Leek, Linda Mcneely. *Excising the Spiritual, Physical and Psychological Self: An Analysis of Female Circumcision in the Works of Flora Nwapa, Ngugi wa Thiong'o, and Alice Walker.* PhD diss. Michigan State U, Ann Arbor: UMI, 1994.

—. 'The Quest for Spiritual/Sexual Fulfilment in Flora Nwapa's *Efuru* and *The Lake Goddess*.' Ed. Marie Umeh. *Emerging Perspectives on Flora Nwapa: Critical and Theoretical Essays.* Trenton, NJ/Asmara, Eritrea: Africa World Press, 1998. 531–548.

Talle, Aud. 'Transforming Women into 'Pure' Agnates: Aspects of Female Infibulation in Somalia Carved Flesh/Cast Selves.' *Gendered Symbols and Social Practices.* Eds. Vigdis Broch-Due, Ingrid Rudie and Tone Bleie. Oxford/ Providence: Berg, 1993. 83-106.

Thiam, Awa. *La Parole aux Négresses.* Paris: Seuil, 1978.

—. 'Portrait de groupe avec drame.' *Jeune Afrique* 1445 (1988): 62-63.

Tucker, Elizabeth. 'The Guéré Excision Festival.' *Time Out of Time: Essays on Festival.* Ed. Alessandro Falassi. Albuquerque: U of New Mexico P, 1987. 276–285.

Tucker, Martin. *Africa in Modern Literature: A Survey of Contemporary Writing in English.* New York: Ungar, 1967.

Turner, Victor. *The Forest of Symbols: Aspects of Ndembu Ritual.* Ithaca/London: Cornell UP, 1970 [1967].

Vergiat, A.M. *Moeurs et coutumes des Manjas.* Paris: Payot, 1937.

Waciuma, Charity. *Daughter of Mumbi.* Nairobi: East African Publishing House, 1974 [1969].

Walker, Alice. *In Search of Our Mothers' Gardens: Womanist Prose.* London: The Women's Press, 1984.

—. *The Color Purple.* London: The Women's Press, 1992 [1983].

—. *Possessing the Secret of Joy.* London: Vintage, 1993 [1992].

Walker, Alice, and Pratibha Parmar. *Warrior Marks: Female Genital Mutilation and the Sexual Blinding of Women.* New York/London: Harcourt Brace, 1993a.

WHO Study Group on Female Genital Mutilation and Obstetric Outcome. 'Female Genital Mutilation and Obstetric Outcome: WHO Collaborative Prospective Study in Six African Countries.' *Lancet* 367.9525 (2006): 1835–41.

Wilentz, Gay. *Binding Cultures: Black Women Writers in Africa & the Diaspora.* Bloomington/Indianapolis: Indiana UP, 1992.

Zabus, Chantal. 'Bouches cousues: L'Autobiographie de l'excisée.' Eds. Marie-Louise Mallet. *L'animal autobiographique: autour de Jacques Derrida.* Paris: Galilée, 1999. 331-352.

Zell, Hans M., and Helene Silver, eds. *A Reader's Guide to African Literature.* London/Nairobi/Ibadan: Heinemann Educational Books, 1972.

Notes to Bishop: 'Oppositional Approaches to FGM in African Literature'
1   For an excellent presentation of the laws of Western (and African) nations concerning

FGM, see 'Laws/Enforcement in Countries where FGM is Commonly Practiced' in Report on Female Genital Mutilation as required by Conference Report (H. Rept. 106-997) to Public Law 106-429 (Foreign Operations, Export Financing, and Related Programmes Appropriations Act, 2001). *Prevalence of the Practice of Female Genital Mutilation (FGM); Laws Prohibiting FGM and their Enforcement; Recommendations on How to Best Work to Eliminate FGM.* Prepared by the Office of the Senior Coordinator for International Women's Issues, Office of the Under Secretary for Global Affairs, US Department of State, February 1, 2000. Updated June 27, 2001. 3 July 2007 <http://www. state.gov/g/wi/rls/rep/ 9303.htm>.

2   Most notably, the Committee on the Elimination of Discrimination Against Women's 1990 declaration against FGM, the United Nations Declaration on the Elimination of Violence Against Women's labelling FGM as 'violence against women' in 1993, and extensive discussion of the matter at the Fourth World Conference on Women in 1995.

3   A well-known example of this backlash can be seen in the varied reactions to Alice Walker and Pratibha Parmar's documentary 'Warrior Marks,' which include many comments such as the following from a review of the film: 'This film has fostered resentment and defensiveness in many African women who have been searching for ways to challenge these practices without becoming outcasts. Thus, despite her laudable intentions, Walker's stance may actually impede efforts to build the critical alliances that can effectively challenge FGM' (James 596).

4   For more recent discussions specifically linking the anti-colonialist concern with FGM, see Obioma Nnaemeka's *Female Circumcision and the Politics of Knowledge: African Women in Imperialist Discourses,* Stanlie James and Claire Robertson's *Genital Cutting and Transnational Sisterhood: Disputing US Polemics,* and several of the articles in Bettina Shell-Duncan and Ylva Hernlund's *Female 'Circumcision' in Africa: Culture, Controversy, and Change.*

5   Although groups such as the National Organisation of Circumcision Information Resource Centres (www.nocirc.org) and Ron Goldman's Circumcision Resource Centre (www.circumcision.org/cht.htm) would not. See bibliography for several texts proposing a similar attitude towards male circumcision.

6   See Carr, 2; Lockhat, 18-20; and Rahman and Toubia, 4–5 for discussions of physical and social/symbolic differences.

7   Thiam worked with Alice Walker and Pratibha Parmar on *Warrior Marks.* P.K.'s narrative became the heart of that documentary.

8   Note that many other writers/editors have since followed this same tactic of presenting interviews and oral histories with diverging or ambiguous viewpoints and attitudes. See Helena Halperin's *I Laugh So I Won't Cry,* Hanny Lightfoot-Klein's *Prisoners of Ritual,* Raqiya Haji Dualeh Abdalla's *Sisters in Affliction* (pages 105–13), and Alice Walker and Pratibha Parmar's *Warrior Marks* among other examples.

9   Note Ousmane Sembène's own transition from fiction to cinema in the 1960's for this very reason.

10 An example of this ambiguity can be seen in the aforementioned deference to men and authority in general – is this motif a positive representation of traditional respect and social structure or a critical revelation of the attitudes that serve as a source for FGM practices?

References

Abdalla, Raqiya Haji Dualeh. *Sisters in Affliction*. London: Zed, 1982.

Amadiume, Ifi. *Re-inventing Africa: Matriarchy, Religion, & Culture*. London: Zed, 1997.

Bâ, Mariama. *Une si longue lettre*. Dakar/Abidjan: Les Nouvelles Editions Africaines, 1980.

Beyala, Calixthe. *Lettre d'une Africaine à ses soeurs occidentales*. Paris: Spengler, 1995.

—. *Tu t'appelleras Tanga*. Paris: Editions Stock, 1988.

Bhabha, Homi. 'Of Mimicry and Man: The Ambivalence of Colonial Discourse.' *October*. 28 (Spring 1984).

Carr, Dara. *Female Genital Cutting: Findings from the Demographic and Health Surveys Program*. Calverton MD: Macro International, 1997.

Chambers, Ross. *Room for Maneuver*. Chicago: University of Chicago Press, 1991.

Committee on the Elimination of Discrimination Against Women, General Recommendation no. 14 (1990).

Darby, Robert. *A Surgical Temptation: The Demonization of Foreskin and the Rise of Circumcision in Britain*. Chicago: University of Chicago Press, 2005.

Denniston, George, Pia Grassivaro Gallo, *et al.*, eds. *Bodily Integrity and the Politics of Circumcision*. New York: Springer, 2006.

Denniston, George C., Frederick Mansfield Hodges, and Marilyn Fayre Milois, eds. *Male and Female Circumcision*. New York: Kluwer Academic/Plenum Publishers, 1999.

Dirie, Waris and Cathleen Miller. *Desert Flower*. New York: HarperCollins, 1998.

El Saadawi, Nawal. *The Hidden Face of Eve*. Boston: Beacon Press, 1980.

Farah, Nuruddin. *Sardines*. Saint Paul: Graywolf Press, 1981.

Goldman, Ronald. *Circumcision: The Hidden Trauma*. Boston: Vanguard, 1997.

Halperin, Helena. *I Laugh so I Won't Cry*. Trenton: Africa World Press, 2005.

James, Stanlie. Rev. of *Warrior Marks*, dir. Pratibha Parmar. *American Historical Review* April 1997: 595–6.

James, Stanlie M. and Claire C. Robertson, eds. *Genital Cutting and Transnational Sisterhood*. Urbana: University of Illinois Press, 2002.

Kenyatta, Jomo. *Facing Mount Kenya: The Tribal Life of Gikuyu*. New York: Vintage, 1965.

Kourouma, Ahmadou. *Les soleils des indépendances*. Paris: Editions du Seuil, 1970.

Lightfoot-Klein, Hanny. *Prisoners of Ritual*. New York: Harrington Park P, 1989.

Lockhat, Haseena. *Female Genital Mutilation: Treating the Tears*. Middlesex: Middlesex University P, 2004.

Nfah-Abbenyi, Juliana Makuchi. *Gender in African Women's Writing*. Bloomington: Indiana UP, 1997.

Nnaemeka, Obioma, ed. *Female Circumcision and the Politics of Knowledge: African Women in Imperialist Discourses*. London: Praeger, 2005.

Oyewumi, Oyeronke. *The Invention of Women*. Minneapolis: U of Minnesota P, 1997.

Pascal, Blaise. *Pensées*. Trans. W. F. Trotter. Grand Rapids: Christian Classics Ethereal Library, 1944.

Parmar, Pratibha, dir. *Warrior Marks*. Women Make Movies. 1993.

Rahman, Anika and Nahid Toubia, eds. *Female Genital Mutilation*. New York: Zed, 2000.

Report on Female Genital Mutilation as required by Conference Report (H. Rept. 106–997) to Public Law 106–429 (Foreign Operations, Export Financing, and Related Programmes Appropriations Act, 2001). 'Laws/Enforcement in Countries where FGM is Commonly Practiced' in *Prevalence of the Practice of Female Genital Mutilation (FGM); Laws Prohibiting FGM and their Enforcement; Recommendations on How to Best Work to*

Eliminate FGM. Prepared by the Office of the Senior Coordinator for International Women's Issues, Office of the Under Secretary for Global Affairs, US Department of State, February 1, 2000. Updated June 27, 2001. 3 July 2007 <http://www.state.gov/g/wi/rls/rep/9303.htm>.

Sembène, Ousmane, dir. *Moolaadé.* New Yorker Films. 2004.

Shell-Duncan, Bettina and Ylva Hernlund, eds. *Female 'Circumcision' in Africa: Culture, Controversy, and Change.* London: Lynne Rienner, 2000.

Sissoko, Cheick Oumar, dir. *Finzan.* California Newsreel. 1990.

Thiam, Awa. *La parole aux négresses.* Paris: Editions Denoël/Gonthier, 1978.

Thiong'o, Ngugi wa. *The River Between.* Portsmouth: Heinemann, 1965.

United Nations General Assembly. Declaration on the Elimination of Violence Against Women, article 2(a) (1993).

Villeneuve, Annie de. 'Étude sur une Coutume Somalie, Les Femmes Cousues.' *Journal de la Societe des Africanistes* (1937) : 7.

Walker, Alice and Pratibha Parmar. *Warrior Marks.* New York: Harcourt Brace & Co., 1993.

Notes to Cage: 'Going Home Again: Diaspora, FGM, and Kinship in *Warrior Marks*'

1   Excerpted from *Black Imagination and the Middle Passage.* Eds. Maria Diedrich, Henry Louis Gates, Jr, and Carl Pedersen. NY: Oxford UP, 1999.

2   An irony here is in unequivocally 'African' activists exercising their claim to a discourse of human rights, not as a 'Western' invention but one with roots of justice in indigenous culture. Note Awa Thiam in *Warrior Marks.* Like Walker, she had also been attacked for talking publicly about excision and called on the carpet for kowtowing to Western influence. Yet she answered Pratibha Parmar's question – 'How do you feel about us coming here and making this film?' with the following: 'You know, I work … in the belief [in] universal sisterhood, that we are all in this together. You in the West may be fighting against other things, but for us, … female genital mutilation [takes] priority. You can help us … put[…] it on the world's agenda' (Lolapress 36).

3   The hardcover was published after the documentary was finished. It features full-text interviews, some reproduced in the film, others not, as well as personal journals of both Walker and Parmar and letter exchanges between them as they prepared to make the documentary. My analysis, then, is centred on both genres, as they are one and the same.

4   Walker's reception in Europe has been stunningly different from its profile in the United States. *Warrior Marks*, for instance, is part of the standard video collection in *Gymnasia* throughout Germany and is approved by the EuroNet FGM, among whose members the following were interviewed or served as consultants for the film: Efua Dorkenoo, Comfort Ottah, Linda Weil-Curiel. See Tobe Levin. 'Alice Walker: Matron of FORWARD.' *Black Imagination and the Middle Passage.* Eds. Maria Diedrich, Henry Louis Gates, Jr., and Carl Pedersen. NY: Oxford UP, 1999. 240-254.

5   That Freud found blinding in literature and dreams to symbolise castration is certainly applicable here.

6   'A raped girl is given one hundred eighty lashes with the whip because she had sex before marriage,' to borrow just one example from Ayaan Hirsi Ali (90).

7   Among many possible illustrations, here's Waris Dirie in her *Brief an meine Mutter* [Letter to my mother] describing post traumatic stress syndrome as a result of infibulation: 'I live through my mutilation over and over, like a movie in my head playing again and again the same horror film. I see myself, five years old, being mutilated. I fever. I freeze. I can't get

any air. I see no way out' (159. Trans. Tobe Levin). Khady makes a similar point: 'My screams still resound in my ears today' (Trans. Rosa von Gleichen. In *Feminist Europa*, 30).

8 For one specific instance of majority support, a Norwegian Church Study (2005) in Eritrea found that 'nowadays... through the various awareness-raising campaigns the significance of infibulation is on the decline though communities still want to continue with clitoridectomy' (qtd. in Kuring, 73).

9 The depiction of circumcised girls as being deceived is part of the culture of silence surrounding the practice, which Nawal El Saadawi, Waris Dirie, Fadumo Korn, and others have written about in their respective autobiographies.

10 In 'Alice Walker in the Bundestag,' a talk delivered at 'The Black World' C.A.A.R. 2005 Conference, Université Francois Rabelais, Tours, France. 22 April 2005, Tobe Levin argues that *Warrior Marks* has been misconstrued as a disrespectful documentary against FGM, whereas it is more accurately viewed as a bio-ethnography of an African American activist.

11 I see an interface here with Paul D of Toni Morrison's *Beloved*, who also caused women to weep by the tenderness of his presence.

12 While research about whether female slaves arrived in the 'New World' with genitalia that had been excised, infibulated, or otherwise operated on is somewhat outside the scope of this project as it is currently framed, I am nonetheless fascinated by the possibility. Therefore, future research will likely include investigation of 'bills of sale' and descriptions of slaves as disseminated at public auctions and between slaveholders to further delve into this issue.

13 The 'Door of No Return' is a significant place in African and African American history as the last stopping point before Africans left the 'slave dungeon' and boarded the slave ship. The 'Door' signifies the uncertainty of the Passage, as Africans did not know where they were journeying, and ultimately, whether they would ever return home.

References

Dawit, Seble, and Salem Merkuria. Editorial. *The New York Times* (7 December 1993): A–27.

Dirie, Waris. *Brief an meine Mutter*. Berlin: Ullstein, 2007.

Friedman, Marilyn. *What Are Friends For? Feminist Perspectives on Personal Relationships and Moral Theory*. Ithaca, NY: Cornell UP, 1993.

Gilroy, Paul. *The Black Atlantic: Modernity and Double Consciousness*. Cambridge: Harvard UP, 1993.

Gourdine, Angeletta. *The Difference Place Makes: Gender, Sexuality, and Diaspora Identity*. Columbus: The Ohio State UP, 2004.

Hirsi Ali, Ayaan. The *Caged Virgin. An Emancipation Proclamation for Women and Islam*. NY: Free Press, 2004.

Khady. *Mutilée*. Paris: Oh! Editions, 2005. Excerpt trans. Rosa von Gleichen in *Feminist Europa. Review of Books*. 5 & 6. 1. 29–31. 18 July 2007. <http://www. ddv-verlag.de/issn_1570_0038_FE%2005_2006.pdf >.

Kuring, Diana. *Weibliche Genitalverstümmelung in Eritrea. Regionale Erklärungen, nationale Ansätze und internationale Standards*. Saarbrücken: VDM Verlag Dr. Müller, 2008.

Levin, Tobe. 'Alice Walker in the Bundestag.' 'The Black World' Collegium for African American Research. Université Francois Rabelais, Tours, France. 22 April 2005. Unpublished conference paper.

—. 'Alice Walker: Matron of FORWARD.' *Black Imagination and the Middle Passage*. Eds. Maria Diedrich, Henry Louis Gates, Jr., and Carl Pedersen. NY: Oxford UP, 1999. 240–254.

Lolapress Europe. 'Identities, Passions and Commitments. An interview with the British Filmmaker Pratibha Parmar.' *Lola Press. International Feminist Magazine.* 12. (Nov. 99–April 2000): 36–41.

Nako, Nontsasa. 'Possessing the Voice of the Other: African Women and the 'Crisis of Representation' in Alice Walker's *Possessing the Secret of Joy.' Jenda: A Journal of Culture and African Women Studies* 1.2 (2001): 1–8.

Nnaemeka, Obioma, ed. *Female Circumcision and the Politics of Knowledge. African Women in Imperialist Discourses.* Westport, CT: Praeger, 2005.

Oyewúmi, Oyèrónké. *African Women and Feminism: Reflecting on the Politics of Sisterhood.* Trenton, NJ: Africa World P, 2003.

Simon, Robert, et al. *Between Hope and Despair: Pedagogy and the Remembrance of Historical Trauma.* Lanham: Rowman & Littlefield, 2000.

Smith, Barbara, ed. *Homegirls: a Black Feminist Anthology.* NY: Kitchen Table: Women of Color P, 1983.

Walker, Alice. *The Color Purple.* NY: Harcourt, Brace Jovanovich, 1982.

—. *Possessing the Secret of Joy.* NY: Harcourt, Brace Jovanovich, 1992.

Walker, Alice and Pratibha Parmar. *Warrior Marks: Female Genital Mutilation and the Sexual Blinding of Women.* New York: Harcourt Brace, 1993.

Notes to Browdy: 'Mother' as a Verb: the Erotic, Audre Lorde, and FGM'

1   See, for example, many of the essays in the recent volume *Decentering the Center: Philosophy for a Multicultural, Postcolonial, and Feminist World,* ed. Uma Narayan and Sandra Harding.

2   The proliferation of names for the 'rite' is far from innocent: female genital mutilation (FGM) is the term used by human rights activists to express their moral outrage at the practice, while FGC, with the 'c' referring either to 'cutting' or 'circumcision,' [or, according to Dr Morissanda Kouyate in Equality Now's journal *Awaken,* 'Female Genital Confusion'] implies a more moderate or ambivalent stance vis-à-vis the practice. See The Bamako Declaration on the Terminology FGM <http://www.iac-ciaf.org/index.php?option=com_content &task=view&id=28&Itemid=44& PHPSESSID=ccab7400b78c4c9a3d1c37b998 17fa52>.

3   For excellent discussions of the human rights dimension in the FGM debate, see Susan Moller Okin, 'Feminism, Women's Human Rights, and Cultural Differences,' in Narayan and Harding, eds.; Rogaia Mustafa Abusharaf's 'Introduction: The Custom in Question' in *Female Circumcision,* ed. R.M. Abusharaf (University of Pennsylvania Press, 2006); and Tobe Levin. 'Female Genital Mutilation and Human Rights.' *Comparative American Studies. An International Journal.* Special Issue on Human Rights. Guest eds. Werner Sollors and Winfried Fluck. Vol. 1 (3) 2003. 285–316.

4   To avoid misunderstanding, only the smallest minority of victims undergoes any sort of anodyne modification. As Ellen Burstyn notes, 'Although in a tiny percentage of cases FGM consists of a small cut to the hood of the clitoris, typically it is much more severe' (Burstyn 2).

5   See the website of Amnesty International for an excellent summary of the problems associated with FGM, as well as its human rights implications. Also of interest is Efua Dorkenoo's *Cutting the Rose: Female Genital Mutilation, the Practice and its Prevention* (London: Minority Rights Group, 1995), revised 2008.

6   *Scoop Independent* provides these recent epidemiological estimates: 'Some 3 million girls

worldwide [risk] FGM each year, and an estimated 120 to 140 million women have already been subject to the practice, which leaves lasting physical and psychological scars and increases the risks of problems during childbirth.' 4 July 2007.<http://www. scoop.co.nz/stories/print.html?path= WO0702/S00087.htm>.

7   How incongruous that the very point of view condemned here as 'imperialistic intervention[s] from meddling Westerners of privilege' is whole-heartedly espoused by the following African activists who, undoubtedly, just as Alice Walker was, would be assimilated to the 'Westerners' camp. Most of these women, adherents of the Bamako Declaration, are organised in the European Network FGM, the IAC, and local NGOs in the European Union: Laila Abdi, Nura Abdi, Ayaan Hirsi Ali, Owolabi Bjalkander, Waris Dirie, Efua Dorkenoo, Etenesh Hadis, Fana Habteab, Faduma Ismail, Adwoa Kluvitse, Khady Koita, Fadumo Korn, Muthoni Mathai, Sarah McCollough, Rahmat Mohammad, Comfort Momoh, Zahra Siad Naleie, Ambara Hashi Nur, Comfort Ottah, Fatou Secka, Berhane Ras-Work, Shamsa Hassan Said, Awa Thiam, Coumba Touré, and of course many more. Google any of these women for details on their activism and the NGOs from whose platforms they oppose FGM.

8   For example, Christine J. Walley, in her contribution to *Genital Cutting and Transnational Sisterhood: Disputing US Polemics*, comments that 'one common trope in much of the Euro-American literature opposing female genital operations has been the tendency to characterise African women as thoroughly oppressed victims of patriarchy and ignorance..., not as social actors in their own right' (34).

9   For instance, 'Many tales warned rebellious adolescents [in Mali among the Dogon] that refusing to accept the custom would lead to the impossibility of marriage – a totally unacceptable consequence, since, until very recently, people could not imagine living unmarried' (Allan et al, 68).

10   Mackie draws attention to similarities between FGM and Chinese foot binding. The only comparable Western practice might be the way many mothers encourage their daughters to diet, telling them that the short-term pangs of hunger are worth the longer-term gain in attractiveness. Just as in the West feminists have focused on body image as an important locus of female empowerment, trying to confront and defuse the popular media conception that 'thin is beautiful,' one line of approach to FGM has been to try to make African women aware that women's genitalia are not ugly or dirty, and need not be excised in order to render girls appealing to men. In both of these cases, evidently, much depends on whether or not men support the feminist effort, but as women are so often the primary carriers of culture, their role is paramount in achieving attitude change.

11   Some approaches discussed by the international activist community include a) programmes to educate communities about the health risks of the practice; b) efforts to remove the procedure from the bush and move it to the clinic where medical personnel operate in aseptic conditions, an alternative, however, unequivocally condemned by the World Health Organisation, UNICEF (United Nations Children's Fund), UNFPA (United Nations Population Fund), other international agencies, the European Union, European Parliament, many European governments and NGOs (see the World Health Organisation's *Female Genital Mutilation. The prevention and the management of the health complications. Policy guidelines for nurses and midwives* [2001]); c) legislation against it, though laws passed in two-thirds of practicing nations are rarely enforced; and d) reward for countries and communities that abandon FGM by increasing international aid.

12 It must be noted, however, that this catalogue seethes with internal contradiction. How, for instance, are equality and hierarchy to be reframed? And if 'sexual restraint' is a value, how could this be reconciled with Audre Lorde's insistence on the importance of sexual freedom for women?

13 Replacement of cutting by a less harmful ritual is also discussed in 'Community-based Efforts to End Female Genital Mutilation in Kenya,' by Asha Mohamud, Samson Radeny and Karin Ringheim, in *Female Circumcision*, ed. R.M. Abusharaf.

14 Details of obstetric and gynaecological perils can be found, among many other sources, in A. El Dareer, *Woman, Why Do You Weep? Circumcision and its Consequences* (London, Zed Press, 1982) and the more recent article "My Grandmother Called it the Three Feminine Sorrows': The Struggle of Women Against Female Circumcision in Somalia,' by Raqiya D. Abdalla, in *Female Circumcision*, ed. R. M. Abusharaf. In addition, on 2 June 2006, the World Health Organisation published in *Lancet* the first broad-based statistical study of maternal hardship: '[It] involved 28,393 women at 28 obstetric centres in six countries, where FGM is common – Burkina Faso, Ghana, Kenya, Nigeria, Senegal and Sudan.' The principal finding is carried in the headline: 'New Study shows female genital mutilation exposes women and babies to significant risk at childbirth.' Investigators revealed that 'FGM put the women's babies in substantial danger during childbirth, [as] there was an increased need to resuscitate babies whose mother had had FGM (66% higher in women with FGM III). The death rate among babies during and immediately after birth is also much higher for those born to mothers with FGM: 15% higher in those with FGM I, 32% higher in those with FGM II, and 55% higher in those with FGM III. It is estimated that in the African context an additional 10 to 20 babies die per 1000 deliveries as a result of the practice.'

15 Balk cites a study of 300 polygynous Sudanese men, in which 20 percent 'stated that they married their second, non-pharaonically circumcised wife because they could not keep up with the ordeal of perforating the progressively toughened 'circumcision' scars... their wives [develop] every time they have a baby' (61). For a first-hand account of the effects of FGM on a young woman's sexuality, see *Aman: The Story of a Somali Girl*, ed. Virginia Lee Barnes and Janice Boddy (Vintage, 1995).

16 Information on Tostan can be found at its well maintained website: www.tostan.org. The programme as carried out in Senegal, Burkina Faso and Mali is discussed in 'Strategies for Encouraging the Abandonment of Female Genital Cutting' by Nafissatou J. Diop and Ian Askew, in *Female Circumcision*, ed. R. M. Abusharaf.

17 The practice has been banned in many other African countries, including Ghana, Guinea, Eritrea, Kenya, Sierra Leone, and Egypt, but official bans are difficult to enforce, which is why the grassroots, attitude-changing approach of Tostan is so important.

18 A remarkable real-life account of such dialogue has been published in *Exciseuse*, by Hawa Gréou with Linda Weil-Curiel and Natacha Henry (2007). 'The first and only exciser convicted and imprisoned in France, Hawa Gréou seeks out the prosecuting attorney and initiates an exceptional conversation. Gréou tells about her own mutilation, about her reasons for excision, and about the thousands of girls mutilated in secret in France. She describes a situation one would never suspect nor, undoubtedly, support' (Trans. Tobe Levin) 4 July 2007 <http://www.city-editions.com/WebPages/DocuSommair.htm>. 2

19 One of the common but (at least from the point of view of professors of literature) rather odd criticisms of Walker's novel is that the African world she created is entirely fictional—M'Lissa and Tashi's language, tribe and country do not really exist. Walker justifies her

creative licence by arguing that she refers to a widespread reality not limited to any one tribe or country on the continent. While recognising the danger of universalism, I find that despite its reduction of M'Lissa and Tashi to archetypal figures, *Possessing the Secret of Joy* is useful in illuminating the way these two women's joint tragedies are manipulated from afar by the patriarchal customs that Tashi will eventually defy.

20 This is not to imply a unitary view among insiders either. Rather, the opposite is the case: there is often dramatic disagreement about FGM among cultural insiders. *The Bamako Declaration*, for instance, scripted by 'radical' African 'positive deviants', claims African 'authenticity' as opposed to other voices, not identified in the document but known to be those of Africans living in the USA, who have lobbied to impose their more 'moderate' views on African campaigners. Oddly, the 'outsiders' to the Bamako Declaration are precisely the writers who claim, in the USA, to be on the 'inside'. In the Bamako Declaration we read about 'African women [living in Africa and throughout the European Diaspora] working against FGM at [a] time when FGM was a taboo, [who feel that] the campaign has been high-jacked by others … not involved at the beginning and who do not appreciate the nature of the struggle.' DECLARATION: on the Terminology FGM; 6th IAC General Assembly, 4 - 7 April, 2005, Bamako/Mali. 06 April 2005. 15 November 2006 <http://www.iac-ciaf.org/index.php?option=com_content&task= view&id=28&Itemid=44&PHPSESSID=ccab7400b78c4c9a3d1c37b99817fa52>. For this reference I am indebted to Tobe Levin, a founding member of the European Network FGM, which works closely with the Inter-African Committee, the group that launched International 'Zero Tolerance' to FGM Day and penned the Bamako Declaration.

References

Abusharaf, Rogaia Mustafa. *Female Circumcision: Multicultural Perspectives.* Philadelphia: U of Pennsylvania P, 2006.

Ahmadu, Fuambai. 'Rites and Wrongs: An Insider/Outsider Reflects on Power and Excision.' *Female 'Circumcision' in Africa: Culture, Controversy, Change.* Eds. Bettina Shell-Duncan and Ylva Hernlund. Boulder, CO: Lynne Rienner, 2000. 283–312.

Allan, Tuzyline Jita et al. 'Introduction.' *Women Writing Africa. West Africa and the Sahel.* Eds. Esi Sutherland-Addy and Aminata Diaw. NY: The Feminist Press at CUNY, 2005.

Balk, Deborah. 'To Marry and Bear Children? The Demographic Consequences of Infibulation in Sudan.' *Female 'Circumcision' in Africa: Culture, Controversy, Change.* Eds. Bettina Shell-Duncan and Ylva Hernlund. Boulder, CO: Lynne Rienner, 2000. 55–72.

Burstyn, Ellen. 'Performed by new immigrants, veiled in deference to a cultural tradition of the developing world, female circumcision is becoming an American problem.' *The Atlantic Monthly.* 1995. 4 July 2007. <http://www.t6heatlantic.com /doc/by/linda_ burstyn>.

Gréou, Hawa, Linda Weil-Curiel and Natacha Henry. *Exciseuse.* Paris: CityEditions, 2007; Website City Editions. 4 July 2007 <http://www.city-editions.com/WebPages/Docu Sommair.htm>.

Jaggar, Alison. 'Globalizing Feminist Ethics.' *Decentering the Center: Philosophy for a Multicultural, Postcolonial and Feminist World.* Eds. Uma Narayan and Sandra Harding. Bloomington: Indiana UP, 2000. 1–25.

James, Stanlie M. and Claire C. Robertson, eds. *Genital Cutting and Transnational Sisterhood.* Urbana and Chicago: U of Illinois P, 2002.

Levin, Tobe. 'Female Genital Mutilation and Human Rights.' *Comparative American Studies.*

An International Journal. Special issue on human rights. Guest eds. Werner Sollors and Winfried Fluck. 1.3 (2003): 285–316.

Lorde, Audre. *The Collected Poems of Audre Lorde.* NY: Norton, 1997.

—. *Sister Outsider.* Freedom, CA: The Crossing Press, 1984.

—. *Zami: A New Spelling of My Name.* Freedom, CA: The Crossing Press, 1982.

Mackie, Gerry. 'Female Genital Cutting: The Beginning of the End.' *Female 'Circumcision' in Africa: Culture, Controversy, Change.* Eds. Bettina Shell-Duncan and Ylva Hernlund. Boulder, CO: Lynne Rienner, 2000. 253–282.

Mohanty, Chandra Talpede. ''Under Western Eyes' Revisited: Feminist Solidarity Through Anti-capitalist Struggles.' *Feminism without Borders: Decolonizing Theory, Practicing Solidarity.* Durham, N.C.: Duke UP, 2003. 221–251.

Narayan, Uma, and Sandra Harding, eds. *Decentering the Center: Philosophy for a Multicultural, Postcolonial and Feminist World.* Bloomington: Indiana UP, 2000.

Okin, Susan Moller. 'Feminism, Women's Human Rights, and Cultural Differences.' *Decentering the Center: Philosophy for a Multicultural, Postcolonial and Feminist World.* Eds. Uma Narayan and Sandra Harding. Bloomington: Indiana UP, 2000. 26-46.

Shell-Duncan, Bettina, and Ylva Hernlund, eds. *Female 'Circumcision' in Africa: Culture, Controversy, Change.* Boulder, CO: Lynne Rienner, 2000.

Shell-Duncan, Bettina, and Ylva Hernlund. 'Female 'Circumcision' in Africa:

Dimensions of the Practice and Debates.' *Female 'Circumcision' in Africa: Culture, Controversy, Change.* Eds. Bettina Shell-Duncan and Ylva Hernlund Boulder, CO: Lynne Rienner, 2000. 1–40.

Shell-Duncan, Bettina, Walter Obungu Obiero and Leunita Auko Muruli. 'Women Without Choices: The Debate over Medicalisation of Female Genital Cutting and its Impact on a Northern Kenyan Community.' *Female 'Circumcision' in Africa: Culture, Controversy, Change.* Eds. Bettina Shell-Duncan and Ylva Hernlund Boulder, CO: Lynne Rienner, 2000. 109-128.

Walker, Alice. *Possessing the Secret of Joy.* NY: Simon and Schuster, 1992.

Walley, Christine J. 'Searching for 'Voices': Feminism, Anthropology, and the Global Debate over Female Genital Operations.' *Genital Cutting and Transnational Sisterhood.* Eds. Stanlie M. James and Claire C. Robertson. Urbana and Chicago: U of Illinois P, 2002. 17–53.

World Health Organisation. *Female Genital Mutilation. The prevention and the management of the health complications. Policy guidelines for nurses and midwives* [2001] 4 July 2007 <http://www.who.int/reproductive-health/publications/rhr_01_18_fgm_policy_guidelines/index.html>.

World Health Organisation. 'New study shows female genital mutilation exposes women and babies to significant risk at childbirth.' *The Lancet.* June 2006. 4 July 2007 <http://www.who.int/mediacentre/news/releases/2006/pr30/en/print.html>.

Notes to Asaah: 'Female Genital Mutilation: Ambivalence, Indictment and Commitment in Sub-Saharan African Fiction'

1   This is a longer version of an earlier article published in *Papers in Modern Languages* (University of Ghana) 1.1 (2007): 11–26.

2   As this chapter shows, the term 'Sub-Saharan fiction,' though often geographically restrictive, culturally engages the attention of critics and readers, African and non-African alike, and by virtue of its style, techniques, themes and preoccupations, is not divorced

from the major currents of world literature.

3   Though officially Senegalese, Awa Thiam acknowledges the hybridity of her roots as she dedicates *La Parole aux Négresses* to relatives all over West Africa. Additionally, she not only takes on board the universal question of female marginalisation but also builds bridges of understanding among women and men of different cultures even as she stresses the peculiarity of women's exclusion in diverse countries.

4   As Chantal Patterson correctly points out, circumcision (removal of the male foreskin) is anatomically different from clitoridectomy/excision/ infibulation (mutilation of the female genitalia): if clitoridectomy, for example, were to be inflicted on a man, it would mean the removal of his glans, his penis and his testicles, thus rendering him amputated for life (162).

5   Page references from Kourouma's first novel are to the translated version *The Suns of Independence*.

6   Jean-Pierre Ombolo reports that although the idea of purification also drives the rare cases of clitoridectomy in the Beti society of Cameroon, it is only hermaphrodites and women, accused of witchcraft, incest and persistent infidelity, who are subjected to 'etsig osot' ('the shearing of the clitoris') as a punitive measure.

7   Page references are to the translated version of Thiam's work, *Black Sisters, Speak Out*.

8   I also appreciate the need for translation of these works into local languages and their adaptation for radio/television transmission in order to achieve greater impact.

References

Abdi, Nura. *Larmes du sable*. Paris: Archipel, 2004.

Amselle, Jean-Loup. *Branchements: anthropologie de l'universalité des cultures*. Paris, Flammarion, 2001.

Andriamirado, Sennen & Renaud de Rochebrune. 'Ahmadou Kourouma: 'Je veux rendre aux Africains leur dignité.' ' [Interview]. *Jeune Afrique* 1558 (7–13 November 1990): 44-49.

Appadurai, Arjun. 'Disjuncture and Difference in the Global Economy.' Eds. Patrick Williams & Laura Chrisman. *Colonial Discourse and Postcolonial Theory: A Reader*. New York: Columbia UP, 1994. 324-39.

Barry, Mariama. *La Petite Peule*. Paris: Mazarine, 2000.

Beyala, Calixthe. *Tu t'appelleras Tanga*. Paris: J'ai lu, 1988.

—. *Lettre d'une Africaine à ses soeurs occidentales*. Paris: Spengler, 1995.

Cissé, Fatou Fanny. *La Blessure*. Abidjan/Montréal: CEDA/ Hurtubise HMH, 2001.

Conteh, Osman. *Unanswered Cries*. Oxford: Macmillan, 2002.

Dirie, Waris with Cathleen Miller. *Desert Flower: The Extraordinary Life of a Desert Nomad*. London. Virago, 1998.

—. *Fleur du desert: Le combat d'un top-model contre l'excision*. Paris: J'ai lu, 2000.

Dirie, Waris. 'My Mother Held Me Down.' BBC. Tuesday, July 10, 2007. 1–3. 19 July 2007. <http://news.bbc.co.uk/2/hi/health/6287926.stm>.

Farah, Nuruddin. *From a Crooked Rib*. London/ Ibadan: Heinemann, 1970.

—. *Sardines*. Saint Paul, MN: Graywolf, 1992 [1981].

Gikandi, Simon. *Reading the African Novel*. London/ Nairobi/Portsmouth, USA: EAEP/Heinemann, 1987.

Gallimore, Béatrice Rangira. *L'Œuvre romanesque de Calixthe Beyala*. Paris: L'Harmattan, 1997.

Herzberger-Fofana, Pierrette. *Littérature féminine francophone d'Afrique noire suivi d'Un*

Dictionnaire des romancières. Paris: L'Harmattan, 2000.

Hickey, Dennis. 'One People's Freedom, One Woman's Pain: Ngugi wa Thiongo, Alice Walker and the Problem of Female Circumcision.' *Ngugi wa Thiongo: Texts and Contexts*. Ed. Charles Cantalupo. Trenton: Africa World Press, 1995. 231–45.

Hussein, Jeylan W. 'The Social and Ethno-Cultural Construction of Masculinity and Femininity in African Proverbs.' *African Study Monographs* 26.2 (2005) : 59-87.

Kâ, Aminata Maiga. *La Voie du salut* suivi du *Miroir de la vie*. Paris: Présence Africaine, 1985.

Kane, Hamidou Cheikh. *L'Aventure ambiguë*. Paris: Julliard, 1961.

Keïta, Fatou. *Rebelle*. 3rd Ed. Paris/Abidjan: Présence Africaine/Nouvelles Editions Ivoiriennes, 2005 [1998].

Kemedjio, Cilas. 'Faire taire les silences du corps noir.' *Présence Francophone* 66 (2006) : 12–36.

Kenyatta, Jomo. *Facing Mount Kenya: The Tribal Life of the Gikuyu*. London: Martin Secker and Warburg, 1938.

Khady. *Mutilée*. Paris: Oh! Editions, 2005.

Kodjo, Edem. ...*Et demain l'Afrique*. Paris: Stock, 1995.

Kouassi, Virginie Affoué. 'Les Femmes chez Ahmadou Kourouma.' *Notre Librairie* 155-156 (2004): 190–94.

Kourouma, Ahmadou. *Les Soleils des indépendances*. Paris: Seuil, 1970 [1968].

—. *The Suns of Independence*. Trans. Adrian Adams. London/Ibadan/Nairobi: Heinemann, 1981.

—. *Monnè, outrages et défis*. Paris: Seuil, 1990.

—. *En attendant le vote des bêtes sauvages*. Paris: Seuil, 1998.

—. *Allah n'est pas obligé*. Paris: Seuil, 2000.

Levin, Tobe. 'Alice Walker in the Bundestag.' CAAR 2005 in Tours. Unpublished paper. (2005): 1–10.

Mambou, Christian. *La Gazelle et les exciseuses*. Paris: L'Harmattan, 2004.

Mbembe, Achille. 'African Modes of Self-Writing.' *Codesria Bulletin* 1 (2000): 4-18.

N'Guessan-Larroux, Béatrice. 'A l'ombre des jeunes filles en pleurs.' *Mots Pluriels* 22 (22 Sept. 2002). 12 April 2007. <http :www.arts.uwa.edu.au/Mots Pluriels/MP2202bnl.html> 1-10.

Ngugi wa Thiong'o. *The River Between*. London: Heinemann, 1965.

Nimako, Annor. *Mutilated*. Tema: Ronna Publishers, 2001.

Nwapa, Flóra. *Efuru*. London: Heinemann, 1966.

Ombolo, Jean-Pierre. *Sexe et société en Afrique noire: l'anthropologie sexuelle beti: essai analytique, critique et comparatif*. Paris: L'Harmattan, 1990.

Ouologuem, Yambo. *Le Devoir de Violence*. Paris: Le Serpent à Plumes, 2003. [1968].

Patterson, Chantal. 'Les Mutilations sexuelles féminines: l'excision en question.' *Présence Africaine* 141(1987): 161-80.

Roventa-Frumasani, Daniela. 'L'Identité féminine dans la presse écrite roumaine: topos et réalité.' *Global Network/ Le Réseau mondial* 12 (2000): 123–36.

Sègla, Aimé & Adékin E. Boko. 'De la cosmologie à la rationalisation de la vie sociale: ces mots idààcha qui parlent ou la mémoire d'un type de calendrier yoruba ancien.' *Cahiers d'Etudes Africaines* 181 (2006): 11–50.

Thiam, Awa. *La Parole aux négresses*. Paris: Denoël, 1978.

—. *Black Sisters, Speak Out: Feminism and Oppression in Black Africa*. Trans. Dorothy S. Blair. London: Pluto, 1986.

Walker, Alice. 'Heaven Belongs to You.' *Re-visioning Feminism around the World*. New York: The Feminist Press, 1995. 62–63.

Notes to Adams: 'The Anti-FGM Novel in Public Education: An Example from Ghana'

1 Ghana has ten administrative regions, three of which are often described as Northern Ghana or as northern regions: Northern Region, Upper East Region and Upper West Region. It bears noting that even in these regions, which coincidentally are (by reason of colonial and postcolonial neglect) the most deprived, not all resident ethnic groups practise female genital mutilation (FGM). Overall, the prevalence rate of FGM in Ghana in 2004, according to UNICEF Multiple Indicator Cluster Surveys, is 5%.

2 Additional works of fiction specifically aimed at youth include Rita Williams-Garcia. *No Laughter Here* (NY: Harper Collins, 2004); Sigrid Weidenweber. *Escaping the Twilight* (Portland, OR: Arnica, 2003); Demba Aboubacar Pamanta's short story *Bermère* (2004) and novella *La Blessure* (Bamako, Mali: Togouna Edition, 2006); the musical written and produced by FORWARD – Germany's African immigrant girls' group with theatre coach Hélène Ekwe and available in DVD, *Im Schatten der Tradition* (2007); the OK featured film *Retten til et fullverdig liv* ['Right to a dignified life'] that covers 'impressions from a theatre group project with young African persons living in Norway' [thank you, Esther Heller, for this information] and described on the website as 'The right to a fully valued life, the film and reference book with suggestions [have been designed to address] the issue of circumcision with young adults from affected groups' (see <http://english.okprosjekt. no/artikkel.asp?AId=183&MId1=54> 21 July 2007); as well as comic books, one in Somali produced by the Finnish Red Cross; *Sara, Daughter of a Lioness*, produced by UNICEF Kenya [thank you, Franziska Gruber, for this detail]; and the DAPHNE sponsored comic in German, French and English, *Diariatou and Tradition*, by Patrick Theunen and El Hadji Sidy Ndiaye (Brussels: GAMS Belgium, 2006). Also marketed to teen-age girls are Pat Lowery Collins. *The Fattening Hut.* (Boston: Houghton Mifflin, 2005), a narrative poem whose heroine 'runs away to escape her tribe's customs of arranged marriages and female genital mutilation' [np] and Cristina Kessler. *No Condition is Permanent.* (NY: Philomel Books, 2000), in which 'shy fourteen-year-old Jodie accompanies her anthropologist mother to live in Sierra Leone, [where] she befriends a local girl but encounters a cultural divide that cannot be crossed' (np). Moreover, Alice Walker's *Possessing the Secret of Joy*, whose heroine Tashi makes life-directing decisions when a teen, is the subject of a chapter on girls in literature. See Verena Stefan. *Rauh, wild und frei. Mädchengestalten in der Literatur.* (Frankfurt: Fischer, 1997). Finally, the New York Public Library put Fadumo Korn with Sabine Eichhorst. *Born in the Big Rains. A Memoir of Somalia and Survival.* Trans. and Afterword Tobe Levin. (NY: The Feminist Press, 2006) on its list of 2006 One Hundred recommended books for youth.

3 The narrative does not state whether Aunt Dora made known her motive in taking Sarah away to Accra. Indeed, the opportunity for the child to be raised and educated by a prosperous, childless aunt in the capital city would, for most families, be welcomed and thus require no further motive to be given.

4 Does 'educated' mean that Sarah possesses the health knowledge to turn her against her people's practice? Because obviously the knowledge did not stop her. Or, does 'educated' mean that Sarah belongs to a social class that is above such customs? Here, too, her class position did not stop her.

5 Ousmane Sembène, in *Moolaadé*, stresses the pain of intercourse for mutilated women in the superimposition of two powerful scenes, the first of clitoridectomy that blends into the marital encounter in which the heroine literally bites her own finger bloody at the moment her husband reaches his brutal climax – reminiscent of the piece of wood

inserted into girls' mouths to prevent them from severing their tongues at the razor's bite. Having used the pinkie to buffer her cries, she rises the morning after and draws a bath, demonstrably nursing her symbolic yet literal wound.

6 A model of such conversion after the fact is the spectacular case of Hawa Gréou, the first sentenced to a firm prison term in France. Upon release, she sought out the prosecuting attorney, Linda Weil-Curiel, to whom she admitted having had a change of heart. She is now among abolition campaigners. Among many additional examples, one more deserves mention here for its particular attractiveness in light of youth culture: the music DVD 'J'abandon' written and performed by Ténin Bomboté (2007).

7 'Women who have themselves undergone FGM are its strongest defenders.' Efua Dorkenoo in *Cutting the Rose*, 67.

8 *Daily Graphic* (Accra), June 7, 2007, p. 17.

References

Bomboté, Ténin. *J'abandon*. Music DVD. Bamako, Mali: Sini Sanuman, 2007.

Collins, Pat Lowery. *The Fattening Hut*. Boston: Houghton Mifflin, 2005.

Conteh, Osman. *Unanswerd Cries*. Oxford: Macmillan, 2002.

Daily Graphic (Accra). 7 June 2007. 17.

Dorkenoo, Efua. *Cutting the Rose. Female Genital Mutilation: The Practice and its Prevention*. (1994). Bloomington: Indiana UP, 2007.

Farah, Nuruddin. *From a Crooked Rib*. London: Heinemann, 1970.

FORWARD – Germany and Hélène Ekwe, dir. *Im Schatten der Tradition*. DVD. FORWARD: Frankfurt am Main, 2007.

Henry, Natacha, Linda Weil-Curiel. *Entretien avec Hawa Gréou. Exciseuse. L'exciseuse de Paris face à l'accusation*. Grainville: City Editions, 2007.

Keïta, Fatou. *Rebelle*. Abidjan: Nouvelles Éditions Ivoiriennes, 1997.

Kessler, Cristina. *No Condition is Permanent*. NY: Philomel Books, 2000.

Khady. *Mutilée*. Paris: Oh! Editions, 2005.

Korn, Fadumo with Sabine Eichhorst. *Born in the Big Rains. A Memoir of Somalia and Survival*. Trans. and Afterword Tobe Levin. NY: The Feminist Press, 2006.

Mambou, Christian. *La Gazelle et les exciseuses*. Paris: L'Harmattan, 2004.

Nimako, Annor. *Mutilated*. Tema, Ghana: Ronna Publishers, 2001.

Pamanta, Demba Aboubacar. *Bermère*. Bamako, Mali: Togouna Edition, 2004.

—. *La Blessure*. Bamako, Mali: Togouna Edition, 2006.

Retten til et fullverdig liv ['Right to a dignified life']. Film. OK Project/ IKM/ Wenche Medbøe/Kreativ Media - Norway. 21 July 2007 <http://www.okprosjekt.no/artikkel.asp?AId=139&MId1=55&Back=1>

Sembène, Ousmane, dir. *Moolaadé*. New Yorker Films. 2004.

Stefan, Verena. *Rauh, wild und frei. Mädchengestalten in der Literatur*. Frankfurt: Fischer, 1997.

Theunen, Patrick and El Hadji Sidy Ndiaye. *Diariatou and Tradition*. Brussels: GAMS Belgium, 2006.

UNESCO. 'Multiple Indicator Cluster Surveys: National Level Data.' Macro International. 23 May 2007 <http://www.measuredhs.com/topics/gender/FGC-CD/start.cfm#DHS%20data>.

UNICEF Kenya. *Sara, Daughter of a Lioness*. Comic. Nd.

Walker, Alice. *Possessing the Secret of Joy*. NY: Simon and Schuster, 1992.

Weidenweber, Sigrid. *Escaping the Twilight*. Portland, OR: Arnica, 2003.

Williams-Garcia, Rita. *No Laughter Here*. NY: Harper Collins, 2004.

Notes to Levin: 'What's Wrong with Mariam? Gloria Naylor's Infibulated Jew'

1   An earlier version of this paper appeared in *Holding Their Own: Perspectives on the Multi-Ethnic Literatures of the United States*. Eds. Dorothea Fischer-Hornung and Heike Raphael-Hernandez. Tübingen: Stauffenberg, 2000. 51-66. Revised version published with permission.

2   See Shaye J. D. Cohen. *Why Aren't Jewish Women Circumcised? Gender and Covenant in Judaism*. Berkeley: U. of California P., 2005.

3   For passionate African-penned diatribes against FGM as a vestige of pre-modern eras, see Comfort Ottah and Ben Osaghae in *Through the Eyes of Nigerian Artists. Confronting Female Genital Mutilation*. Accessed 13 September 2007. http://www.forward-germany.org/uploads/images/FORWARD%20 Broschure%20Nigerian%20Artists.pdf

4   Although the Bamako Declaration appears earlier in this work, I would emphasize the following passages here underscoring that the authors are exclusively African veterans of the anti-FGM struggle: 'We recognize that while it may be less threatening for non-Africans to adopt other less confrontational terminology in order to enter into dialogue with communities, it is imperative that the term FGM [be] retained. *The term FGM is not judgemental. It is instead a medical term that reflects what is done to the genitalia of girls and women. It is a cultural reality. Mutilation is the removal of healthy tissue. The fact that the term makes some people uneasy is no justification for its abandonment.*

We would highlight that...FGM was adopted [by] consultation and consensus [among...] African experts [at] the first technical working group meeting held in Geneva in 1995 and gained...world-wide currency and acceptance. The Beijing conference also adopted and used...female genital mutilation. ...FGM has been adopted and endorsed by the European Union [and] the African Union; [it] is currently utilized in all their documentation including the most recent Additional Protocol to the African Charter on Human and Peoples' Rights, on the Rights of Women [Maputo].

While we appreciate the efforts made in response to FGM on the continent and the Diaspora, it is patronizing and belittling to African women and girls to have outsiders define their oppression. Indeed what gives anyone but Africans the right to change a term agreed upon by the largest group of African activists on this issue in the world? This is at best paternalism and is a sad reflection of how, after many years of African women working against FGM at the time when FGM was a taboo, the campaign has been high-jacked by others...not involved at the beginning and who do not appreciate the nature of the struggle.'

5   Afro-centric student unions provided the annual venues for hundreds of speeches by Leonard Jeffries, Steve Cokeley, Khalid Abdul Muhammad or Louis Farrakhan. And although 'headlines in the general and Anglo-Jewish press have provided an impression that anti-Semitism and related issues of bigotry on campus are more prevalent than they actually are' (Ross & Schneider 269), the Anti-Defamation League's Audit of Anti-Semitic Incidents recorded an increase in hate speech from 1988 to 1993 of 126 percent (Ross & Schneider 269), with institutions of higher learning having 'emerged in the 1990s as...major sites for the introduction and dissemination of anti-Semitism into American society' (Ross & Schneider 268). Thus Naylor's misleading representation, in 1992, of Jews as mutilators merits critical appraisal.

6   Though insiders know FGM is happening in Germany, this particular case was uncorroborated at the time.

7   I contextualise this event in 'Female Genital Mutilation: Campaigns in Germany.'

Engendering Human Rights: Cultural and Socio-Economic Realities in Africa. Ed. Obioma Nnaemeka. NY: Palgrave Macmillan at St Martin's Press, 2005. 285–301.

8   Naylor's publicists provided this disturbing internet description of *1996*: 'After having published several critically acclaimed novels like *The Women of Brewster Place* and *Mama Day*, author Gloria Naylor bought a house on St. Helena Island off the coast of South Carolina. She intended to relax, write in peace, and enjoy life and gardening but [a Jewish neighbour, who felt threatened by the presence of a Black next door], ruined her tranquillity. When this neighbour's fears spurred a massive covert surveillance operation against Naylor in 1996, the year became one of discomfort and confusion for [her]. This is her account of invasion of privacy in the extreme.' To what extent is the neighbour's Jewishness at fault? 12 September 2007 http://books.google.com/books?id= 5UCJAAAACAAJ&dq=inauthor:Gloria+inauthor:Naylor

9   To be clear about this, 'up until ten years ago, [interview in Israel with Reke Mullu, 1987] clitoridectomy was performed on girls in Ethiopia. Most people say ... at the age of 11, but one person interviewed said it took place in infancy. The operation was performed by a *kinterkoraj*, a woman trained like a *mohel* (ritual circumciser of infant Jewish boys). ... According to Ambaw, genital mutilation is more an Ethiopian practice than a Jewish one and is no longer done at all in Israel' (King 8). Similarly, an article authored by R.H. Belmaker et al on the 'Disappearance of Female Genital Mutilation from the Bedouin Population of Southern Israel' has been accepted by *The Journal of Sexual Medicine* (2008).

10 See also Shalva Weil. 'Ethiopian Jewish Women: Trends and Transformations in the Context of Transnational Change.' *Nashim: A Journal of Jewish Women's Studies & Gender Issues.* 8. (Fall 2004): 73-86.

11 This includes Ethiopians, Sudanese, Somalis, Eritreans, and some groups in Nigeria and Mali.

References

Abdi, Mariam Sheikh. *A Religious Oriented Approach to Addressing FGM/C among the Somali Community of Wajir, Kenya.* US AID & Population Council, 2007.

Azodo, Ada Uzoamaka. 'Editor's Recapitulation. Representation(s) of the the Ivorian Novel: From Ahmadou Kourouma's *The Suns of Independence* (1968) to Fatou Keita's *Rebellious Women* (1998).' *Gender and Sexuality in African Literature and Film.* Eds. Ada Uzoamaka Azodo and Maureen Ngozi Eke. Lawrenceville: Africa World Press, 2007. 189–196.

Azoulay, Katya Gibel. *Black, Jewish and Interracial. It's Not the Color of Your Skin, but the Race of Your Kin, and Other Myths of Identity.* Durham: Duke U.P., 1997.

Beck-Karrer, Charlotte. *Löwinnen sind sie. Gespräche mit somalischen Frauen und Männern über Frauenbeschneidung.* Bern: eFeF: Verein Feministische Wissenschaft, 1997.

Belmaker, R.H. et al. 'Disappearance of Female Genital Mutilation from the Bedouin Population of Southern Israel.' *The Journal of Sexual Medicine.* 2008. [Viewed in proof.]

Belmaker, R.H. 'Re: Ethiopian Jews and FGM.' E-mail to the author. 6 March 1998. belmaker@bgumail.bgu.ac.il

Berman, Paul, ed. *Blacks and Jews. Alliances and Arguments.* NY: Delacorte, 1994.

Cohen, Shaye. Email to Sylvia Fishman. 26 August 2007. Email forwarded to Tobe Levin 26 August 2007.

—. *Why Aren't Jewish Women Circumcised? Gender and Covenant in Judaism.* Berkeley: U. of California P., 2005

Daly, Mary. *Gyn/Ecology. The Metaethics of Radical Feminism.* Boston: Beacon, 1978.

Erickson, Peter. Rev. of *Bailey's Cafe. Kenyon Review* 15, Summer 1993. rpt. in *Gloria Naylor. Critical Perspectives Past and Present.* Eds. Henry Louis Gates, Jr. and K.A. Appiah. NY: Amistad, 1993. 32–34.

Fowler, Karen Joy. Rev. of *Bailey's Cafe. The Chicago Tribune*, October 4, 1992. rpt. in *Gloria Naylor. Critical Perspectives Past and Present.* Eds. Henry Louis Gates, Jr. and K.A. Appiah. NY: Amistad, 1993. 26-28.

Gates, Henry Louis, Jr. 'The Uses of Anti-Semitism.' *Blacks and Jews. Alliances and Arguments.* Ed. Paul Berman. NY: Delacorte, 1994. 217–223.

Gilman, Sander. *The Jew's Body.* NY: Routledge, 1991.

Göttinger, P. (10.7.1996) 'Awa, 17: 'Ich wurde Beschnitten', in *BRAVO! Girl* 15: 10-11.

Grisaru, Nimrod, Simcha Lezer, and R.H. Belmaker. 'Ritual Female Genital Surgery Among Ethiopian Jews.' *Archives of Sexual Behavior.* 26.2 (1997): 211–215.

Harel, D. 'Medical Work among the Falasha of Ethiopia.' *Israel Journal of Medical Science* 3 (1967) : 483–490.

Heschel, Susannah. 'Configurations of Patriarchy, Judaism, and Nazism in German Feminist Thought.' *Gender and Judaism. The Transformation of Tradition.* Ed. T.M. Rudansky. NY: NYU P, 1995. 135–154.

The Holy Scriptures according to the Masoretic Text. Philadelphia: The Jewish Publication Society of America, 1917.

Hosken, Fran. 'Canada: Female Genital Mutilation Workshop Manual.' *WIN News.* 24. 4. (1998): 33–35.

Inter-African Committee. DECLARATION: on the Terminology FGM; 6th IAC General Assembly, 4–7 April, 2005, Bamako/Mali. 06 April 2005. 15 November 2006 <http://www.iac-ciaf.org/index.php?option=com_content&task=view&id=28&Itemid=44&PHPSESSID=ccab7400b78c4c9a3d1c37b99817fa52>.

Ismael, Edna Adan. Interview with the author. Dakar, Senegal. Nov. 1997.

'Jammeh Says His Government Will Not Ban FGM.' Copyright © 1999 Spice News Services. Distributed via Africa News Online <www.africanews.org> 2 February 1999. <http://www.hollyfeld.org/ftp/archives/fgm-l>.

Kassi, Bernadette K. 'Représentation(s) de l'Excision dans le roman ivoirien: des *Soleils des indépendances* (1968) à *Rebelle* (1998) de Fatou Keita.' *Gender and Sexuality in African Literature and Film.* Eds. Ada Uzoamaka Azodo and Maureen Ngozi Eke. Lawrenceville: Africa World Press, 2007. 177–188.

King, Andrea. 'Is Israel Really Liberating for Ethiopian Women?' *Lilith.* 18. (Winter 1987–88/ 5746): 8–12.

Eine Klasse der Oberstufe Suhr [Schulhaus Ost, Oberstufe / Sek. 3a Herr Basler, 5034 Suhr, CH]. Letter to the author. 1996.

Levin, Meyer. *The Falashas.* Video. 1973. Ergo media. 1987.

Levin, Tobe. 'Women as Scapegoats of Culture and Cult: An Activist's View of Female Circumcision in Ngugi's *The River Between.' Ngambika. Studies of Women in African Literature.* Eds. Carole Boyce Davies and Anne Adams Graves. Trenton: Africa World P, 1986. 205–221.

—. 'Female Genital Mutilation: Campaigns in Germany.' *Engendering Human Rights: Cultural and Socio-economic Realities in Africa.* Ed. Obioma Nnaemeka. NY: Palgrave Macmillan at St Martin's Press, 2005. 285–301.

Montgomery, Maxine Lavon. 'Authority, multivocality, and the new world order in Gloria

Naylor's *Bailey's Cafe.* *African American Review.* Spring 1995. 12 September 2007 <http://findarticles.com/p/articles/mi_m2838/is_n1_v29/ai_ 17276614>.

Naylor, Gloria. *Bailey's Cafe.* NY: Harcourt, Brace, Jovanovich, 1992.

—. *Linden Hills.* NY: Penguin, 1985.

—. *Mama Day.* NY: Vintage, 1989.

—. *The Men of Brewster Place.* NY: Vintage, 1998.

—. *1996.* Chicago: Third World P, 2005.

—. *The Women of Brewster Place.* NY: Viking, 1982.

Reinharz, Shula, Tobe Levin & Joy Keshi Walker, eds. *Through the Eyes of Nigerian Artists. Confronting Female Genital Mutilation.* 13 September 2007. <http://www.forward-germany.org/uploads/images/FORWARD %20Broschure%20Nigerian%20Artists.pdf>.

Rifkind, Donna. Rev. of *Bailey's Café. The Washington Post.* October 11, 1992. rpt. in *Gloria Naylor. Critical Perspectives Past and Present.* Eds. Henry Louis Gates, Jr. and K.A. Appiah. NY: Amistad, 1993. 28–30.

Robinson, Lori S. 'Finding Fair Settlement.' *Emerge.* February 1995. 16.

Ross, Jeffrey A. and Melanie L. Schneider. 'Antisemitism on the Campus: Challenge and Response.' *Antisemitism in America Today. Outspoken Experts Explode the Myths.* Ed. Jerome R. Chanes. NY: Birch Lane Press, 1995. 267–291.

Teaching About Violence Against Women. An Interdisciplinary Resource Guide. May 1993. 3 March 1998. <http://www.inform.umd.edu:8080/der.../Teaching Guide/2genital-mutilation>.

United Nations. World Health Organisation. Division of Family Health. 'Female Genital Mutilation: Actions for Eradication.' *Female genital mutilation/ Mutilations sexuelles féminines.* Geneva: WHO/FHE/94.4. 31 July 1994: J1–J2.

Wakefield, Dan. Rev. of *Bailey's Cafe. The New York Times Book Review,* October 4, 1992. rpt. in *Gloria Naylor. Critical Perspectives Past and Present.* Eds. Henry Louis Gates, Jr. and K.A. Appiah. NY: Amistad, 1993. 30–32.

Walker, Alice and Pratibha Parmar. *Warrior Marks.* Video. Our Daughters Have Mothers. 1993.

Walther, Wiebke. *Women in Islam. From Medieval to Modern Times.* Princeton: Marcus Wiener, 2006.

Weil, Shalva. 'Ethiopian Jewish Women: Trends and Transformations in the Context of Transnational Change.' *Nashim: A Journal of Jewish Women's Studies & Gender Issues.* 8. (Fall 2004): 73–86.

Wilentz, Gay. 'Healing the Wounds of Time.' *The Women's Review of Books.* 10.5 (Feb. 1993): 15–16.

Wood, Rebecca S. ''Two Warring Ideals in one Dark Body'. Universalism and Nationalism in Gloria Naylor's *Bailey's Cafe.' African American Review.* 30.3 (Fall 1996): 381–395.

References to Sarkis: 'Somali Womanhood: A Revisioning'

Ahmed, Christine Choi. 'Finely etched chattel: The invention of a Somali woman.' *The Invention of Somalia.* Ed. Ali Jamale Ahmed. Lawrenceville, NJ: Red Sea Press, 1995. 157–89.

Bestemann, Catherine. 'Polygyny, women's land tenure, and the 'mother-son partnership' in Southern Somalia.' *Journal of Anthropology Research.* 51.3 (1995): 193–213.

Dirie, Waris. *Brief an meiner Mutter.* Berlin: Ullstein, 2007.

—. with Jeanne d'Haem. *Desert Dawn.* London: Virago, 2004.

—. *Desert Children*. London: Little Brown, 2007.

Dirie, Waris, and Cathleen Miller. *Desert flower: the extraordinary journey of a desert nomad.* NY: William Morrow, 1998.

Ghorashi, Halleh. 'Why Ayaan Hirsi Ali Is Wrong.' *Signandsight.com.* 14 March (2007) 29 August 2007 <http://www.signandsight.com/features/1250.html>

Helander, Bernard. *The Slaughtered Camel: Coping with Fictitious Descent among the Hubeer of Southern Somalia.* Uppsala: Acta Universitatis Upsaliensis, 2003.

Hirsi Ali, Ayaan. *The Caged Virgin: an Emancipation Proclamation for Women and Islam.* NY: Free Press, 2006.

—. 'Islamic Reformation will come from Europe.' *New Perspective Quarterly.* 6 September (2006). 15 September 2006 <http://www.digitalnpq.org/archive/ 2006_winter/hirsi_ali. html>.

—. *Infidel.* NY: Free Press, 2007.

Kandiyoti, Deniz. 'Bargaining with Patriarchy.' *Gender Society* 2.3 (1988): 274–90.

Kapteijns, Lidwien. 'Gender Relations and the Transformation of the Northern Somali Pastoral Tradition.' *The International Journal of African Historical Studies.* 28.2 (1995): 241–259.

— and Maryan Omar Ali. *Women's voices in a man's world: women and the pastoral tradition in Northern Somali orature, c. 1899-1980.* Portsmouth, NH: Heinemann, 1999.

Korn, Fadumo and Sabine Eichhorst. *Born in the Big Rains: a Memoir of Somalia and Survival.* Trans. and Afterword Tobe Levin. New York: Feminist Press at CUNY, 2006.

Lewis, I. M. *A Modern History of Somalia: Nation and State in the Horn of Africa.* London: Longman, 2004 [1995].

—. *Peoples of the Horn of Africa: Somali, Afar and Saho.* London: International African Institute, 1955.

Samatar, Abdi Ismail. 'Destruction of State and Society in Somalia: Beyond the Tribal Convention.' *The Journal of Modern African Studies.* 30.4 (1992): 625–641.

Tripodi, Paolo. 'Back to the Horn: Italian Administration and Somalia's Troubled Independence.' *The International Journal of African Historical Studies.* 32.2/3 (1999): 359–380.

Walker, Alice. *Possessing the Secret of Joy.* NY: Harcourt, Brace, Jovanovich, 1992.

Notes to Herzberger-Fofana: 'Excision and African Literature: an activist's annotated bibliographical excursion'

1   This is the first English translation of chapter 4, 'Littérature Africaine' in Herzberger-Fofana's on-line publication, *Les Mutilations Génitales Féminines (MGF).* <http://aflit.arts.uwa.edu.au/MGF1.html>

2   In line with this volume's debt to activism, I should mention one example (among many) of linking economic development to FGM. In 1998, Joy Keshi (Ashibuogwu) Walker enlisted the talents of artists in Nigeria to create a travelling exhibition of artworks against female genital mutilation whose theme 'The Suffering, The Sorrow, the Setback' gestured toward the deceleration of progress in a population systematically debilitating half its number. Enter into google: 'Through the Eyes of Nigerian Artists.'

3   See Awa Thiam and Fran Hosken. *The Hosken Report* and all issues of the quarterly *WIN News* published from 1975 to 2003. With regard to Hosken's commitment to eradicating FGM, the *Boston Globe* wrote: 'One such battle [as a controversial figure] occurred in the 1970s, when Mrs. Hosken was accused by anthropologists of committing cultural

genocide by criticising Africans for countenancing female circumcision. She was undeterred by such criticism, having visited hospitals where the practice was not only routine, but subsidised by US aid, her son said. 'She was a woman of privilege who had the money and opportunity to help other women who had neither.'

4   'A review of country-specific Demographic and Health Surveys (DHS) shows FGM prevalence rates of 97 percent in Egypt,' though this figure dates from 1995 (*Demographic*). More recently, German activist Rüdiger Nehberg has achieved success at the legal level in that a Fatwa against FGM has been issued by Egyptian clerics. See Bundesministerium für wirtschaftliches Zusammenarbeit und Entwicklung (BMZ) 'Fatwa gegen Verstümmelung.' See also 'Empfehlungen der Islamischen Konferenz – im Werte einer Fatwa am 24–25 November 2006,' Prof. Dr Ali Goma'a, Grand Mufti, Al-Azhar University, Cairo.

5   Given the racist exhibition of 'The Hottentot Venus,' Saarjite Baartman's 'steatopygia' (large buttocks), this sensitivity is not in the least surprising. Krista A. Thompson (1998) wrote, 'The spectacle of Baartman's body, however, continued even after her death at the age of twenty-six. Pseudo-scientists interested in investigating 'primitive sexuality' dissected and cast her genitals in wax. Baartman, as far as we know, was the first person of Khosian-descent to be dismembered and displayed in this manner. Anatomist Georges Curvier presented Baartman's dissected labia before the Académie Royale de Médecine, in order to allow them 'to see the nature of the labia' (Gilman 235). Curvier and his contemporaries concluded that Baartman's 'oversized primitive' genitalia were physical proof of the African women's 'primitive sexual appetite.' Baartman's genitalia continued to be exhibited at Le Musée de l'Homme, the institution to which Curvier belonged, long after her death.' ("Exhibiting 'Others' in the West").

6   For details on Walker's controversial reception after *Warrior Marks* see Tobe Levin. 'Alice Walker: Matron of FORWARD.'

References

AAWORD. 'A Statement on Genital Mutilation.' *Third World. Second Sex. Women's Struggles and National Liberation.* Ed. Miranda Davies. London: Zed, 1983. 217–220.

Abdalah, Dualeh Raqiya Haji. *Sisters in Affliction. Circumcision and infibulation.* London: Zed Press, 1983.

Barry, Kesso. *Kesso, Princesse Peule.* Paris: Seghers, 1988.

Beyala, Calixthe. *Tu t'appelleras Tanga.* Paris: J'ai Lu, 1988.

La Commission pour l'Abolition des Mutilations Sexuelles, Linda Weil-Curiel, Mathieu Pasquini. *La Suite du Pari de Bintou and Bintou in Paris.* Cartoonist Vincent Martin. 22 August 2007. http://www.cams-fgm.org/bd/intro.php

El Dareer, Asma. *Woman, Why Do You Weep?* London: Zed P, 1982.

'Demographic and Health Survey – Egypt.' (1995). Calverton, MD: Macro International Inc. 171. In Reymond, Laura, Asha Mohamud, Nany Ali, compilers. *Female Genital Mutilation – The Facts.* Funding provided by the Wallace Global Fund. 23 July 2007 http://www.path.org/files/FGM-The-Facts.htm

Dirie, Waris. *Brief an meiner Mutter.* Berlin: Ullstein, 2007.

— with Corinna Milborn. *Desert Children.* Trans. Sheelagh Alabaster. London: Virago, 2005.

— with Cathleen Miller. *Fleur du désert. Du désert de Somalie au monde des top-models, l'extraordinaire combat d'une femme hors du commun.* Trans. Josiane & Alain Deschamps. Paris: Albin Michel, 1998.

Dorkenoo, Efua. *Tradition! Tradition.* London: FORWARD, 1983.

'Dossier sur l'excision.' *Le Monde.* 14 October 1997/10 January 1998/22 August 1998/ 10 October 1998.

'L'excision dans les sociétés africaines.' *Le Matinal.* 4 November 1998. 3.

'Excision, le combat des Africaines.' *Marie-Claire* 399. (November 1985). 57.

Farah, Nuruddin. *From a Crooked Rib.* London: Heinemann, 1986.

Fofana, Aicha. *Mariage, on copie.* Bamako: Jamana, 1994.

Gilman, Sander L. 'Black Bodies, White Bodies: Toward an Iconography of Female Sexuality in Late Nineteenth-Century Art, Medicine, and Literature.' *Race, Writing and Difference.* Eds. Henry Louis Gates Jr. and Kwame Anthony Appiah. Chicago: U. of Chicago P., 1986.

Herzberger-Fofana, Pierrette. *Littérature féminine francophone d'Afrique noire.* Paris: Harmattan, 2000.

—. *Les Mutilations Génitales Féminines (MGF).* Erlangen: AFARD/AAWORD (Association des Femmes Africaines pour la Recherche et le Développement/ Association of African Women for Research and Development, European Section) Section Europe & FORWARD-Germany, 2000.

—. *Les Mutilations Génitales Féminines (MGF).* Retrieved 16 September 2007. <www.afrology.com> Click on société.

—. *Les Mutilations Génitales Féminines (MGF).* Retrieved 22 July 2007. <http:// www.arts.uwa.edu.au/AFLIT/MGF1.html>.

—. Rev. of Waris Dirie. *Fleur du Désert. Du désert de Somalie au monde des top-models, l'extraordinaire combat d'une femme hors du commun.* Trans. Josiane & Alain Deschamps. Paris: Albin Michel, 1998. In: *Mots Pluriels* 10. (May 1999). 15 Oct. 2007. <http://www.arts.uwa.edu.au/MotsPluriels/MP1099phfwaris.html>

—. Rev. of Waris Dirie. *Nomadentochter.* Berlin: Ullstein, 2004. 16 Sept. 2007. <http://www.afrikanet.info/index.php?option=com_content&task=view&id=704&Itemid=83.

—. 'Sembène Ousmane, Avocat de la cause féminine a tiré sa révérence (1923-2007).' 16 Sept. 2007. <www.grioo.com> <www.afrology.com>. <www.senkto.com> <www.renaf.com>

—. 'Sembène Ousmane, l'Aîné des Anciens.' 16 September 2007. <www.grioo.com>.

Hosken, Fran P. *The Hosken Report. Genital and Sexual Mutilation of Females.* Lexington, MA: WIN News, 1979.

'Jammeh says his Government will not ban FGM.' *Afrique-Info-Service SYFEV-Enda.* Spice News Service. 22 Jan. 1999.

Kâ, Aminata Maïga. *La Voie du salut* followed by *Le miroir de la vie.* Paris: Présence Africaine, 1985.

Kahn, Joseph P. 'Fran P. Hosken, 86; activist for women's issues globally.' *The Boston Globe.* 12 Feb. 2006. 23 July 2007. <http://www.boston.com/news/globe/ obituaries/articles /2006/02/12/fran_p_hosken_86_activist_for_womens_issues_globally/>.

Kassindja, Fauziya and Layli Miller Bashir. *Niemand sieht dich, wenn du weinst.* [*Do They Hear You When You Cry?*] München: Blessing Verlag, 1998.

Keita, Fatou. *Rebelle.* Paris, Dakar and Abidjan: Présence africaine/ Nouvelles Éditions Ivoiriennes, 1998.

Khady. *Mutilée.* Paris: Oh! Editions, 2005.

Korn, Fadumo with Sabine Eichhorst. *Born in the Big Rains. A Memoir of Somalia and Survival.* Trans. and Afterword Tobe Levin. NY: The Feminist Press, 2006.

Levin, Tobe. 'Alice Walker: Matron of FORWARD.' *Black Imagination and the Middle Passage.* Eds. Maria Diedrich, Henry Louis Gates, Jr., and Carl Pedersen. NY: Oxford UP, 1999. 240–254.

—. 'Creative Writing of FGM as an Act of Violence and Human Rights Abuse.' Ed. Levin, Tobe, *Violence: 'Mercurial Gestalt.'* Amsterdam: Rodopi, 2008. 111–122.

'Mariama Lamizana.' *Amina.* 328. (August 1997). 32.

Mbacké, Mame Seck. *Le froid et le piment. Nous travailleurs émigrés.* Dakar: NEA, 1983.

Ndiaye, Adja Ndèye Boury. *Collier de chevilles.* Dakar: NEA, 1984.

Nwapa, Flora. *Efuru.* London: Heinemann, 1966.

Parmar, Pratibha, dir. and Alice Walker. *Warrior Marks.* Video. Our Mothers Have Daughters. 1983.

Pimsleur, Julie and Kirsten Johnson. *Bintou in Paris.* Video. Paris: Commission pour l'Abolition des Mutilations sexuelles, 1994.

Pliya, Jean qtd. in 'L'excision dans les sociétés africaines.' *Le Matinal.* 4 November 1998. 3.

El Saadawi, Nawal. *God Dies by the Nile.* London: Zed Books, 1986.

—. *The Hidden Face of Eve.* London: Zed Press, 1987.

—. *Women at Point Zero.* Zed Press: London, 1983.

Sembène, Ousmane, dir. *Moolaadé. Bann der Hoffnung.* Film. Dakar & Paris: Filmi Doomirew & Ciné Sud Promotion, 2004.

Sister Marie-André. *Femmes d'Afrique noire.* Paris: Payot, 1939.

Sovide, Valentin. 'Excisée ou dépravée.' *La Nation* [Bénin]. (27 Nov. 1998): 1.

'A Statement on Genital Mutilation.' *Third World: Second Sex, Women's Struggles and National Liberation.* Ed. Davies, Miranda. London: Zed P, 1983. 217.

Tchak, Sami. *La sexualité féminine en Afrique.* Paris: L'Harmattan, 1999.

Thiam, Awa. *La parole aux Négresses.* Paris: Denoël, 1978.

Thompson, Krista A. "Exhibiting 'Others' in the West." 23 July 2007. <http://www.english.emory.edu/Bahri/Exhibition.html >.

de Villeneuve, Annie. 'Etude sur une coutume somalienne: les femmes cousues.' *Journal de la Société des Africanistes.* (1937): 30.

Walker, Alice. *Possessing the Secret of Joy.* NY: Simon and Schuster, 1992.

Waris Dirie Foundation Website. 15 Oct. 2007 <http://www.waris-dirie-foundation.com/>.

Weil-Curiel, Linda. 'La Suite du Pari de Bintou.' 23 July 2007 <http://www.cams-fgm.org/bd/credits.php>

Notes to Mathai: 'Who's Afraid of Female Sexuality?'

1 The use of the term *circumcision* does not in any way imply a comparison to male circumcision but is applied as used in the community.

2 The house of Mumbi is another way of referring to the Kikuyu people. Mumbi is said to have been the Mother of the Kikuyus and Gikuyu the father.

3 *Ugali*, a kind of national dish in Kenya, is a solid mass of white maize floor cooked in water.

4 Interview conducted by the author in 2002.

5 The traditional parliamentary group of elders among the Tigania Meru.

6 That women also support men in this line of argument is not new, but why women in patriarchal societies maintain a system that oppresses them is another story altogether. Still, it's worth mentioning here that when I probed a bit more into Mama K's marital experience, asking, 'Did you feel it was good even though you passed there?' she answered, 'Yes.' If women deny the intended effect of FGM – to interfere with their sexual pleasure – motivation to resist is weak.

References

Ajulu, R. 'Thinking Through the Crisis of Democratisation in Kenya: A Response to Adar and Murunga.' *African Sociological Review.* 4.2 (2000): 135–157.

'KENYA Rights activists decry Mungiki circumcision threat.' *OCHA IRIN.* 15 September 2007 <http://www.irinnews.org/report.asp?ReportID=27467.htm>

Kenyatta, Jomo. *Facing Mount Kenya. The Tribal Life of the Gikuyu.* London: Heinemann, 1989. 130–154.

Mathai, Anna M. (Muthoni). 'FGM: A threat to the health of the African woman and girl-child.' *Einschnitte; Materialband zu Female Genital Cuttings* (FGC). Eds. Diaby–Pentzlin & Göttke. Eschborn: GTZ, 1999. 13–20.

—. 'Strategies for Change in Kenya.' *Einschnitte; Materialband zu Female Genital Cuttings* (FGC). Eds. Diaby–Pentzlin & Göttke. Eschborn: GTZ, 1999. 144–153.

Mathai, Muthoni. *Sexual decision making and AIDS in Africa: A look at the social vulnerability of women in Sub-Saharan Africa to HIV/AIDS. A Kenyan Example.* Kassel: Kassel UP, 2006.

Mungiki – religious cults and sects. In: 'The Shadowy World of Mungiki.' *The Nation/Africa News Online* (Kenya). 24 April 2000. 15 September 2007 <http://www.africanews.org/east/kenya/stories/20000424/20000424_feat8.html>; <http://www.apologeticsindex.org/news/an200425.html#30>

Notes to Abdi: 'Desert Tears'

1   Excerpts from Nura Abdi and Leo Linder. *Tränen im Sand.* [Desert Tears] Bergisch Gladbach: Ehrenwirth, 2003. In *Feminist Europa. Review of Books.* Vol. 3, No. 1, 2004.

References

Abdi, Nura and Leo Linder. *Tränen im Sand.* [Desert Tears] Bergisch Gladbach: Ehrenwirth, 2003. In *Feminist Europa. Review of Books.* Vol. 3, No. 1, 2004.

Index

AAWORD, xv, 145-146, 210, 211, 214
Abdalla, Raqiya Haji Dualeh, 193, 198
Abdi, Maryam Sheikh, 117, 181
Abdi, Nura, viii, ix, 3, 14, 75, 85, 86, 91, 173, 179, 183, 187, 197, 201
Abusharaf, Rogaia Mustafa, 196, 198, 199
Accad, Evelyne, 29,187
Accra 93-97,103, 111, 181, 203, 204
Achebe, Chinua, 28,187
Afar, 128, 129, 199, 209
AIDS, 14,156, 162,163,165-172,179, 213, 214
Allas, Yasmine, 23,187
Amselle, Jean-Loup, 77, 201
André, Sister-Marie, 143, 212
Anti-Semitism, 115,116,119, 120, 123, 205-207
Armah, Ayi Kwei, 78, 179,187
Assaad, Marie xiv, 178
Azoulay, Katya Gibel, 124, 204

Bâ, Mariama, 65, 193
Babikar Badri Women's Studies Centre, Omdurman, xiv
Barre, Siad, 128, 138
Bamako Declaration xvi, 124, 177, 178, 196, 197, 199, 205
Bambara, 9, 36
Barry, Kesso, 154,183
Barry, Mariama, 11, 29, 75, 85, 88, 150, 180, 187, 201
Bashir, Layli Miller, 199, 211
Beck-Karrer, Charlotte, 121, 206
Benin, 61, 142, 152, 212
BENKADI, e.V. Kultur Raum Afrika, 8, 180
Berman, Paul, 116, 207
Beta Israel, 113, 117-119, 125
Beti, 201, 202
Bettelheim, Bruno, 188
Beyala, Calixthe, 11, 23, 25-27, 75, 85, 86, 151,188, 193, 201, 202, 210
Bintou in Paris, 146, 147, 210, 212

Black Atlantic (The), 52-54, 56, 195
Brahimi, Denise, 183, 188
Brown, Lloyd, 21,188, 209
Burkina Faso, v, 49, 61, 113, 143, 148,154,178, 179,198

Cameroon, x, 201
CAMS (Commission pour l'Abolition des Mutilations Sexuelles), xv, 8, 146, 147, 181, 210
Carr, Dara, 182, 188, 192, 193
Cazenave, Odile, 183, 188
Chambers, Ross, 41, 42, 193
Circling Song, 24, 25, 189
Circumcision, female, xi, xvi, xviii, 39, 68, 79, 81, 98, 101, 113, 114, 117, 136, 156, 158-161, 165, 177, 178, 181-183, 188, 189, 191-193, 196, 198, 199, 202, 207, 210
Circumcision, male, xvi, 49, 114, 116, 118, 192, 212
Cissé, Fatou Fanny, 85, 201
Clitoridectomy xiv, xvi, 2, 7, 12-14,16, 25, 30, 56, 64, 65, 75, 78-80, 85, 86, 103, 119, 124, 143,144,148, 151, 159, 161, 162, 167, 170, 171, 177, 182, 185, 201, 204, 206
Clitoris, xv, xvi, 12, 17, 23, 41, 58, 59, 65, 68 70, 82, 83, 88, 90,105, 118, 135, 143, 149, 151, 152, 160, 170, 177, 196, 201
Clarke, Breena, 31
Collins, Pat Lowery, 203, 204
Comic books, 7, 203
Confucius, 77
Conteh, Osman, 11, 88, 91, 180, 201, 204
Creider, Jane Tapsubei, 183, 188
Cuny, Mary-Thérèse, 91, 189
Cutting the Rose, 188, 197, 204

Dabla! Excision, 6, 178, 181
D'Almeida, Assiba Irène, 188
Daly, Mary, 66, 121,185, 188, 207
DAPHNE program of the European

Union, 7, 203
Dareer, Asmael, xiv, 35, 149, 186
Darod, 128, 129,133
Daughter of Mumbi, 17-20,191
Davies, Carole Boyce, ix, 189, 190, 208
Defibulation, 123, 138
Desert Children, 1,136, 152, 180, 199
Devoir de violence (Le), xxi, 84, 186, 190, 202
Diallo, Khadidiatou, xx, 7
Dickerson, Glenda, 31, 32, 33, 188
Diop, Aminata , 57, 187
Dirie, Waris, xx, 3, 12, 14, 40, 75, 85, 86, 91, 127, 129-131, 133, 135, 136, 138-142, 152, 153, 180, 183, 188, 193-195, 197, 201, 209, 211, 212
Dogon, 9, 82, 197
Dorkenoo, Efua, xv, xx, 2, 3, 4, 57, 149, 178, 180, 184, 186, 188, 194, 197, 204, 211

Efuru, 21, 25, 80, 142, 151, 185, 190, 191, 202, 212
Egypt, 28, 32, 114, 144, 177, 181, 184, 198, 210
Eichhorst, Sabine, 131, 138, 189, 203, 204, 209, 212
Ekwe, Hélène, 6, 203, 204
Eritrea, 150, 177, 179, 188, 191, 195, 198
Ethiopia, 105, 106, 117,118, 128, 150, 177, 206, 207
Exciser, 9, 17, 81, 139, 198
Excision, v, vii, viii, x, xv, 2, 3, 5-8, 11, 15-27, 29-37, 39, 43, 46, 48, 49, 51, 55, 68, 69, 75, 81-86, 89, 90, 103, 110, 135, 142-148, 150-154, 169, 185-189, 191, 194, 198, 199, 201, 209, 211, 214, 215

Facing Mount Kenya, vii, 15, 17, 39, 79, 159, 160, 182, 183, 189, 193, 202, 213
Farah, Nuruddin, 11, 23, 24, 25, 28, 29, 75, 84, 91, 150, 185, 189, 193, 201, 204, 211
Female Genital Cutting, xii, 178, 181, 182, 188, 193, 198, 200
Female Genital Excision, vii,15-17, 19-23,25, 27,29-31,34-37,178,182-188

Female Genital Mutilation (FGM), v, vii, xi, 1, 3-5, 38, 52, 65, 66, 75, 88
Female Sexuality, vii, 12, 14, 24, 64, 68, 69, 71, 82, 85, 116, 156, 162, 165, 170, 189, 211, 212
Finzan, 36, 38, 49, 50, 179, 188, 191
Fire Eyes, 26, 178, 190
Fofona, Aicha, 151, 211
FORWARD, 10, 211
Friedman, Marylin, 195
From a Crooked Rib, 23, 25, 84, 92, 93, 150, 189, 201, 204, 211
Fulda-Mosocho-Project, 9, 180

Gallimore, Rangira Béatrice, 75, 85, 202
Gambia (The), 57, 62, 124,153
Gates, Henry Louis, Jr., xx, 116, 181, 190, 194, 196-198, 211, 212
Gender-based Violence (GBV), ii, ix, 81, 90
Ghana, 12, 61, 93-95, 103, 108, 110, 121, 181, 185, 198, 200, 203, 204, 215
Gikandi, Simon, 90, 201
Gikuyu, 18, 19, 20, 39, 78, 79, 82, 88, 184,187,188, 193, 202, 212, 213
Gilman, Sander, 120, 207, 210, 211
Gilroy, Paul 53, 56, 195
Gogh, Theo van, 14, 127, 134
Gorée Island, 59, 61, 62
Gourdine, Angeletta, 52
Gréou, Hawa, 3, 180, 198, 199, 204
Groult, Benoite, 5
GTZ (German Association for Development Cooperation), xi, 6, 213

Halpular, 150
Hawiya, 138
Helander, Berland, 132, 209
Henry, Henry, 180, 198, 199, 204
Herzi, Hagi-Dirie, 29, 32,189
Hirsi Ali, Ayaan , xx, 4,14, 126, 133, 140, 194, 197, 209
HIV, xii, 88,165, 213
Horn of Africa, 22, 65, 128, 129,150, 209
Hosken, Fran, xv, 143, 184, 185, 189, 210, 211
House of Slaves, 59, 60, 61, 62

Human Rights, vii, x, xv, 1, 5, 11, 15, 16,
32, 38, 63, 65, 66, 72, 76, 78, 83, 92, 112,
136, 139, 141, 147, 182, 187, 189, 194,
196, 200, 206, 208, 212
Huxley, Elspeth, 16, 17, 19, 184,189

Infibulation, 2, 5, 12, 13, 15, 16, 24, 26,
29, 31-33, 39, 55, 56, 64, 65, 67, 69,75,
84-86, 103,105, 112-114, 117, 119, 120,
126, 127, 129, 136, 139, 143-145, 149,
150, 177, 179, 182, 183,185, 186, 191,
195, 199, 201, 210
INTEGRA, 6
Inter-African Committee (IAC), xvi, 3, 65,
87, 180, 199, 207
Irene Koso-Thomas, xv, 177, 181
Isegawa, Moses, 186,189
Ismail, Edna Adan, xiv, 87, 197, 209

James, Stanlie M., 189, 192, 193, 200
*Jenda: A Journal of Culture and African
Women Studies,* 2, 181, 196
Johnson, Kirsten, 212

Kâ, Aminata Maiga, 22, 85,150, 151
Kane, Cheik Hamidou, 80, 202, 214
KANU, 158
Kassindja, Faussiya, 183, 189, 211
Keïta, Fatou, 12, 34, 75, 85, 89, 91,155,189,
202, 204, 207, 212
Kenya ,vii, xii, 9, 15-17, 19, 32, 39, 79, 112,
117, 128, 144, 150, 158-161, 165, 177,
182, 183, 185, 189, 193, 198, 202, 205,
206, 212, 213
Kenyatta, Jomo, 15-17, 23, 39, 79, 80, 144,
156, 159, 160, 184, 189, 193, 202, 213
Kessler, Cristina, 203, 204
Kodjo, Edem, 76, 202
Koita, Khady, xx, 155, 183, 197
Kono, 69
Korn, Fadumo, ii, xx, 3, 12, 127, 129, 131,
133, 135, 136, 138-141, 183, 189, 195,
203, 204, 209, 212
Kourouma, Ahmadou, xxi, 11, 23, 25,
48,75, 80, 81, 83-85, 201, 202
KPU, 158
Kul, Bafing, 8,146

Lancet, 69, 179, 182, 191, 199, 220
Levin, Meyer, 123, 207
Lewis, Joan, 128, 129, 130, 141
Lightfoot-Klein, Hanny, 186,189,193
Likimani, Muthoni, 17-20, 22, 189
Linder, Leo C., xviii, ix, 173, 179, 187, 213
Lorde, Audre, 13, 54, 64, 67, 69, 70, 74,
196, 200

Male Genital Mutilation (MGM), 39
Mali, 4, 6, 36, 49, 57, 85, 178, 180, 191,
197-199, 203, 204, 206, 207
Malicounda, 71, 72
Malinké, 48, 82
Malti-Douglas, Fedwa, 184, 190
Mambou, Christian, 88, 202, 204
Maran, René, 190
Mbacké, Mame Seck, 154
Mbembe, Achille, 77, 202
Mende, 82
Menstruation, 185
Meru, 161, 213
Middle Passage, 52, 53, 57, 60, 62, 181,
194, 196, 212
Mike, Chuck, 6
Miller, Cathleen, 91, 188, 193, 201, 209,
211
Mire, Soraya, 4, 36, 178, 181, 190
Mogadishu, 136, 139
Moolaadé, v, 4, 9, 36, 40, 49-51, 148, 154,
181, 191, 194, 202, 212
Muiritu, 157
Mumbi, 158, 160, 212
Mungiki, 160, 161, 165, 171, 213
Mutilated, 12, 87, 88, 92-94, 99, 110, 155,
181, 185, 202, 204
Mutilée, 2, 23, 91, 93, 155, 180, 183, 189,
195, 202, 204, 212

Naylor, Gloria, 13, 15, 31, 112, 114-121,
125, 190, 206-208
Nawal el Saadawi, xiv, 24, 25, 27, 29, 144,
146, 149, 184-186, 188,190, 193,195,
212
Ndiaye, Adja Ndèye Boury, 154, 212
Ngugi, wa Thiong'o, 11, 12, 16-20, 22, 40,
44, 75, 78-81, 92, 124, 144, 181, 187,

190, 191,194, 202
Nigeria, 6,10, 106,178, 198, 206, 209
Nimako, Annor, 11, 93
Njau, Rebecca, 21, 22, 185, 190
Nkashama, Pius Ngandu, 183,190
Nnaemeka, Obioma, xx,181-183, 190, 193, 196, 206, 208
Nwapa, Flora, 12, 20, 21, 22, 92,142-144, 151, 185, 190, 191, 202, 212

Ogunyemi, Okonjo Chikwenye, 183, 190
Ombolo, Jean-Pierre, 201, 202
Oppositional narrative, x, 40, 41, 44, 48, 49, 51
Ottah, Comfort, xvi, xvii, xx, 177, 178, 181, 194, 197, 205
Ouologuem, Yambo, xxi, 84, 85, 186, 190, 202
Oy?wùmi, Oyèrónké, 2, 47, 181, 193, 196

Parmar, Pratibha, 57-61, 181, 186, 190-194, 196, 208, 212
Pamanta, Demba Aboubacar, 204
Performance Studio Workshop, 6
Pomerance, Erica, 6, 178, 181
Possessing the Secret of Joy, 2, 15, 29-32, 34, 55, 67, 73, 120, 124, 144, 150,179, 181, 182, 186, 187, 191,196, 199, 200, 203, 205, 209, 212
Pulaar, 9

Rebelle, 34, 89, 90-93, 151, 155, 189, 202, 204, 207, 212
Rendille, 70
Rifaat, Alifa, 23, 24, 190
River Between (The), 18-20, 32, 40, 43, 78, 80, 124, 144, 183, 187, 189, 190, 194, 202, 207
Robertson, Claire C., 182, 189, 193, 200
Roventa-Frumasani, Daniela, 78, 202

Sarakole, 9
Savané, Marie-Angélique, xiv
Scar (The), 20-22, 25, 34, 35, 185, 186, 190
Sembène, Ousmane, v, xi, 4, 10, 36, 49, 50, 148, 149, 154, 181, 191, 194, 204, 211, 212

Senegal, xi, 6, 12, 43, 55, 57, 59, 61, 62, 71,191, 198, 207
Senouofo, 9
Shakespeare, William, 114, 208
Sierra Leone, xv, 61, 69, 180, 198, 203
Simon, Robert, 63, 196
Sini Sanuman, 9, 180, 204
Sissoko, Cheick Oumar, 36, 49,189,194
SISTER FA, 8
SISTERHELP, 6
Smith, Barbara, 52, 54
Soleils des indépendances (Les), xxi, 25, 40, 48, 80, 81, 91, 92, 151, 181, 189, 190, 194, 202, 204
Somalia, ii, ix, xi, 23, 33, 85, 88, 106, 127-129, 131, 133, 134, 136, 138, 150, 177, 183, 190, 191, 198, 203, 204, 209, 212
Stefan, Verena, 203, 204
Strong-Leek, Linda McNeely, 183, 191
Sudan, xiv, 150, 177, 178, 180, 198, 199

Tchak, Sami, 212
Temne, 88
Tent of the Living God, 160, 161, 165, 171
Thahu, 79
Theunen, Patrick, 7,182, 203, 204
They Shall be Chastised, 17-20, 189
Thiam, Awa, xiv, xv, xx, 2, 8, 15, 45, 75, 145, 185, 194, 197, 201
Thiam, Khady, 2
TOSTAN, 6, 71, 72, 198
Trevarthen, Anne, 188
Turigu, 157

UK Female Genital Mutilation Act of 2003, 10
Urinary tract infections, xvii

Villeneuve, Annie de, 46, 143
VVF (Vesico-Vaginal Fistula), 8

Waciuma, Charity, 17-19, 22, 191
Walker, Alice, xx, 1,12, 36, 54, 64, 67, 121, 141, 149, 150, 152, 177, 181, 191, 192, 194-197, 202, 212, 214
Walker, Joy Keshi (Ashibuogwu), 187, 209
Walther, Wiebke, 114, 208

Warrior Marks, vii, xvi, 2, 3, 4, 12, 46, 52,
    53, 55-57, 62, 67, 121, 145, 149, 150,
    177, 178, 181, 186, 190-196, 208, 210,
    212
Weidenweber, Sigrid, 203
Weil-Curiel, Linda, xx, 8, 146, 180-182,
    194, 198, 199, 204, 210, 212
Wilentz, Gay, 123, 124, 183, 191, 208
Williams-Garcia, Rita, 182, 203, 205

Williams-Okorodus, Godfrey, xiii, xx, 10
Women in Africa and the African
    Diaspora (WAAD), 10, 187
'Womanism', 54, 178

Yalomba, Adama, 9

Zabus, Chantal, 6, 178, 182, 183, 191